Women, Employment and Organizations

The shift in women's social and economic position has been one of the key revolutions in industrialized societies over the past century, largely as a consequence of their increased employment participation. This book examines the main labour market and organizational issues in relation to women's employment in the twenty-first century. Bringing together the latest European and North American research, it explores:

- the causes and explanations of women's employment patterns and the policy responses of the social partners;
- the persistence of gender segregation, the gender pay gap and the prevalence of part-time working among women;
- how employers are responding to gender equality issues – the shift from 'equal opportunities' to 'diversity management' and 'work–life balance' policies;
- the prospects for and limitations of trade unions advancing gender equality.

Women, Employment and Organizations concludes that the rise in women's employment poses challenges for the liberal state, in terms of who cares for children and the elderly, as well as for social justice and wider issues such as falling birth rates. It is essential reading for students and lecturers in Business Studies, Sociology, Social Policy and Gender Studies, as well as for policy-makers.

Judith Glover is Professor of Employment Studies at the School of Business and Social Sciences, Roehampton University, UK.

Gill Kirton is Senior Lecturer in Employment Relations at the School of Business and Management, Queen Mary University of London, UK.

Women, Employment and Organizations

Judith Glover and Gill Kirton

Routledge
Taylor & Francis Group

LONDON AND NEW YORK

First published 2006
by Routledge
2 Park Square, Milton Park, Abingdon, Oxon OX14 4RN

Simultaneously published in the USA and Canada
by Routledge
270 Madison Ave, New York, NY 10016

Routledge is an imprint of the Taylor & Francis Group, an informa business

© 2006 Judith Glover and Gill Kirton

Typeset in Times New Roman by
GreenGate Publishing Services, Tonbridge

Printed and bound in Great Britain by
TJ International Ltd, Padstow, Cornwall

British Library Cataloguing in Publication Data
A catalogue record for this book is available from the British Library

Library of Congress Cataloging in Publication Data
A catalog record has been requested for this book

ISBN10: 0-415-32838-1 (hbk)
ISBN10: 0-415-32839-X (pbk)
ISBN10: 0-203-36693-X (ebk)

ISBN13: 978-0-415-32838-8 (hbk)
ISBN13: 978-0-415-32839-5 (pbk)
ISBN13: 978-0-203-36693-6 (ebk)

Contents

Tables

Acknowledgement

The authors and publishers are grateful to the following for their kind permission:
The Future Foundation for Table 6.1.

Chapter 1

Women, employment and organizations

Changes and challenges

Introduction

One of the key revolutions in industrialized societies over the past century, and perhaps particularly the past half century, is the shift in women's social and economic position. Many women are well qualified, some highly so; the full-time homemaker model has largely been replaced by the dual role of earner and caregiver; women, particularly highly qualified ones, are delaying or turning their back on childbirth; single-adult households, the great majority of which are headed by women, are now common, some as a result of high divorce rates. OECD (2002: 69) reports that women account for 45 per cent of the UK workforce aged 15 to 64. The level is somewhat higher in the Nordic countries[1] (47–48 per cent) and the United States (47 per cent). The increase in women's participation in the labour market is a particularly significant feature of the economies of industrialized countries (Garcia *et al.* 2003).

Improving women's labour force participation rate is a major goal of the European Union's European Employment Strategy. At the Lisbon Summit in March 2000 it was agreed that the percentage of working-age women in employment should increase to more than 60 per cent in 2010 (Plantenga 2004). The European Commission in its 2005 'Growth and Jobs' paper insists that 'the huge potential of women in the labour market remains to be fully exploited' in the context of building economic growth and setting national targets for employment growth (European Commission 2005: 24). Sen (1999) argues that if women's freedom to work outside the home is increased, this will increase their freedom in domains such as the home, healthcare, education, reproductive control and social and political life, with important individual and collective advantages. The UK Equal Opportunities Commission believes that equality for women and men is in everyone's interests: individuals, employers and society as a whole because, it says, gender equality helps to make the economy strong, helps to reduce poverty, including poverty for children, reduces the damage that discrimination causes in individuals' lives, means everyone has a fair stake in society and in the decisions that affect them, and leads to better services (EOC 2003). These are the underpinning assumptions of this book as it explores women's employment and the theoretical and practical challenges for management.

Yet, there is a lag between the reality of these life patterns and societal institutions and cultural beliefs (Giele and Holst 2004). The institutional context in which families and individuals live has changed rather little: workplaces, schools, service providers and so on all assume that a full-time homemaker is available (Moen 2003). Probably this lag is to be expected, since social change is unlikely to come about smoothly or quickly. Depending on the perspective, there will be both winners and losers. A second lag referred to by Giele and Holst relates to policy; there exists a disparity between 'private needs and public willingness to provide social support' (Giele and Holst 2004: 3). Employment is one of the arenas where the lags referred to by Giele and Holst are found.

Against this context, this book explores the primary macro (labour market) and micro (organizational) level issues in relation to women's employment in the twenty-first century. At the macro level, the persistence of occupational segregation, the gender pay gap, and the prevalence of part-time working among women are given detailed attention. Bridging the macro and micro levels of analysis is a discussion of women in the professions and management – more women are entering both spheres, but gender segregation and a pay gap persist. At the micro level, we consider how organizations are currently responding to gender equality issues with a discussion of the shift from 'equal opportunities' to 'diversity management'. There is also an examination of the concept of 'work–life balance' as a government and organizational policy response to political, economic and social changes. Finally, the prospects for and limitations of trade unions in advancing the gender equality project are discussed. Running through the chapters is the 'choice'/constraint debate that has preoccupied scholars of women's employment over the past decade. We summarize this debate towards the end of this chapter. Each chapter is self-contained with its own introduction, conclusion and references; however, the themes are interlinked, as is evident from the discussion below, and there are signposts throughout to other relevant chapters.

The approach in this book is to cast a critical eye on policy development by locating the UK in a wider context. The aim is not to compare women's employment patterns in different types of social/welfare regimes; nevertheless, one country's approach to social, political and economic issues is best understood by putting it alongside other countries. The principal weight of data, evidence and argument centres in this book on the UK at the end of the twentieth century and the beginning of the twenty-first century. However, attention is systematically given to other social and employment regimes: the liberal (individualist) regime exemplified by the US, as well as the Nordic countries, exemplifying the social democratic approach to political ideology and welfare.

The themes and issues outlined below and discussed in further detail in the chapters that follow pose challenges for the theory and practice of organizations and management. The evidence points to an increasing diversity of female employment preferences, career patterns and trajectories. However, the perspective of this book is that women make employment choices within a context of constraint; one of the theoretical challenges of the twenty-first century is to interpret and understand women's employment in ways that are sensitive to the complexity of the lived realities of being female. Another theoretical challenge is to make sense of institutional and organizational responses to the 'problem' of women's employment. In practice it is clear that women are an important source of labour for many industries, organizations and occupations in advanced industrialized economies. It is no longer tenable to construct workers as genderless beings free of the trappings of domestic life; rather government and organizational policies need to be sensitive to gender and other cross-cutting demographic characteristics and their impact on employment.

There is perhaps inevitably resistance to change from institutions, work organizations, families and individuals, some of whom see a diminution of power and influence on an individual or collective level. One clear and far-reaching example of this resistance is the relatively unchanging domestic division of labour (gender roles within the household). We explore this issue in Chapter 7. Depending on levels of optimism or pessimism, this is seen by Anderson et al. (1994) as 'lagged adaptation' and by Hochschild (1989) as the 'stalled revolution'. The question here is whether the gender regime – exemplified at least partly by the domestic division of labour – sets out clear gender roles for women and men. Attempts to measure the domestic division of labour show that in all industrialized countries there is a tendency for a traditional gendered division of labour to persist (Garey 1999; Gershuny 2000; Pilcher 2000; Bianchi and Mattingly 2004; Sullivan 2000; Fisher and Layte 2002). However, countries with less traditional gender role attitudes overall, such as the Nordic ones, are associated with a less traditional division of domestic labour (Crompton et al. 2003).

Women's employment: a changing landscape

Women are now well represented in the UK labour force, as in most industrialized countries. In 2003, the *Labour Force Survey* showed that 70 per cent of working-age women in the UK were in employment, compared with 47 per cent in 1959, the first year for which comparable estimates are available (ONS 2004: 127). Ethnic differences should be noted: in 2003, the *Labour Force Survey* showed that the labour force participation of white women of working age was 74 per cent, of black Caribbean women 72 per cent and of Bangladeshi women 22 per cent (2004: 127). Black Caribbean women are more likely to work full-time than white women (Holdsworth and Dale 1997).

Historians are generally in agreement that the post-Second World War period marked a major change in women's employment patterns (Lewis 1984; Summerfield 1984). The 1940s and 1950s in the UK were times of economic expansion with the new engineering and electrical industries developing. In the face of labour shortages, women were seen as an available pool of labour. In the

UK, unprecedented numbers of married women, many of them with children, entered the labour force. Crucially, in terms of understanding present-day employment patterns, women were encouraged into a particular form of labour market participation – as part-time workers. In explaining the particular prevalence of part-time working in the UK, Summerfield cites post-war policy documents that provide evidence of a duality of thinking that persists to this day. Post-war governments acknowledged the need to boost the economy and saw women as an untapped pool of labour, but also insisted on women's responsibility as homemakers. It was therefore argued that part-time working enabled women to fulfil their responsibilities as wives, mothers and workers. Summerfield (1984) cites a 1949 Royal Commission Report that welcomed the idea of women combining these roles, urging employers to devise work that would allow them to do this.

The acceptance of women's economic role was also obvious in the Factories (Evening Employment) Act of 1950. 'Twilight shifts' were encouraged: these allowed women to care for their children during the day and then to go out to work once the children were in bed, when household childcare (grandparents, fathers) would take place. In this way, a separate, part-time, labour force of women was created by employers (Blossfeld 1997). Burchell *et al.* (1997) conclude that this post-war increase in part-time working has done little to challenge the position of men within the labour market or the position of women within the home, in terms of their traditional domestic roles. In the labour market, men were largely untouched by women's participation, since the jobs that women entered were highly sex-segregated and low paid. Burchell *et al.* conclude that although the post-war entry of women into the labour market gave women some economic freedom as well as an alternative identity to that of wife and mother, it largely amounted to the taking on of an additional role. The issue of how many roles this totals has been the subject of some debate, covered in Chapter 7.

In the UK the rate of total and full-time employment has increased over the past 40 years, although full-time employment plateaued in the 1990s; part-time employment has carried on rising. In the US, by contrast, full-time employment has carried on rising, with part-time employment showing a plateau over the past 30 years or so. The prevalence of part-time working in the UK forms the backdrop to the current rhetoric and related policies on 'work–life balance', where the argument is that good quality part-time work is a positive benefit for women as it enables them to balance their work and caring roles. However, this does not mean that employer strategies are simply responding to women's preference for part-time work. It is clear that employers deliberately construct many 'women's jobs' as part-time in order to provide 'structured flexibility', particularly in industries such as retail (Grant *et al.* 2005). Part-time employment also provides employers with cost advantages. For example, meal breaks are rarely paid for and part-time workers are likely to receive less training (Purcell 2000). Women who 'choose' to work part-time in order to balance work and home responsibilities usually pay a high price. They are likely to experience 'downward occupational mobility' on moving to part-time work, mainly into female-typed areas involving lower pay, loss of status and poorer conditions of employment (Grimshaw and Rubery 2001; Harkness 2002; Walby and Olsen 2002; Grant *et al.* 2005). This has longer-term consequences, as women who work part-time often encounter financial hardship, especially after divorce and retirement (Ginn *et al.* 2001). Senior and management level jobs are rarely constructed as part-time jobs (Grant *et al.* 2005).

Across Europe, women are participating in the labour market on a more continuous basis, less interrupted than in the past by childbearing and child rearing (Rubery *et al.* 1998). In 2002 72 per cent of women in the UK who were at work during their pregnancy returned to work within 10 to 11 months, compared with only 24 per cent in 1979 (WEU 2004). In European Union countries, around half of women with a child aged under six are in part-time employment (OECD 2001). OECD reports that those who are not in paid work say they want to move into employment during the next few years but state a preference for part-time working of relatively long hours. Levels of education also make a difference to labour force participation: the employment rates of well educated mothers are considerably higher than those of less well educated mothers in almost all countries and this gap is increasing.

A changing economy

A key element of the 'new economy' of the twenty-first century is the intensification of work (Green 2001). 'Knowledge work' has developed strongly and information and communication technologies (ICTs) have blurred the boundaries of work and non-work in both time and space. The concept of 'greedy organizations' is an element of the new economy and this is developed further in Chapter 7. This notion has developed from Coser's (1974) idea of 'greedy institutions' that seek undivided loyalty, such as the institutions (in the sociological sense) of paid work and the family. Epstein *et al.* (1998) have built on Coser's work by introducing the concept of 'greedy jobs'. As an example, management jobs can be greedy in various ways, perhaps especially in relation to time, but also in terms of space (through employers' assumptions of geographical mobility and willingness to take work home). The intensification of work has brought about long hours, with the UK being a particularly obvious example of this. Many workers are constantly 'on call'. Because of the persistence of traditional gender roles in the home (see below), women may be 'on call' from both the institutions of paid work and that of the family/household. For Guest (2002) the key developments in employment are the speed of communications, information load/overload, long hours including weekend and evening work, the pace of technical change, a focus on quality because of a need to ensure customer satisfaction in increasing competition, deadlines – and the implications of all of this for time and personal stress/pressure. It is essential that we add to all of this the reality that the role of paid work is only one of several roles that many women perform. We discuss this further in Chapter 7.

A further aspect of the 'new economy', discussed in Chapter 4, is that Europe-wide, there is a shift from jobs organized on a relatively permanent and full-time basis, towards casualized, less standard and insecure forms of employment, including part-time and temporary work (Plantenga 2004; Piore 2004). Further, service sector work in many countries including the UK has generally increased and employment in manufacturing and production has decreased over the past couple of decades. This restructuring of the economy has benefited women to the extent that much of the increase in jobs has been in areas traditionally dominated by women (Hibbett and Meager 2003). However, much of the growth has been in low-skill, low-status part-time work, meaning that for many women in the UK part-time work is less of a choice than the only available option (Purcell 2000).

In most industrialized countries, women's economic activity is clearly related to their parental status; motherhood affects the form that employment takes, as well as patterns of unemployment/labour market inactivity. In the UK this is not only an effect that takes place at the time of childbirth, but also at the time of children going to school (Brewer and Paull 2006). At its most obvious, there is a strong tendency for part-time working to be much more prevalent for mothers than for women who do not have children. However, this varies considerably between countries. For example, the effect of children on women's employment is much greater in the UK than in North America (Harkness and Waldfogel 1999). Particularly focusing on the long-term effects of women's employment patterns, Ginn *et al.* (2001) argue that in the UK it is the advent of motherhood which is the single factor most associated with women's poverty in old age. They conclude that those women with the best economic prospects in old age are in a child-free marriage. The category that is most likely to be economically disadvantaged in old age is that of single mothers.

In almost all countries, there has been an increase in formal childcare arrangements. On average around a quarter of children under three are in formal childcare in OECD countries, although there is a lot of variation between countries (OECD 2001). For children between three and the mandatory school age, formal childcare covers three-quarters of children, this time with rather little variation between countries. It appears that there is a rather universal cultural norm of formal childcare for children aged three and older, but considerably less so for younger children. This is an example of the lag referred to by Giele and Holst (2004). Societal institutions and cultural beliefs are at odds with the reality of life and employment patterns for women and families.

Changing households

Household types have undergone considerable change. Table 1.1 compares the evolution over ten years of four different types of two-parent families. We focus on the UK, but the US is included for comparative purposes.

Major social change is evident here. In the UK of the mid-1980s, only 7 per cent of couple families with a child under the age of six were of the dual breadwinner type, where both parents are in full-time employment (Type 1). By the end

Table 1.1 Trends in employment patterns in four family types, US and UK, 1984 and 1999, expressed as a percentage of two-parent families with a child under six years

	Two-parent household Type 1		Two-parent household Type 2		Two-parent household Type 3		Two-parent household Type 4	
	1984	1999	1984	1999	1984	1999	1984	1999
UK	7%	20%	23%	38%	55%	29%	13%	7%
US	26%	37%	16%	19%	44%	35%	5%	3%

Key: household types
1 Dual earners full-time
2 Male breadwinner full-time, woman part-time worker
3 Male breadwinner full-time, woman out of the labour force
4 Both out of the labour force
Source: OECD 2001, *Employment Outlook*, extracted from table 4.2, p. 135.

of the twentieth century, this figure had trebled. Marked increase has also taken place in households where there is a child under the age of six and where the man works full-time and the woman part-time, although this remains the most common type of household for couple families with a young child in the UK. The type of household that was the most common in post-war Britain where there was a young child – the traditional male breadwinner type, Household Type 3 – has halved. By 1999, this type of family was less common than Household Type 2.

This picture of two-adult families only tells a part of the story; it is obviously important to complete it by looking at one-parent families, again for the UK and the US. OECD provides data for three types of family where the parent is a woman with a child under six. Here there are three types of family: where the woman is 1) working full-time, 2) working part-time and 3) not in the labour force.

Again major social change is evident. In the UK the most common employment pattern for single mothers with a child under six years remains being out of

Table 1.2 Trends in employment patterns in three family types, US and UK, 1984 and 1999, expressed as a percentage of single mothers with a child under six years

	One-parent household Type 1		One-parent household Type 2		One-parent household Type 3	
	1984	1999	1984	1999	1984	1999
UK	6%	13%	13%	22%	81%	66%
US	34%	49%	10%	17%	56%	34%

Key
1 The woman is working full-time
2 The woman is working part-time
3 The woman is not in the labour force
Source: OECD 2001, *Employment Outlook*, extracted from table 4.2, p. 135.

the labour force (66 per cent), but this has reduced from a massive 81 per cent in 1984. There is a doubling of the proportion of such women who are in full-time working. We would not expect to see large amounts of part-time working in the United States, given the tax and social insurance system that militates against part-time working, but Table 1.2 shows that in the US just under half of single mothers are in full-time working. This is a major contrast from 1984, when most were out of the labour force.

Until recent times, many welfare regimes have made the assumption that caring work within the immediate and sometimes not-so-immediate family, sometimes referred to as 'familism' (Esping Andersen 1999), will be carried out by women, largely free of charge. If women are no longer able or willing to do such work because much of their time is increasingly taken up in paid work, substitute care will need to be found. This can come either from the market or from the state. Seen in the context of the ageing of the population, which increases the need for caring work, this conundrum has been the subject of considerable debate. Yet a return to 'familism' is likely to be wishful thinking. A response from the state and/or the market is therefore required, if unacceptable burdens are not to be put on women who are in paid work, in the context of the persistence of a traditional domestic division of labour.

A move towards the market?

The deregulation and market-led values of the 1980s onwards have taken hold in many European countries, perhaps especially the UK, and primarily but not exclusively within the private sector. At the same time many European Union countries experienced an increase in regulation in terms of social and employment policy, affecting both private and public sector employment. At the beginning of the twenty-first century, however, faced with low levels of productivity and an inability to compete with the US economy, there are signs of the European Union backing away from regulation. We may now be in a period of 'hands-off' governance: the European Commission (2005) says that the 'one size fits all approach' to social policy is no longer relevant; member states should develop their own 'best policy mix'. This is a clear message that the days of European Directives being handed down to member states in spirit *and* letter are disappearing. The liberal model of individualism, as exemplified by the UK and in a rather more extreme form by the US, may be on the reascendent. The European Commission argues that a generous – and therefore costly – social protection regime is increasingly seen as a barrier to economic growth and the achievement of high levels of employment (European Commission 2005). Workers should be adaptable and labour markets flexible: 'Adaptability is a key element of productivity and job creation; both employees and employers should be able to "anticipate, trigger and absorb change"' (European Commission 2005: 26).

So the EU appears to be gradually distancing itself from the more generous French and German social models towards a UK model of deregulation and reliance on the market – which is an attenuated form of US market-led individualism. This has implications, clearly, for women's employment, since it implies that some of the policies of recent decades that seek to ease the relationship between paid work and unpaid domestic commitments could lose political support. There has long been an undercurrent of resistance to many of these policies from some elements of the business community – and we may be seeing a swing towards these influential opinions.[2]

Policy-makers in western welfare states appear to be moving towards a new set of assumptions (Lewis and Giullari 2005). The 'full adult worker model' has three main characteristics: that citizens should be self-sufficient, self-provisioning and in employment. A consequence of this is that caring work is seen as less the responsibility of the state, and more a self-provisioning responsibility – located in the market and/or the family. If governments are assuming that individuals take care of themselves, and presumably those around them, there are major consequences for women, since care work is largely seen as their responsibility. This needs to be seen alongside the reality of very limited change in all industrialized countries in the domestic division of labour, as Chapter 7 explores and as we briefly discussed above. As Lewis and Giullari argue, an assumption of self-provisioning increases markedly the 'time squeeze', something that underlies almost all aspects of women's employment.

But this new climate does not imply a wholesale adoption of the market. The European Union's commitment to the moral arguments of equal opportunities for women and men remains visible: social partners (trade unions, employer organizations and government) should be committed to eliminating inequalities, particularly the gender pay gap (European Commission 2005: 24). The widespread and obdurate nature of the gender pay gap is the focus of Chapter 3. This issue, along with an 'opportunity gap', is a key aspect of the 2006 UK government's Women and Work Commission report, which we discuss in the concluding chapter. Furthermore, the European Commission General Framework for Equal Treatment and Occupation Directive, adopted by the UK government in October 2000, outlaws workplace discrimination on grounds of age, religion, disability and sexual orientation and requires the UK to have legislation in place by December 2006.

The European Union's attempt to hold together a dual polity involving both the moral arguments of equal opportunities and the bottom line of productivity/policy effectiveness is clearly evident here. Similarly the UK government's Equality Bill, expected to take effect in 2007, will introduce a gender equality duty for all public authorities in Great Britain; all public authorities will be legally bound to promote gender equality. This leaves open the question of how private sector employers deal with such issues. The 'diversity' approach, rather than one based on 'equality', may be seen by the private sector as the way forward, although many public sector organizations have also substituted diversity for equality, as Chapter 6 explores.

Demographic concerns

In most industrialized countries the birth rate is considerably below the level at which population replacement takes place (OECD 2001). At the same time, populations are ageing. This has created major concern in industrialized countries about a looming demographic crisis, where the working population is not large enough to support the non-working population.

There has been a tendency amongst women in the UK to delay having children (Dench *et al.* 2002) but this is most obvious amongst highly qualified women (Rendall *et al.* 2005). Fifty years ago in the US 75 per cent of women were mothers by age 25, compared to a current figure of 50 per cent (Gornick and Meyers 2003). Esping Andersen *et al.* (2002) have argued that the only logical policy solution is a considerable increase by governments in their investment in services for children. The implication here is that if they receive such support, women will have more children. The link between government subsidy of childcare, either directly or through the tax system, and the level of women's labour force participation is unclear. In the Nordic countries this does seem to be the case, but a counter-example is the United States, which shows high levels of female participation, largely full-time, but with minimal public subsidy of childcare. The relationship is undoubtedly more complex than policy-makers may assume. For example, as Duncan and Edwards (1999) point out, individual and collective 'moral rationalities' – behaviour that is underpinned by a view of what is morally 'right' – vary between social groups. Pfau-Effinger (2005) makes the same point about different countries.

The decline in the fertility rate has come about at the same time as an increase in the rate of women's employment, although the nature of the causality is unclear. A decline in the fertility rate may have been caused by a complex range of factors, including better contraception, a rise in the cost of living, women's increasing political and financial independence, their increased education and governments' encouragement of women's entry to the labour force. It seems simplistic to argue that an increase in women's employment has caused a decline in the fertility rate. A counter-example is that in the Nordic countries, with their high labour force participation rate of women, the fertility rate shows some evidence of a slight increase (OECD 2001). We could tentatively conclude that the gender regime in the Nordic countries allows women to undertake paid work without major consequences for either their own employment prospects or the welfare of their families. This would reinforce the conclusion that state investment in caring for children is the only way to ensure that an increasingly large labour force with a high presence of women does not bring about perverse effects on social inclusion and specifically the welfare of children (Esping Andersen *et al.* 2002). Nevertheless, policies do not necessarily bring about social change; if the 'moral rationalities' of citizens (see Duncan and Edwards 1999) militate against particular forms of behaviour, policies will not bring about their desired outcomes. Dex (2003) argues that there are barriers to extending formal childcare provision, not least that parents want to see their children. This implies that the long-hours culture that is particularly obvious in countries such as the UK and the US would need to change.

Convergence, divergence and polarization

There is strong evidence of women's position in the labour market converging across EU states (Rubery *et al.* 1998; OECD 2001: Table 4.1). Countries where women's employment rate has been low are catching up quite rapidly with those with a higher employment rate. The convergence of women's labour force participation rates, argue Rubery *et al.*, is largely due to the growth of female dominated employment sectors. However, it does not follow that a trend towards convergence across countries leads to the desegregation of the labour market or that gender equality is being achieved. There is some evidence of an increase in women's concentration in particular sectors and occupations – and in a growing number of part-time jobs. However, there is conflicting evidence about whether occupational sex segregation is increasing or decreasing. There is also debate about whether sex segregation necessarily matters in terms of women's employment prospects. Chapter 2 covers these issues.

Some other aspects of the labour market suggest convergence between women and men (Rubery *et al.* 1998). An increasing (although still markedly small) proportion of men is found in part-time jobs; there is an increasing proportion of working-age men who are out of the labour market and combined with the increasing tendency for women to be in the labour market, this has decreased the gap between women's and men's labour force participation; women are less likely to exit to have children. Also, interestingly, a convergence in women's and men's employment patterns at the beginning and end of employment has been observed (Rubery *et al.* 1998). On entry to the labour market, men's employment behaviour is often rather like women's – both accept in more or less equal measures part-time and temporary jobs; these possibly act as bridges into full-time work. After statutory retirement age men are participating more in gender-atypical work. But between these two age-related extremes, women's and men's employment patterns remain by and large distinct, as indicated in the UK by women's propensity for part-time work discussed in Chapter 4. Thus, it is important to examine employment participation by age, insofar as available data allow for this.

Increasingly there appears to be polarization between those women who have educational, social and cultural capital, and those women who do not. In the UK, women's social class background clearly patterned their labour force participation in the first half of the twentieth century, but its effect is thought to have lessened from the 1950s onwards (Lewis 1997). However, there is evidence of a growing polarization in industrialized countries between women with different levels of education and therefore between many younger and older women (Glover and Arber 1995; Burchell *et al.* 1997; Blau and Ehrenburg 1997; McRae 2003). This polarization is at its most obvious when pay is examined; there are increasingly clusters of highly paid women and low-paid women. In the UK, those with high levels of qualification are much less likely to work part-time and are considerably more likely to have uninterrupted employment (Burchell *et al.* 1997). Because of high levels of education, women have started to challenge men for entry into more prestigious occupations. Thus this is a major change from the post-war scenario, as discussed in Chapter 5. On a global scale, polarization – this time between North and South – can be seen even more starkly, with the conditions brought about by globalization having negative effects on women in the South (Koggel 2003).

Women's economic insecurity in old age

Women are the main victims of poverty in old age in many industrialized societies (Ginn *et al.* 2001). Yet those welfare regimes that have traditionally provided relatively generous social protection (such as the Nordic countries) are increasingly seen in European policy terms as unsustainable. The liberal model of welfare is increasingly encouraging citizens to protect themselves in old age, but this marketized approach to pensions is not to the advantage of women. This is particularly obvious in the US (Street and Wilmoth 2001) as well as the UK. Women are particularly vulnerable to a pension shortfall (Ginn *et al.* 2001) and this is even greater for black and minority ethnic women (Fawcett Society 2005). One cause is women's longevity: on average women live longer than men and this makes them particularly vulnerable, since they are spending fewer years in the labour market than men. Another is that women are less likely to be in paid employment than men, particularly at certain times of their lives. Furthermore, they are more likely to work part-time and/or in low-paid occupations and thus they have lower lifetime earnings than men (Falkingham and Rake 2001). Just 2 per cent of 21- to 45-year-old women are saving for their old age (Rake and Jayatilaka 2002). Low-earning women are particularly unlikely to have a final say in a couple's financial decisions, yet policy-makers assume that households share money fairly (Falkingham and Rake 2001). Despite the fact that in the European Union, part-time workers can no longer be excluded from occupational pension schemes, many part-time workers do not belong to occupational pension schemes (Ginn *et al.* 2001).

Focusing on occupational pension schemes in the UK, Gough (2001) argues that these are founded on an assumption of long-term service with one employer together with a high salary prior to retirement. This is the traditional male model of employment. Because women have lower lifetime earnings than their male counterparts and because they tend to have interrupted employment patterns, the premise underpinning occupational pension schemes works against them. In addition, because they tend to live longer than men, their lower starting pension is gradually reduced in real terms by the effects of inflation. Thus, Gough concludes that the inequalities of the workplace are projected into old age through the mechanism of the occupational pension scheme. It is important to remember, nevertheless, that many fewer women than men have access to occupational pension schemes because of the nature of their employment. There is also evidence that women do not take advantage of occupational pension schemes in the same way as men.

Gough (2001) argues that schemes should be more flexible to allow for women to take employment breaks without incurring major financial penalties in old age. There is some evidence in the UK that a rethink is happening in relation to the state pension, in recognition of older women's poverty. The Blair government is considering the introduction of a pension based on residence rather than employment-related contributions (*The Guardian*, 29 January 2005). Thus it is recognizing that a system based on national insurance contributions is heavily weighted against those who are not in employment because of their caring roles and those without continuous full-time employment, both groups in which women figure prominently.

The discovery of the likelihood of poverty in old age appears to be something which comes as a surprise to many women, as Peggs (2000) shows. This raises the question of whether employers have a role to play here in pointing this out to women through encouraging them to join pension schemes as Gough (2001) advocates; or whether there is an assumption amongst employers that long-term issues such as this should be left to individuals, or indeed to politicians.

Employment-supporting policy: flexibility

Flexibility – defined in this book mainly as time flexibility – covers a range of policies that seek to address the 'time squeeze'. Many industrialized countries have seen an increase in flexible working policies aimed at and mainly taken up by women.

Specifically, entitlement to maternity and childcare leave has increased in almost all countries; in many OECD countries, the maximum leave exceeds one year (OECD 2001). However, there are large variations between countries both in terms of how long the benefits last and also about whether the leave is paid or not. There has been an increase in many countries in the entitlement for fathers, but generally the take-up rate is low, except where there is full earnings replacement, as sometimes happens in public sector employment. A family-friendly work environment – defined as measures that complement statutory requirements – is more likely to exist in large firms and where the employees have high skill levels, and it is also more prevalent in the public sector (OECD 2001).

Flexibility in time use may not bring higher benefits to the individual worker or guarantee gender equality. One theme that emerges at various points in this book is whether 'employment-supporting policies' that seek to ease the relationship between paid work and unpaid domestic work (so-called 'work–life balance' policies) can mark women out as in need of special help and in the long run be against their interests. This would happen if policies that are framed as ostensibly gender neutral (i.e. aimed at a general category of parents) are in reality only taken up by women. Flexible working policies have the potential to reduce the stress of individual employees and therefore improve their quality of life in the short term, but may bring about little change in organizational culture (Lewis 1997). The main form of flexible working is part-time working and this is a form of working that has not provided the same opportunities as full-time working, with major long-term consequences in the form of poverty in old age. Such forms of working are, however, popular with many women (Dex 2003). Thus, the issue is how to balance short-term gains in terms of quality of life with likely long-term disadvantages in terms of economic security. These disadvantages do not only impact upon individuals and households; they also have financial implications for the state because of its role of ensuring that poverty does not reach unacceptable standards (Himmelweit 2002).

A further possible negative aspect of 'work–life balance' policies is that employers may hesitate to hire or promote women since they might believe that a long period of training and acquisition of firm-specific human capital may be wasted if some women decide to 'choose' a family career over a work one. This view reflects Hakim's (2000) argument in favour of different employer policies for different groups of women, even involving different career tracks for those who are family-centred and those who are work-centred. Of course these views, if made explicit, would be discriminatory and thus liable to fall foul of legislation. In the post-equal opportunities legislation era, such views may have gone underground – but they are likely to still exist (see Collinson *et al.* 1990) and thus, ironically, may be more difficult to detect than prior to the legislation.

There is broad agreement in industrialized countries in Europe on what constitutes women-friendly policy: affordable childcare, paid maternity and parental leave, provision for absence when children are ill, and the ability to work school hours (Esping Andersen *et al.* 2002). There is sometimes a tendency for politicians to focus on childcare, probably because there are clear policy instruments available, unlike the drivers of cultural change. Ken Livingstone, Mayor of London, focuses particularly on a lack of high-quality affordable childcare, arguing that this is acting as a serious brake on the London economy, since in his view it is preventing women from returning to the workforce (Greater London Authority 2005). Kingsmill (2001), in a report commissioned by the UK Department for Trade and Industry (DTI), recommended a more comprehensive 'optimal conditions environment' for employees. The conditions referred to here are paid paternity leave, extended maternity leave, paid adoption leave, crèche facilities, various flexible working arrangements and a career break scheme. Human resource management was singled out in this report as particularly important because of its role of conducting internal audits and reviews to monitor this environment.

It follows logically that at times of scarcity of skilled labour, employers will find some means of retaining highly qualified women, such as flexible working policies. But policies that are based on labour shortages may only be favoured when there are shortages of highly skilled labour; they may be less prevalent when highly skilled labour is not in short supply (McGlynn 2003). The implication of McGlynn's argument is that so-called 'work–life balance policies' need to be based on the moral arguments of equal opportunities, as well as the 'bottom line'

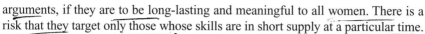

arguments, if they are to be long-lasting and meaningful to all women. There is a risk that they target only those whose skills are in short supply at a particular time.

However, in practice, despite all the rhetoric in the UK about flexibility being good for business, in 2004 75 per cent of women and 85 per cent of men did not have access to flexible working patterns such as flexitime, term-time working and job-sharing (WEU 2004) that would open up more genuine choices for parents, both women and men, about how to balance the need to earn with the need/wish to care for children.

Organizational and trade union responses to the changing landscape

While some of the policies designed to increase and improve women's earnings and employment prospects are clearly located at the level of the state, it is the case that other actors in the employment relationship – namely, employers and trade unions – also have a role to play. In the UK employing organizations have traditionally attempted to guarantee women's equality under the auspices of 'equal opportunities' (EO) policies. Most organizational EO policies were compliant with the Sex Discrimination Act (1975) and Equal Pay Act (1970) and claimed to eliminate discrimination and unfair treatment on the basis of sex. Some organizations, particularly in the public sector, sought to go further than the rather minimalist legal requirements and actually promote women's equality by implementing a range of 'family-friendly' initiatives and developing specific policies to prevent and protect women against sexual harassment. Others went further still and developed 'positive action' initiatives, such as training programmes to increase women's representation in management or in particular occupations/professions (Kirton and Greene 2005).

Policy action was justified on grounds of a combination of legal necessity, business benefits and social justice. The popularity of EO policies, especially the more proactive kind, was arguably always greatest with public sector and a minority of large private sector employers. But during the 1990s against the changing political, economic and social context described above, EO policies began to fall out of favour among employing organizations and there was a turn towards 'diversity management'. Diversity management makes a specific appeal to business, claiming that increasing and valuing workforce diversity can enhance organizational performance. In policy terms, it is unclear what diversity management means, although many of the elements of traditional EO policies seem also to be contained within diversity policies. Nevertheless, critics have argued (e.g. Kirton and Greene 2006) that diversity management might signal a retreat from a commitment to social justice and that a more prominent focus on business need might be detrimental to the gender equality project. The orientation of policy-making and what it means is discussed in detail in Chapter 6.

With regard to the role of trade unions in pursuing a gender equality agenda generally and more specifically in tackling some of the policy issues discussed here, membership has been falling across much of the industrialized world, so that unions often find themselves marginalized in the organizational policy-making process and the wider polity. It is only relatively recently that British unions have addressed women's equality in a concerted and reasonably coherent manner. Most large unions are now seeking to attract women members and in some cases it is women who are holding up membership levels, while male membership declines. The changed political, economic and social context has meant that many unions have developed policies on issues such as 'work–life balance' and part-time working that they had previously neglected. It is argued that the presence of a Labour government, combined with the promotion at European Union level of joint engagement – labour–management cooperation – have created a more hospitable context for equality bargaining in the UK (Colling and Dickens 2001). It falls to unions to take advantage of this by ensuring that their internal structures and institutions provide strong support for women's equality. Certainly, many unions have redressed the previously under-represented nature of leadership within their own ranks and trade union women are now articulating their demands (Healy and Kirton 2000). The obstacles and opportunities facing trade unions in relation to pursuing a gender equality agenda are discussed in Chapter 8.

Women's decision-making: choice or constraint?

A major debate over the past decade or so in the study of women's employment has centred around so-called 'preference theory'. Women, says Hakim (1996), can be divided up into those who prioritize their domestic work and those who prioritize their paid work. Occupational segregation has developed because some lower status and lower paid jobs allow for the 'marriage career'. This is why, claims Hakim, female-dominated occupations have a lot of part-time work, not much in the way of unsocial hours, a lack of resistance to insecurity and low rates of trade union membership. Hakim proposes three qualitatively different types of women, each of which demonstrates a preference for a different type of work–life balance: home-centred (20 per cent of women), adaptive (60 per cent of women)[3] and work-centred (20 per cent). She also says that whilst most women prefer some sort of work–life balance, most men are work-centred. Her estimates of the variation of work–life preferences amongst men are 10 per cent home-centred, 30 per cent adaptive and 60 per cent work-centred.

Considerable opposition has been sparked off by these views. Hakim's work, say Sommerlad and Sanderson (1998) has given academic respectability to some employers' perspectives on women's lack of commitment. Others have taken issue with Hakim because of the unproblematic way in which Hakim uses the concept of 'choice', since she implies that women are free to choose between these two roles (see for example Ginn et al. 1996, McRae 2003, Procter and Padfield 1999). At the very least we should be talking about a concept of constrained choice, thereby acknowledging the complexity of decision-making about employment

(Devine 1994). For example, the aim of retaining a perceived balance between paid and unpaid work could be one of the factors that intervenes in women's decision-making when they are considering employment changes that involve increases in time spent on paid work, as well as spatial changes (Glover 2002). In many ways, this can be seen as a 'rational choice', but not in the sense that the term is used by neo-classical economists. The term 'rational' should be reclaimed, argues Nelson (1993), so that it describes the complexity of the context within which women take decisions. These ideas are explored further in Chapter 7 and Chapter 5.

Winners and losers?

The changes surrounding women's greater employment participation have brought about what could be seen as winners and losers. On the positive side, white, highly qualified (probably child-free) women who are willing and able to meet the expectations of the male norm of full-time, continuous employment and of privileging work over home and family, appear to be winning to some extent. These women have increased their share of managerial and professional work and seem to be breaking through the 'glass ceiling'. However, their relative success carries a social and personal price. As their employment position improves, the gendered competition for jobs intensifies and this could provoke a white male backlash that organizations may respond to by taking a more cautious approach to initiatives to enhance women's position. Further, black and minority ethnic women often perceive a 'concrete ceiling' or 'concrete walls' as standing in their way (Bell and Nkomo 2001). Thus the picture for highly qualified black and minority ethnic women looks less positive.

Professional and managerial women's relatively high pay enables them to buy in substitute care and household labour. This substitute domestic labour is usually provided by less well qualified, often minority ethnic women who can command only low pay and poor conditions (Hochschild 2001). In addition, the equality policies that have assisted highly qualified women's advancement in the workplace usually have little to offer lower skilled women. It could also be argued that the social and economic polarization of women has become an issue obscured by contemporary gender-neutral discourses such as 'work–life balance'. The effects of poorly paid, low-hours jobs on women's long-term financial security are particularly serious, with consequences for individuals, households and the welfare state.

The arithmetic of many families has clearly changed since the mid-twentieth century (Moen 2003). Moen's argument is that prior to this time, families were often composed of two adults with one work career and one family career. In recent times, two-adult families are more likely to contain three jobs – two work careers plus one family career. Marx argued that the health and welfare of the (male) workforce was sustained by the efforts of wives and mothers. In what could be seen as a modern version of this, Jones (2004) argues that employers can no longer expect a 'two for the price of one' offer. By employing one person (usually a man), employers were in the past able to get another person (a wife and often a mother) free. She would do the domestic work that freed men up to spend long hours in paid work. Since women, many of whom will be mothers, are forecast to make up 80 per cent of the workforce growth to 2010, this position is no longer sustainable. These changes have many implications for employment policy-making at the level of the state and organizations and these are discussed in more detail in the chapters that follow.

Notes

1   Despite many similarities in terms of approaches to social policy in the Nordic countries, there are differences between these countries. Policies that impinge upon women's employment in the Norwegian welfare state are different from the Danish and Finnish welfare states because in Norway the family is much more strongly supported as a provider of social care (Leira 1998; Pfau-Effinger 2005). Family policies in Norway are founded on the dual breadwinner/dual carer model, argues Pfau-Effinger, and on the dual breadwinner/state carer family model in Denmark and Finland.
2   The Confederation of British Industry, which is one of the main bodies in the UK representing employers, has voiced its opposition to the Blair administration's wish to extend parental leave, on the grounds of administrative burdens. The Federation of Small Businesses talks of an 'administrative nightmare' and the costs of finding and replacing staff on parental leave (*The Guardian*, 24 December 2005).
3   A further criticism of Hakim's typology is that her category of 'adaptive' women is too large (Nolan 2005; MacRae 2003). For such a category to be of analytical use it needs to be broken down into further categories that shed more light on whether women regard paid work or domestic commitments as central.

References

Anderson, M., Bechhofer, F. and Gershuny, J. (eds) (1994) *The Social and Political Economy of the Household*, Oxford: Oxford University Press.

Bell, E. and Nkomo, S. (2001) *Our Separate Ways: Black and White Women and the Struggle for Professional Identity*, Boston, MA: Harvard Business School Press.

Bianchi, S. and Mattingly, M. (2004) 'Time, work and family in the United States', in J. Giele and E. Holst (eds) *Changing Life Patterns in Western Industrial Societies*, Oxford: Elsevier, 95–118.

Blau, F. and Ehrenberg, R. (eds) (1997) *Gender and Family Issues in the Workplace*, New York: Russell Sage.

Blossfeld, H.-P. (1997) 'Women's part-time employment and the family cycle: a cross-national comparison', in H.-P. Blossfeld and C. Hakim (eds) *Between Equalization and Marginalization*, Oxford: Oxford University Press, 315–24.

Brewer, M. and Paull, G. (2006) *Newborns and New Schools: Critical Times in Women's Employment*, London: Institute for Fiscal Studies on behalf of the Department for Work and Pensions.

Burchell, B., Dale, A. and Joshi, H. (1997) 'Part-time work among British women', in H.-P. Blossfeld and C. Hakim (eds) *Between Equalization and Marginalization*, Oxford: Oxford University Press, 210–46.

Colling, T. and Dickens, L. (2001) 'Gender equality and trade unions: a new basis for mobilization?' in M. Noon and E. Ogbonna (eds) *Equality, Diversity and Disadvantage in Employment*, Basingstoke: Palgrave.

Collinson, D., Knights, D. and Collinson, M. (1990) *Managing to Discriminate,* London: Routledge.

Coser, L. (1974) *Greedy Institutions: Patterns of Undivided Commitment*, New York: Free Press.

Crompton, R., Dennett, J. and Wigfield, A. (2003) *Organizations, Careers and Caring*, Bristol: Policy Press and Joseph Rowntree Foundation.

Dench, S., Aston, J., Evans, C., Meager, N., Williams, M. and Willison, R. (2002) 'Key indicators of women's position in Britain', London: DTI Women and Equality Unit.

Devine, F. (1994) 'Segregation and supply: preferences and plans among "self-made" women', *Gender, Work and Organization*, 1 (2): 178–94.

Dex, S. (2003) 'Families and work in the twenty-first century', Bristol: Policy Press and Joseph Rowntree Foundation.

Duncan, S. and Edwards, R. (1999) *Lone Mothers, Paid Work and Gendered Moral Rationalities*, Basingstoke: Macmillan.

EOC (2003) *75 Years on: Equality for Women and Men Today?* Manchester: Equal Opportunities Commission.

Epstein, C. F., Seron, C., Oglensky, B. and Saute, R. (1998) *The Part-time Paradox: Time Norms, Professional Lives, Family, and Gender*, London: Routledge.

Esping Andersen, G. (1999) *Social Foundations of Postindustrial Economics*, Oxford: Oxford University Press.

Esping Andersen, G., Gallie, D., Hemerijck, A. and Myles, J. (2002) *Why We Need a New Welfare State*, Oxford: Oxford University Press.

European Commission (2005) *Growth and Jobs: Working Together for Europe's Future*, Brussels: European Commission.

Falkingham, J. and Rake, K. (2001) 'Modelling the gender impact of British pension reforms', in J. Ginn, D. Street and S. Arber (eds) *Women, Work and Pensions*, Buckingham: Open University Press, 67–85.

Fawcett Society (2005) *Black and Ethnic Minority Women in the UK*, London: Fawcett Society.

Fisher, K. and Layte, R. (2002) *Measuring Work–Life Balance and Degrees of Sociability: A Focus on the Value of Time Use Data in the Assessment of Quality of Life*, Colchester: University of Essex.

Garcia, B., Anker, R. and Pinnelli, A. (eds) (2003) *Women in the Labour Market in Changing Economies: Demographic Issues*, Oxford: Oxford University Press.

Garey, A. (1999) *Weaving Work and Motherhood*, Philadelphia: Temple University Press.

Gershuny, J. (2000) *Changing Times: Work and Leisure in Postindustrial Society*, Oxford: Oxford University Press.

Giele, J. and Holst, E. (2004) 'New life patterns and changing gender roles', in J. Giele and E. Holst (eds) *Changing Life Patterns in Western Industrial Societies*, Oxford: Elsevier, 3–22.

Ginn, J., Street, D. and Arber, S. (eds) (2001) *Women, Work and Pensions*, Buckingham: Open University Press.

Ginn, J., Arber, S., Brannen, J., Dale, A., Dex, S., Elias, P., Moss, P., Pahl, J., Roberts, C., Rubery, J. and Walby, S. (1996) 'Feminist fallacies? A reply to Hakim on women's employment', *British Journal of Sociology*, 47 (1): 167–74.

Glover, J. (2002) 'The "balance model": theorising women's employment behaviour', in A. Carling, S. Duncan and R. Edwards (eds) *Analysing Families*, London: Routledge, 251–67.

Glover, J. and Arber, S. (1995) 'Polarization in mothers' employment', *Gender, Work and Organization*, 2 (4): 165–79.

Gornick, J. and Meyers, M. (2003) *Families That Work: Policies for Reconciling Parenthood and Employment*, New York: Russell Sage Foundation.

Gough, O. (2001) 'The impact of the gender pay gap on post-retirement earnings', *Critical Social Policy*, 21 (3): 311–34.

Grant, L., Yeandle, S. and Buckner, L. (2005) *Working Below Potential: Women and Part-time Work*, Manchester: Equal Opportunities Commission.

Greater London Authority (2005) *Women in London's Economy*, London: Greater London Authority.

Green, F. (2001) 'It's been a hard day's night: the concentration and intensification of work in late twentieth-century Britain', *British Journal of Industrial Relations*, 39 (1): 53–80.

Grimshaw, D. and Rubery, J. (2001) *The Gender Pay Gap: A Research Review*, Manchester: Equal Opportunities Commission.

Guest, D. (2002) 'Perspectives on the study of work–life balance', *Social Science Information*, 41 (2): 255–79.

Hakim, C. (1996) *Key Issues in Women's Work*, London: Athlone Press.

Hakim, C. (2000) *Work–Lifestyle Choices in the 21st Century: Preference Theory*, Oxford: Oxford University Press.

Harkness, S. (2002) *Low Pay, Times of Work and Gender*, Manchester: Equal Opportunities Commission.

Harkness, S. and Waldfogel, J. (1999) *The Family Gap in Pay: Evidence from Seven Industrialized Countries*, London: Centre for Analysis of Social Exclusion.

Healy, G. and Kirton, G. (2000) 'Women, power and trade union government in the UK', *British Journal of Industrial Relations*, 38 (3): 343–60.

Hibbett, A. and Meager, N. (2003) 'Key indicators of women's position in Britain', *Labour Market Trends*, October, 503–11.

Himmelweit, S. (2002) 'Making visible the hidden economy: the case for gender-impact analysis of economic policy', *Feminist Economics*, 8 (1): 49–70.

Hochschild, A. (1989) *The Second Shift*, Harmondsworth: Viking Penguin.

Hochschild, A. (2001) *The Time Bind: When Work Becomes Home and Home Becomes Work*, New York: Henry Holt.

Holdsworth, C. and Dale, A. (1997) 'Ethnic differences in women's employment', *Work, Employment and Society*, 11 (3): 435–57.

Jones, A. (2004). *Work–Life Diversity: Rising to New Challenges*, paper presented at the Department for Trade and Industry Employment Relations Seminar Series, London.

Kingsmill, D. (2001). *Kingsmill Review of Women's Pay and Employment*, London: Stationery Office.

Kirton, G. and Greene, A. M. (2005) *The Dynamics of Managing Diversity* (2nd edn), Oxford: Elsevier.

Kirton, G. and Greene, A. M. (2006 forthcoming) 'The discourse of diversity in unionized contexts: views from trade union equality officers', *Personnel Review.*

Koggel, C. (2003) 'Globalization and women's paid work: expanding freedom?' *Feminist Economics*, 9 (2–3): 163–83.

Leira, A. (1998) 'The modernization of motherhood', in E. Drew, R. Emerek and E. Mahon (eds) *Women, Work and Family in Europe*, London: Routledge, 159–69.

Lewis, J. (1984) *Women in England 1870–1950: Sexual Divisions and Social Change*, London and New York: Harvester/Wheatsheaf.

Lewis, J. and Giullari, S. (2005) 'The adult worker model family, gender inequality and care: the search for new policy principles and the possibilities and problems of the capabilities approach', *Economy and Society*, 34 (1): 76–104.

Lewis, S. (1997) '"Family friendly" employment policies: a route to changing organizational culture or playing about at the margins?', *Gender, Work and Organization*, 4 (1): 13–23.

McGlynn, C. (2003) 'The status of women lawyers in the United Kingdom', in U. Schultz and G. Shaw (eds) *Women in the World's Legal Professions*, Oxford and Portland, OR: Hart Publishing, 139–56.

McRae, S. (2003) 'Constraints and choices in mothers' employment careers: a consideration of Hakim's preference theory', *British Journal of Sociology*, 54 (4): 317–38.

Moen, P. (2003) *It's About Time: Couples and Careers*, Ithaca, NY: IRL Press.

Nelson, J. (1993) 'The study of choice or the study of provisioning? Gender and the definition of economics', in M. Ferber and J. Nelson (eds) *Beyond Economic Man*, Chicago: University of Chicago Press.

Nolan, J. (2005) *Job Insecurity, Gender and Work Orientation: An Exploratory Study of Breadwinning and Caregiving identity: GeNet Working Paper 2005/6*, ESRC Gender Equality Network.

OECD (2001) *Employment Outlook*, Paris: OECD.

OECD (2002) *Employment Outlook*, Paris: OECD.

ONS (Office for National Statistics) (2004) *UK 2004*, London: TSO.

Peggs, K. (2000) 'Which pension? Women, risk and pension choice', *Sociological Review*, 48 (3): 349–64.

Pfau-Effinger, B. (2005) 'Culture and welfare state policies: reflections on a complex interrelation', *Journal of Social Policy*, 34 (1): 3–20.

Pilcher, J. (2000) 'Domestic divisions of labour in the twentieth century: "change slow a-coming"', *Work, Employment and Society*, 14 (4): 771–80.

Piore, M. (2004) 'The reconfiguration of work and employment relations in the United States', in J. Giele and E. Holst (eds) *Changing Life Patterns in Western Industrial Societies*, Oxford: Elsevier, 23–44.

Plantenga, J. (2004) 'Changing work and life patterns: examples of new working–time arrangements in the European member states', in J. Giele and E. Holst (eds) *Changing Life Patterns in Western Industrial Societies*, Oxford: Elsevier, 119–35.

Procter, I. and Padfield, M. (1999) 'Work orientations and women's work: a critique of Hakim's theory of the heterogeneity of women', *Gender, Work and Organization*, 6 (3): 152–62.

Purcell, K. (2000) 'Gendered employment insecurity?' in E. Heery and J. Salman, (eds) *The Insecure Workforce*, London: Routledge, 112–39.

Rake, K. and Jayatilaka, G. (2002) *Home Truths: An Analysis of Financial Decision Making Within the Home*, London: Fawcett Society.

Rendall, M., Couet, C., Lappegard, T., Robert-Bobée, I., Rensen, M. and Smallwood, S. (2005) 'First births by age and education in Britain, France and Norway', *Population Trends*, 121 (Autumn): 27–34.

Rubery, J., Smith, M., Fagan, C. and Grimshaw, D. (1998) *Women and European Employment*, London: Routledge.

Sen, A. (1999) *Development as Freedom*, New York: Anchor Books.

Sommerlad, H. and Sanderson, P. (1998) *Gender, Choice and Commitment: Women solicitors in England and Wales and the Struggle for Equal Status*, Aldershot: Ashgate.

Street, D. and Wilmoth, J. (2001) 'Social insecurity? Women and pensions in the US', in J. Ginn, D. Street and S. Arber (eds) *Women, Work and Pensions*, Buckingham: Open University Press, 120–41.

Sullivan, O. (2000) 'The division of domestic labour', *Sociology*, 34 (3): 437–56.

Summerfield, P. (1984) *Women Workers in the Second World War: Production and Patriarchy in Conflict*, London: Croom Helm.

Walby, S. and Olsen, W. (2002) *The Impact of Women's Position in the Labour Market on Pay and Implications for UK Productivity*, Report to Women and Equality Unit. London: Department of Trade and Industry.

WEU (2004) *Interim Update of Key Indicators of Women's Position in Britain*, London: Women and Equality Unit.

Chapter 2

Gender segregation

Introduction

Scholars around the globe debate the significance of gender segregation for the continuance of economic indicators of women's inequality, such as the gender pay gap and lower pension entitlements. Women's labour market participation has increased considerably in the post-war period, particularly that of married women and mothers, such that the gender gap in employment rates has narrowed in many contexts. In Britain, for example, 70 per cent of women are now economically active (that is either in employment or actively seeking work), compared with 83 per cent of men (EOC 2005). In 1951, 26 per cent of women were economically active (Walby 1997). Women's activity rate in Britain now appears to have plateaued – there has been only a 3 per cent increase in the past 15 years (Hibbett and Meager 2003). Women are concentrated in a limited range of occupations and industries, in the public sector, in small private sector firms and in particular modes of employment such as part-time work (Fagan and Burchell 2002). Gender segregation can be examined along a number of possible dimensions including industry, sector and occupation. This chapter focuses on occupational sex segregation, but touches on other dimensions for the purposes of contextualization and illustration.

Industrial segregation

Analysing gender segregation by industry is a useful way of obtaining an overview within different national contexts. Table 2.1 presents women's employment by broad industrial category in the 15 countries that were members of the European Union prior to May 2004 (EU15). The broad European patterns are largely replicated in Britain (EOC 2005). Women fill most of the jobs in four categories that rely heavily on the use of part-time workers. Therefore industrial gender segregation is closely associated with part-time work. Over half of all employed women work in just two categories – sales, hotels and catering, and health and education (Fagan and Burchell 2002). Thus any changes in labour market and employment conditions in these two industries impact particularly on women. Women's concentration in a small number of industries leaves them potentially vulnerable when economic change occurs (e.g. industrial downturns; public sector cutbacks).

Sectoral gender segregation

It is also particularly notable that 32 per cent of women compared with 19 per cent of men in Europe are employed in the public sector (Fagan and Burchell 2002). In Britain in 2005, 36 per cent of employed women were in the public sector, compared to 25 per cent of men; this is an increase from 1998 when the equivalent figures were 32 and 19 per cent (authors' calculations from ASHE 2005). Therefore the state has a significant influence on women's working conditions and women are particularly vulnerable to public sector cutbacks. In the US women are also concentrated in the public sector (OECD 2001) and a similar picture exists in the Nordic countries (Anker 1998). This has been typically cited as an important contributory factor in explaining women's economic inequalities, since public sector pay is typically lower than in the private sector. However, very recent figures from the UK show that women's pay in the public sector is on average higher than in the private sector (ASHE 2005). In Sweden, however, Gornick and Jacobs (1998) estimate that the gender pay gap is increased by about 10 per cent by the combined effects of women's over-representation in the public sector and the low wages of the public sector.

There is evidence of a race and ethnic dimension to sectoral gender segregation. Black Caribbean women are over-represented in public health and education services compared to white women's over-representation in the private services sector where the growth has been mainly in part-time jobs, a more common form of working for white women (TUC 2002). At a European level women migrants are prominent in several of the so-called '3D' jobs – dirty, degrading and dangerous – in sectors including domestic work, textiles, hotels and catering, and agriculture (Kofman 2003).

Table 2.1 Women's employment by industry in the EU15, 2002

Sector	% Women
Health and social work and education	75
Sales, hotels and catering	53
Other community, social and personal service activities	56
Financial intermediation	42
Public administration and defence; compulsory social security	44
Manufacturing	27
Transport, storage and communications	25
Utilities	16
Agriculture, hunting, forestry and fishing	34
Construction	9
Extraction	16
Private households	95

Source: adapted from Fagan and Burchell (2002).

As interesting as it is to examine gender segregation at the industry/sector level, doing so cannot reveal the *type* of jobs that women hold. To do this, we need to look at gender segregation at the occupational level.

Occupational segregation

The tendency for women and men to work in different occupations is 'extensive in every region, at all economic development levels, in all political systems and in diverse religious, social and cultural environments' (Anker 1998: 403). While there have been significant increases in the proportion of women in higher level jobs, horizontal occupational sex segregation (discussed below) is one of the most enduring features of the US and European labour markets (Reskin and Hartmann 1986; Gonas 2004). For example, in Britain nearly half of all employed women work in three typically low-paid occupational groups that are at least two-thirds female (personal service; administrative and secretarial; sales and customer service) (EOC 2005).

Occupational segregation is conventionally considered to have two dimensions: horizontal and vertical (Hakim 1979). Horizontal segregation is the tendency for women and men to be concentrated in different occupations. Female dominated and male dominated occupations are the result. Vertical segregation is the tendency for women and men to be concentrated in different jobs within occupations, with advantage running from low to high. Vertical segregation is argued to refer to the element of gender inequality in segregation, while horizontal segregation refers to difference without making a statement about inequality (Blackburn and Jarman 2005).

Some occupations that do not appear to be gender segregated can nevertheless be internally segregated (Crompton and Harris 1998). Clear examples here are medicine and law (Epstein *et al.* 1998; Riska 2001; Schultz and Shaw 2003). We discuss this issue further in Chapter 5.

There is general agreement that the more detailed the job categories, the more occupational segregation is revealed (Baron and Bielby 1986; Anker 2000; Robinson *et al.* 2005). This is a major issue which must cast considerable doubt on how confident we can be about attempts to measure the phenomenon. The problem can be illustrated as follows: at the least level of detail an occupational classification will show that women are reasonably well represented among professionals. However, investigation using more detailed data will typically show that most women professionals are either teachers or located in the medical, dental and veterinary occupations. Further segregation is revealed with even more detailed data, since most women medical, dental and veterinary workers are nurses, and the majority of women teachers are in the pre-primary and primary school sectors. In the US, in 2004 women held half of all management and professional occupations (Chao and Utgoff 2005). However, within this broad category, internal segregation is clear. Only 27 per cent of IT occupations and 8 per cent of electrical engineering jobs – clearly important categories in the knowledge economy – were held by women and 29 per cent of physicians and surgeons were women. By contrast, although 49 per cent of law professionals were women, only 29 per cent of lawyers were women, whilst 86 per cent of paralegals and legal assistants were women.

Occupations can also be segregated by race and ethnicity which can then intersect with gender segregation, such that occupations that are both gendered and racialized can be identified. Some healthcare occupations in the UK are good examples of this. However, it is argued that gendered divisions in the labour market are stronger than differences between women of different ethnic origins (Modood and Berthoud 1997). Nonetheless, as shown below, some ethnic differences are evident. One significant problem with assessing the extent of ethnic differences within women's employment is the lack of detailed data available. In the UK, the data sources on occupational segregation tend to focus either on gender or on race. There is a helpful tendency in the US government labour force statistics to disaggregate data by both of these variables.

One way forward in terms of getting a more accurate picture of horizontal segregation is the use, if available, of data at the level of workplaces and firms. The growing practice, particularly in the UK public sector, of gender audits may be particularly important in this respect. The 'gender duty' on all public authorities in the UK, due to come into effect in 2007, may yield better data at the level of the workplace. It will be particularly important that these data are made available for public inspection.

Gender segregation is not a static phenomenon, but a dynamic social process. This is particularly evident from the changing ethnic structure of some occupations. For example, the number of overseas nurses in the UK has risen dramatically as a consequence of labour shortages and active recruitment from the Philippines, India and South Africa (Kofman 2003). This type of change is hidden from most official statistics.

Horizontal occupational segregation: the evidence

The evidence presented in this chapter is largely focused on the UK, but as stated above, gender segregation is a global phenomenon. International comparisons can provide useful insights into the processes, policies and practices that produce and sustain gendered occupations. However, precise comparisons between countries are not straightforward, given the use of different occupational classifications. Although we concentrate here on the UK patterns, it is helpful to contextualize the discussion by providing some details about other national contexts. This raises the issue of how to compare occupational segregation cross-nationally. The use of a harmonized classification is no guarantee that the categories are being understood in exactly the same way. Job titles are the product of national economic, social and demographic histories and the corralling of them into international classifications does not change this (Glover 1996). Nor do all countries 'buy into' the international classifications: the International Standard Classification of Occupations (ISCO-88, ILO 1990) is typically used in Europe, but not in the

US. Nevertheless, international classifications of course have their uses in terms of showing broad trends and patterns.

Horizontal occupational segregation levels have historically been high in the Nordic countries; nevertheless they have declined in Sweden during the past decades, although less in the public than in the private sector (Nermo 1996). In a comparison of 14 EU member states, Rubery *et al.* (1998) report some increase in segregation, with women becoming even more concentrated in particular sectors and occupations. This process has been reinforced by the growth of part-time jobs, which are largely taken up by women. In the US, some decline in horizontal occupational segregation is reported (Chao and Utgoff 2005), alongside some resegregation (Jacobsen 1994; Reskin and Roos 1990).

Table 2.2 shows British women's percentage share of occupational groups. As can be seen, three occupational groups, employing nearly half of all women, are at least two-thirds female. Similarly half of all men are employed in three occupational groups – managers and senior officials, process, plant and machine operatives, skilled trades – that are at least two-thirds male. This alone indicates a significant degree of horizontal segregation in Britain. Interestingly, gender parity is almost achieved in two occupational groups – professional and associate professional and technical, highlighting the changed nature of some women's labour market position. It is argued (Walby 1997) that this pattern is evidence of increased polarization among women, between those who are highly qualified and now able to access higher level occupations and those who are less well qualified and remain in highly segregated feminized employment.

Because of the coexistence of occupational segregation by race, the table below needs to be read with caution as the data are not sensitive to ethnic differences. For example, black Caribbean, black African and Pakistani women are all less likely than white women to be in professional and managerial positions

Table 2.2 Women and men in occupational groups in Britain, 2004

Occupational group	% Women
Managers and senior officials	33
Professional	42
Associate professional and technical	48
Administrative and secretarial	80
Skilled trades	8
Personal service	84
Sales and customer service	69
Process, plant and machine operatives	15
Women as % of workforce	46

Source: adapted from EOC (2005) www.eoc.org.uk, Standard Occupational Classification (SOC).

(Cabinet Office 2003). It should be noted though that the difference between black–Caribbean and white women is only two percentage points (13 per cent of black–Caribbean women are professionals and managers compared with 15 per cent of white women). In contrast, Chinese and Indian women are more likely than white women to work at these levels. It is also important to note that some minority ethnic women's employment is invisible within official national labour market statistics because of their tendency to be employed as homeworkers. In the UK this applies particularly to Pakistani and Bangladeshi women (Holdsworth and Dale 1997). Homeworking could be considered as another form of occupational segregation by gender and race. In the US, Asian women were more likely than white, black or Hispanic women to work in management and professional occupations (44 per cent, compared with 39, 31 and 22 per cent respectively) (Chao and Utgoff 2005). Hispanic and black women were more likely than white or Asian women to work in service occupations.

Table 2.3 examines horizontal sex segregation in three of the Nordic countries. It is clear from Table 2.3 that similar patterns are found in Britain and in the Nordic countries. Most obviously, women are concentrated in clerical, service and elementary[1] occupations; men are concentrated in craft and manufacturing work. Table 2.3 also gives information about over- and under-representation; this is done by comparing the figures in each of the broad occupational groups with the overall representation of women in the labour force (the bottom line of the table). Table 2.4 gives the picture for the US.

From Table 2.4 we can see that with only one group more than two-thirds female, occupational segregation appears somewhat less marked in the US compared with

Table 2.3 Representation of women in occupational groups, 2001, Nordic countries

Categories	Finland	Norway % Women	Sweden
Legislators, senior officials, managers	27	26	30
Professionals	50	41	50
Associate professionals	54	52	47
Clerks	81	69	72
Service workers, shop and market sales workers	79	73	78
Skilled agricultural and fishery workers	34	24	25
Craft and related workers	9	8	6
Plant and machine operators and assemblers	20	17	18
Elementary occupations	59	60	66
Women as a % of the labour force	48	47	48

Source: extracted from United Nations Economic Commission for Europe
www.unece.org/stat Indicator Work & the Economy – Employment by Occupation (ISCO-88) and
OECD 2002: 69.

Table 2.4 Representation of women in occupational categories, US, 2002

Occupational group	% Women
Executive, administrators and managerial	45
Professional speciality	55
Technical and related support	56
Sales	49
Administrative support, including clerical	79
Precision production, craft and repair	9
Operators, fabricators and labourers	23
Service occupations	60
Farming, forestry and fishing	22
Total % of women in the labour force	47

Source: US Census Bureau, Current Population Survey, March 2002, extracted from Tables 11 and 12, www.census.gov/population/socdemo/gender/.

Britain. However, despite problems in making direct comparisons, broadly similar patterns can be seen in the UK, the Nordic countries and the US. Women are over-represented in clerical, administrative and service occupations, and men over-represented in production occupations. The 'professional' category is less easy to come to a conclusion on; it appears that women in the UK are less well represented in this category than in the other countries and American women are generally somewhat better represented in the higher level occupational groups. Chao and Utgoff (2005) report an increase in women's representation in these groups. But the US classification does not have a specific category for Associate Professional, whilst the SOC classification does. Nevertheless, this structural reason cannot be used when comparing the Nordic countries and the UK, since the ISCO classification does have an Associate Professional category. The Nordic countries have a higher representation of women in the Professional category than the UK does. This may relate to the historically high level of participation in higher education in the Nordic countries, whilst the UK until recently has had low female participation. A further reason is that the Nordic countries have high levels of female representation in the public sector, within which many professional occupations are found, particularly relating to health (Melkas and Anker 1998; Gornick and Jacobs 1998).

Moving beyond Europe and North America, Anker's work shows some interesting patterns that relate to cultural contexts; for example, in OECD countries almost 100 per cent of typists are women, whilst in the Middle East and Africa, the figure is around 60 per cent; hairdressers are almost always women in OECD countries, but they are rarely so in the Middle East and Africa (Anker 1998: Figure 11.2). These differences demonstrate that there is nothing inherently feminine or masculine about particular occupations and that occupational segregation by gender is produced and sustained by historical, social, cultural and economic processes that are specific to national contexts. Nevertheless, some universals are clear: the broad occupational category of 'architects, engineers and related technical workers' is heavily male-dominated globally.

Occupational sex segregation is persistent and one reason appears to be that organizational decision-makers tend to select applicants of their own sex (Reskin and Roos 1990). Collinson *et al.* (1990) investigated recruitment practices in traditionally male and female occupational groups. Their empirical material revealed how recruiters reproduce and rationalize sex discrimination in selection. But this can also be due to the nature of the recruitment pool. A longitudinal study of just under 1500 Swedish workplaces and all of their employees showed that sex segregation is reproduced across generations of workers (Bygren and Kumlin 2005). The 'established demography' – the sex composition of the labour pool from which workers are recruited – can produce sex bias in the recruitment of new employees. If the pool is mostly composed of men, it is likely to be reproduced in the recruitment process, unless there are specific positive action measures and quotas to be filled. There are clearly implications here for organizations, but also for educators. If an occupation is not sex-diverse, or more generally socially diverse, employers will be severely constrained in their recruitment strategies. Bygren and Kumlin's conclusion has important policy implications for those who seek to change the sex composition of workplaces, since it implies that the sex composition of the occupation *as a whole* must change first.

It is important though not to construct employees as merely passive victims of management practices. From the supply point of view, but in a context of gender segregation, it is possible that some people are attracted to organizations with large numbers of people like themselves. This implies that change will only occur when a certain critical mass of one sex or another has been arrived at both in the organization and in the occupation. Dale *et al.* (2005) find that women who succeed in non-traditional skill areas are particularly resilient and determined. The question for organizations and policy-makers is how the cycle of occupational segregation can be broken, and whether it is necessary to do this. We now examine this issue.

Does gender segregation matter?

Vertical sex segregation, where women are concentrated in low level positions and men in high level positions, inevitably has consequences for women's employment, in terms of pay and prospects. Even when women's qualifications are in applied subjects that are particularly relevant to the labour market, such as Languages, Engineering and Business Studies, substantial numbers of women graduates in the UK are employed in routine manual and non-manual jobs (Purcell 2002). Male graduates with similar qualifications are much more likely to work in higher level managerial and professional occupations. The Appendix of Chapter 5 gives an analysis of vertical sex segregation in higher education employment in the UK, showing that women are concentrated in the lowest level and least secure academic positions. Maume (2004) shows in a study of managerial attainment in the US that vertical segregation operated in different ways for different social groups. Senior positions in management were most likely to be held by white men, and least likely to be held by black women; interestingly, young black men showed career success, although still falling short of parity with white men. Vertical segregation is still strong in Nordic countries (Melkas and Anker 1998). Research from Sweden shows that the few women who reached top positions are usually in administrative support functions – accounting, personnel or public relations (Swedish Institute of Occupational Health 1995). It is also easier for women to reach top positions in the public sector. In the Nordic countries women's careers usually tail off at middle level management or 'expert' positions (ILO 1997). It is relatively easy, therefore, to come to the conclusion that vertical segregation has negative consequences for women's employment prospects and pay, both in the short term and the long term.

The question of whether horizontal occupational segregation is an issue of concern is however not particularly straightforward to answer. On the one hand, say Rubery *et al.* (1998), segregation has underpinned women's employment growth, since the sectors that have grown in the post-war economy are those that are seen as suitable for women's employment. With reference to Nordic labour markets, Melkas and Anker (1998) argue that occupational segregation can protect women's employment from competition and maintain the demand for women's labour. However, at the same time it is a basis for women's inequality (Rubery *et al.* 1998). This is because it has fostered the development of a particular sort of employment form that does not measure up to the yardstick of men's employment patterns – uninterrupted over the life course, and long-hours employment. Rubery *et al.* argue that women's employment patterns come to be seen as 'atypical'. This has enabled the growth of low wages and in particular has fostered the growth of part-time working. Clear patterns across industrialized countries indicate that men are over-represented in managerial and craft occupations; these are traditionally the best paid of the white-collar and blue-collar workforces (Reskin and Roos 1990: 5). Generally, the higher the representation of women in an occupation, the lower the pay in industrialized countries (Le Grand 1991; Rubery 1992; Kilbourne *et al.* 1994; Tomaskovic-Devey *et al.* 1996; Falkingham and Rake 2001).

Anker argues from an economic perspective that the consequences of horizontal segregation for the labour market are often harmful: it is a major source of labour market rigidity and economic inefficiency (Anker 1997). This is because large numbers of workers are excluded from a majority of occupations; thus it is wasteful of human resources, increases labour market inflexibility, and reduces an economy's ability to adjust to change. Rigidly sex segregated labour markets also have consequences for the moral arguments of equal opportunities: they reduce choice and opportunity for both women and men (Collinson *et al.* 1990). High levels of segregation are considered to be a significant factor in the gender wage gap (Reskin and Roos 1990; Rubery 1992) and cause inequalities in power, skill and earnings (Blackburn and Jarman 1997). It follows from this that the policy challenge is to reduce occupational sex segregation. But, asks Charles (2003), how does this square with evidence that occupational sex segregation is less obvious in 'gender-traditional' countries such as the southern European countries and Japan, and more obvious in 'gender-progressive' countries such as Sweden and the US? Charles' study of ten national labour markets is revealing, emphasizing the importance of making a distinction between manual and non-manual occupations. In the 'gender-progressive' countries, there were relatively low levels of vertical sex segregation in non-manual occupations and relatively high levels in manual occupations. But in the context of post-industrial sectoral change – a decline in manufacturing and a growth of the service sector – horizontal segregation was greater in these countries.

A particularly interesting aspect of Scandinavian labour markets is their high level of horizontal occupational segregation by sex. There is a rather traditional picture of 'who does what', alongside a strong public commitment to gender equity and to full employment for all citizens. Furthermore, there is a relatively small gender pay gap. It could be hypothesized that countries with high levels of female participation would be less segregated; however, Jarman et al. (1999) report no such trend. Indeed, in many countries where women are a substantial part of the labour force, it can be shown that they are not spread through the occupations but are highly concentrated in a few, as in Sweden and Finland (Hakim 2004). Anker (1997) argues that public commitment to these goals directly affects the sex segregation of occupations, since it leads to the creation of many public sector jobs that help women combine their family and work responsibilities. In 1990 approximately 10 per cent of women workers in Finland and Norway and 19 per cent of women workers in Sweden were in one of the following public sector occupations: child day-care centre worker, social worker, municipal home-help, and assistant nurse/attendant. Since these occupations are very highly feminized (in numerical terms), this substantially increases occupational segregation by sex in Scandinavia and in part explains why such segregation is higher than in other European countries. However, the key difference is that the occupations where women are concentrated are not necessarily poorly paid. This example illustrates that horizontal sex segregation in employment is not automatically a negative thing for women's employment prospects and opportunities. Yet, scholars and policy-makers persist in regarding occupational sex segregation as an indicator of women's economic disadvantage (Charles 2003).

Reskin and Roos (1990) make a clear connection between occupational sex segregation and unequal pay. This is a fundamental point, since if it can be shown that occupational sex segregation automatically brings about unequal pay between men and women, this represents a clear justification for policies that tackle occupational sex segregation. Yet Crompton (1999) points out that the link between occupational sex segregation and unequal pay cannot be established unequivocally.

She points particularly to the high level of occupational segregation in the Nordic countries, where the pay gap is particularly narrow. The conclusion from this is that the phenomenon of male dominated and female dominated occupations need not necessarily be the subject of policy change, if it does not inevitably lead to pay inequalities. This has led several commentators to conclude that the crucial issue for policy-makers is that of pay, and not necessarily that of horizontal occupational sex segregation.

In the US context, there has been a high degree of convergence in the industries and occupations that white and black women are employed in. Black women were once largely concentrated in household service work and manufacturing, whereas they are now more likely to be employed as clerical or service workers in the service industries where white women are also concentrated. However, some occupational segregation by race remains and it is thought to explain two-thirds of the racial gap among women in earnings (Kim 2002).

The crux of the matter is whether horizontal sex segregation leads to financial disadvantage, both in the short and long term. Recalling women's concentration in the public sector, one way of looking at this is to compare average pay in the public and private sectors. Comparing hourly pay, data for the UK show perhaps counter-intuitively that the median earnings for women in the public sector were higher than in the private sector (ASHE 2005). However, in the top decile – which represents the higher paid managerial and professional jobs – median hourly pay was similar. Long-term financial disadvantage – where women have little pension provision in old age – is also less likely for public sector employees (Ginn *et al.* 2001). Further, the coincidence of a high concentration of female workers and low pay has important implications where there is an earnings-related element in the pension system (Falkingham and Rake 2001). Where occupational pensions are a major part of overall pension provision, the occupational segregation of women is important. This is because women tend to be located in small firms and in sectors such as retail which are less likely to offer occupational pension coverage (Le Grand 1991; Ginn *et al.* 2001). In addition, in a study of the Swedish labour market, Hultin (2003) concludes that women in female-dominated occupations have poor chances of advancement. Therefore women are at risk of remaining stuck in low level, low pay work.

Jarman *et al.* (1999) argue, somewhat against the grain, that high levels of segregation could contribute towards reducing gender-based inequalities, for example in all-female job ladders where women supervise other women, the creation of female zones of influence protected from male applicants, female-friendly workplaces and work policies and women's trade unions. Evidence for such phenomena is hard to find, although they may be suggested here in a utopian way. There is no certainty that female-dominated occupations would command equal pay or equal status with male-dominated ones; indeed all of the historical evidence is against this. As Rubery *et al.* (1998) say, employment opportunities for women can and have been created, but it does not follow that these bring about equal pay for work of equal value.

It can be argued, therefore, that a high level of horizontal gender segregation is not necessarily and in itself bad for women (Anker 2000; 1998). However, it can produce gender differences in working conditions. For example, women are more likely to be working in jobs dealing directly with customers and the public often associated with high levels of stress, intimidation and harassment (e.g. call centre work; nursing). In white-collar work, women are often employed in occupations at greater risk of ergonomic hazards. These factors are associated with women's greater susceptibility to work-related ill-health (Fagan and Burchell 2002).

What processes bring about gender segregation?

The establishment of how job segregation comes about is clearly a complex task, involving both demand and supply factors. One way to examine this interplay of demand and supply is to examine what happens when new jobs are created, as Skuratowicz and Hunter (2004) did in their case study of job segregation in an American bank at a point when banks in different locations were being restructured and new jobs created. This research showed a four-step feedback process that touches reciprocally on both labour supply and demand. First, managers built gendered assumptions into the job descriptions of some types of these new and restructured jobs, but not into others; these assumptions included breadwinning, competition and nurturing. Employees then responded to the cues in gendered ways, especially when part-time working was allowed in some posts but not in others. Managers recruited in a way that was consistent with these assumptions and what they and the employees saw as choices; both parties then legitimized gendered norms about the new positions. Crucially, at no point was there any suggestion of deliberate discrimination: almost all employees received their first choice of job and the principle of meritocracy was believed to be upheld. Thus, the complex nature of the creation and persistence of job segregation is revealed.

In terms of labour supply, rational choice arguments about women's preferences are often cited (see Hakim 2004). The argument here is that women prefer certain types of occupation such as those with flexible hours or those occupations which are relatively easy to interrupt for a period of time to bear or rear children. These occupations tend to be female-dominated, and/or located in the public sector. Women continue to qualify themselves for careers within spheres of work traditionally seen as 'female'. As a result they follow financially less rewarding career paths premised on assumptions about women's domestic roles (Lyon 1996). Thus, the 'choice'/constraint debate, outlined in the introductory chapter, is highly relevant when considering explanations of how occupational segregation by sex comes about. As we explored in the introductory chapter, the 'choice' explanation has attracted a substantial critique arguing that a proper understanding requires that women's employment preferences and choices are located within the social structural conditions in which they are made. Whether these conditions mitigate against subsequent change is something that organizations may want to consider, as we discuss below.

An understanding of the phenomenon of occupational segregation requires a historical examination of social and economic factors; these shape what comes to be viewed as women's and men's work (Milkman 1987; Reskin and Roos 1990). Taking the example of highly qualified women in the natural sciences, Rossiter's data from the nineteenth and twentieth centuries in America show that certain sciences became established as suitable for women, resulting in clear patterns of horizontal segregation (Rossiter 1982, 1995). Within some sciences, there was also territorial demarcation. For example, in psychology, women tended to work in clinical areas, child psychology or social welfare, while men tended to be in academic psychology. Within biochemistry, women were generally employed in nutrition, a field that was largely demoted in mid-century to home economics. Engineering, closed to women before the Second World War, opened up to women post-war, but women worked as 'engineering aides', where there was no clear career ladder. Here we see a combination of internal and vertical segregation. One view is that an advantaged group (for example white men) seeks to preserve privileged status by exerting social closure (Tomaskovic-Devey and Skaggs 1999). The concept of exclusionary closure describes the mobilization of power by a dominant group in order to claim resources and opportunities – and therefore financial and status rewards – for itself. It does this by formally regulating the supply of its own labour and by creating a monopoly over skills and knowledge. Thus, exclusionary shelters are created for the dominant group. This does not stop qualified 'outsiders' from entering, but they are likely to be in lower level positions. This perspective, which has much to offer the explanation of vertical and horizontal segregation, has its roots in the thinking of Parkin (1979) and was effectively used by Witz (1992) in an examination of the history of women's entry into the medical profession.

Gender segregation: an issue for organizations?

Labour shortages in some occupations might lead human resource managers to think beyond the traditional sex-typing of particular jobs and skills and to develop recruitment practices designed to attract the under-represented sex. They might also see the training and development function as a way of diverting women and men from traditional 'choices'. Although this might ultimately help to tackle horizontal and vertical segregation, it begs the question of whether these changes would occur if there were not labour shortages. Organizations might however be keen to follow good practice guides such as those produced by equality bodies (e.g. the UK Equal Opportunities Commission), which contend that gender equality and diversity are good for business. It is possible that the development of systems that rank organizations according to a series of 'women-friendly' criteria will have a considerable effect on organizational practice. For example, the UK's Department for Trade and Industry runs a website that singles out those companies – often major FTSE 100 'household names' – that focus on aspects which will be to the advantage of women's employment (www.wherewomenwanttowork.com). However, it is not obvious from this site that the issue of occupational segregation is a focus; women are asked to identify which aspects of employment they particularly value from a list that mentions flexible working, role models, networking, equal pay and training. The issue of horizontal segregation is unlikely to be a focus, since women's occupations may be seen by organizations as something that has been 'chosen' long before recruitment. However, vertical segregation, with its link with equal pay, is clearly an organizational issue.

One way of looking at occupational sex segregation is from the viewpoint of diversity. As discussed in Chapter 6, organizations are now exhorted to become more diverse in order to improve performance. Therefore, it may particularly concern employers that their organizations contain pockets that are sex-segregated, possibly preventing them from making full use of workforce diversity. On the other hand, within a diversity paradigm employers are encouraged to 'utilize difference' where it would be beneficial – and this could end up being a case *for* sex segregation. The diversity approach could be seen as conservative in the sense that the use of existing difference could confirm gender role stereotypes and the assumption of essential social difference between women and men.

Williams and O'Reilly (1998) review the reasons in the literature for the benefits of diversity within the organization. They argue that it helps integration and communication and reduces conflict levels. There may be some link here with the literature on mixed classrooms. Research in this area has moved beyond the view that the integration of girls with boys creates better behaviour by the boys whilst lowering the achievement levels of girls (Jackson and Smith 2000). But there is evidence that girls' communication skills are being used in classrooms to enable boys' achievements through for example placing girls next to boys so that girls' superior language skills will 'rub off' on boys (Warrington and Younger 2003; Francis and Skelton 2005). Translating this to the workplace, it might be possible to argue that women are positioned within organizations in pastoral roles that stereotype them in assumptions about their caring characteristics. The workplace may run more smoothly and the bottom line of productivity is therefore improved, but the women's employment prospects may be worse. As Kilbourne *et al.* (1994) argue, feedback mechanisms from women's status in the home and the larger social context have a reciprocal relationship with their status in the workplace. Women's apparent aptitude for conflict resolution roles, as cited above by Williams and O'Reilly, is unlikely however to lead to advancement or involve access to strategic positions within the organization.

We have cited research indicating that left to itself, the workforce will reproduce itself in terms of demographic characteristics. This implies that organizations will need to construct interventionist policies and practice in order to break down occupational segregation. Equality policies have been widely used for around two decades in an effort to increase opportunities for women, but it is likely that the formalization of recruitment and selection practices advocated by such policies can have only limited impact on the employment decisions and outcomes that reproduce occupational sex segregation (Collinson *et al.* 1990). A longer term view and strategy to tackle this deeply embedded phenomenon is undoubtedly necessary.

Maume (2004) argues that longitudinal data are needed to underpin the development of policies. Collected over the entire course of careers, a data set that includes measures of employer behaviour and organizational practices would be necessary. The criteria used by supervisors to reward and promote workers, results from annual evaluations, employees' use of mentor programmes and so on are all crucial variables in trying to discover how equality and inequality are created and sustained over time. However, it seems unlikely that such a long-term perspective on the gathering of complex information, with considerable resource implications, could be envisaged by most organizations, unless it was made obligatory by governments.

An interesting perverse effect of overcoming vertical segregation may be the creation of a 'glass cliff'. Ryan and Haslam (2005) showed that firms that were doing badly tended to appoint women into leadership roles rather than men. In these circumstances, women can be appointed precisely because they are different, the usual model not having proved effective. These jobs had a high risk of failure, since in the likelihood of a poor performance spiralling downwards, there is a clear scapegoat. Thus, the glass ceiling can be understood in these circumstances as the 'glass cliff', a concept that we discuss further in Chapter 5. Ryan and Haslam conclude that firms need to manage diversity better, by examining the way they are supporting the role and not judging performance on the basis of traditional, masculine measures.

Conclusions

Occupational segregation by sex – whether vertical or horizontal – is pervasive and long-lasting, both temporally and spatially. It can be defined in terms of occupation, industry and sector and it can affect ethnic groups differently. However, an examination that goes beyond Europe and North America shows that there is nothing inherently feminine or masculine about different occupations; they are produced and sustained in different historical, cultural and economic contexts.

Focusing on occupations, vertical segregation – the tendency for women to be located at the lower levels of job hierarchies – can be shown to lead to the gender pay gap and therefore to women's short-term and long-term financial insecurity. As we discuss in Chapter 3, this is not to the advantage of individuals, households or governments. But the effects of horizontal segregation – the tendency for women and men to be located in different occupations – are more difficult to discern. We conclude that there is no clear evidence that a high level of horizontal segregation is necessarily and of itself bad for women's employment. Organizations that seek to change segregation patterns will probably focus on vertical segregation, because of its links with the gender pay gap. It is unlikely that they will tackle horizontal segregation, since it is probably assumed that this relates to women's 'choice'.

Here again, as in many parts of this book, the 'choice'/constraint issue comes to the fore. It is possible to argue, as McGlynn (2003) does, that Hakim's espousal of 'preference theory' has given academic legitimacy to employers' views that employment decisions are firmly in the individual's court. On this basis, interventions from employers might seem inappropriate. However, as Maume (2004) argues, there is a need for long-term data-gathering at the level of the firm, in order to throw light on such things as the criteria used by supervisors to reward and promote workers, results from annual evaluations, and employees' use of mentor programmes. Despite the undoubted resource implications of such serious data-gathering, these are all crucial variables in trying to discover how equality and inequality are created and sustained over time.

Note

1   Elementary occupations consist mainly of 'simple and routine tasks which mainly require the use of hand-held tools and often some physical effort'. Most occupations in this major group require skills at the first ISCO skill level (primary education which generally begins at the age of five, six or seven and lasts about five years) (ILO 1990: 249). It is a major category for women, since it includes domestic and hotel cleaning jobs.

References

Anker, R. (1997) 'Theories of occupational segregation by sex: an overview', *International Labour Review*, 136 (3): 315–17.

Anker, R. (1998) *Gender and Jobs: Sex Segregation of Occupations in the World*, Geneva: International Labour Office.

Anker, R. (2000) *Gender: A Partnership of Equals*, Geneva: International Labour Office.

ASHE (Annual Survey of Hours and Earnings) (2005), <www.ons.gov.uk>.

Baron, J. and Bielby, W. (1986) 'Men and women at work: sex segregation and statistical discrimination', *American Journal of Sociology*, 91 (January): 759–99.

Blackburn, R. and Jarman, J. (1997) 'Occupational gender segregation', *Social Research Update*, 16.

Blackburn, R. and Jarman, J. (2005) *Segregation and Inequality: GeNet Working Paper 2005/3*, ESRC Gender Equality Network.

Bygren, M. and Kumlin, J. (2005) 'Mechanisms of organizational sex segregation', *Work and Occupations*, 32 (1): 39–65.

Cabinet Office (2003) *Ethnic Minorities in the Labour Market*, London: Cabinet Office.

Chao, E. and Utgoff, K. (2005) *Women in the Labor Force: A Databook*, Washington: Department of Labor.

Charles, M. (2003) 'Deciphering sex segregation: vertical and horizontal inequalities in ten national labor markets', *Acta Sociologica*, 46 (4): 267–87.

Collinson, D., Knights, D. and Collinson, M. (1990) *Managing to Discriminate*, London: Routledge.

Crompton, R. (ed.) (1999) *Restructuring Gender Relations and Employment*, Oxford: Oxford University Press.

Crompton, R. and Harris, F. (1998) 'Gender relations and employment: the impact of occupation', *Work, Employment and Society*, 12 (2): 297–316.

Dale, A., Jackson, N. and Hill, N. (2005) *Women in Non-traditional Training and Employment*, Manchester: Equal Opportunities Commission.

EOC (2005) *Facts about Men and Women in Great Britain*, Manchester: Equal Opportunities Commission.

Epstein, C. F., Seron, C., Oglensky, B. and Saute, R. (1998). *The Part-time Paradox: Time Norms, Professional Lives, Family, and Gender*, London: Routledge.

Fagan, C. and Burchell, B. (2002) *Gender, Jobs and Working Conditions in the European Union*, Dublin: European Foundation for the Improvement of Living and Working Conditions.

Falkingham, J. and Rake, K. (2001) 'Modelling the gender impact of British pension reforms', in J. Ginn, D. Street and S. Arber (eds) *Women, Work and Pensions*, Buckingham: Open University Press, 67–85.

Francis, B. and Skelton, C. (2005) *Reassessing Gender and Achievement*, London: Routledge.

Ginn, J., Street, D. and Arber, S. (eds) (2001) *Women, Work and Pensions*, Buckingham: Open University Press.

Glover, J. (1996) 'Epistemological and methodological considerations in secondary analysis', in L. Hantrais and S. Mangen (eds) *Cross-National Research Methods in the Social Sciences*, London: Pinter, 28–38.

Gonas, L. (2004) 'Gender segregation and the European employment strategy: levels and divisions', *European Journal of Industrial Relations*, 10 (2): 139–59.

Gornick, J. and Jacobs, J. (1998) *Gender, the Welfare State and Public Employment*, Luxembourg: Luxembourg Income Study.

Hakim, C. (1979) *Occupational Segregation*, London: Department of Employment.

Hakim, C. (2004) *Key Issues in Women's Work* (2nd edn), London: Glasshouse Press.

Hibbett, A. and Meager, N. (2003) 'Key indicators of women's position in Britain', *Labour Market Trends*, October, 503–11.

Holdsworth, C. and Dale, A. (1997) 'Ethnic differences in women's employment', *Work, Employment and Society*, 11 (3): 435–57.

Hultin, M. (2003) 'Some take the glass escalator, some hit the glass ceiling', *Work and Occupations*, 30 (1): 30–61.

ILO (1990) *ISCO-88: The International Standard Classification of Occupations 1988*, Geneva: International Labour Organization. See also <http://www.warwick.ac.uk/ier/isco/frm–is88.html>.

ILO (1997) *Breaking through the Glass Ceiling: Women in Management*, Geneva: ILO.

Jackson, C. and Smith, I. D. (2000) 'Poles apart? An exploration of single-sex and mixed-sex educational environments in Australia and England', *Educational Studies*, 26 (4): 409–22.

Jacobsen, J. (1994) 'Sex segregation at work: trends and predictions', *The Social Science Journal*, 31 (2): 153–69.

Jarman, J., Blackburn, R., Brooks, B. and Dermott, E. (1999) 'Gender differences at work: international variations in occupational segregation', *Sociological Research Online*, 4.

Kilbourne, B., Farkas, G., Beron, K., Wier, D. and England, P. (1994) 'Returns to skill, compensating differentials, and gender bias: effects of occupational characteristics on the wages of White women and men', *American Journal of Sociology*, 100 (3): 689–719.

Kim, M. (2002) 'Has the race penalty for black women disappeared in the United States?' *Feminist Economics*, 8 (2): 115–24.

Kofman, E. (2003) *Women Migrants and Refugees in the European Union*, paper presented to OECD–European Commission Conference: The Economic and Social Aspects of Migration, Brussels.

Le Grand, C. (1991) 'Explaining the male–female wage gap: job segregation and solidarity wage bargaining in Sweden', *Acta Sociologica*, 34: 261–78.

Lyon, E. (1996) 'Success with qualifications: comparative perspectives on women graduates in the labour market', *Higher Education*, 31: 301–23.

McGlynn, C. (2003) 'The status of women lawyers in the United Kingdom', in U. Schultz and G. Shaw (eds) *Women in the World's Legal Professions*, Oxford and Portland, OR: Hart Publishing, 139–56.

Maume, D. (2004) 'Is the glass ceiling a unique form of inequality?' *Work and Occupations*, 31 (2): 250–74.

Melkas, H. and Anker, R. (1998) *Gender Equality and Occupational Segregation in Nordic Labour Markets*, Geneva: International Labour Organization.

Milkman, R. (1987) *Gender at Work: The Dynamics of Job Segregation by Sex During World War Two*, Chicago: University of Illinois Press.

Modood, T. and Berthoud, R. (1997) *Ethnic Minorities in Britain: Diversity and Disadvantage*, London: Policy Studies Institute.

Nermo, M. (1996) 'Occupational sex segregation in Sweden, 1968–1991', *Work and Occupations*, 23 (3): 319–32.

OECD (2001) *Employment Outlook*, Paris: OECD.

OECD (2002) *Employment Outlook*, Paris: OECD.

Parkin, F. (1979) *Marxism and Class Theory: A Bourgeois Critique*, London: Tavistock.

Purcell, K. (2002) *Qualifications and Careers: Equal Opportunities and Earnings among Graduates* (Working Paper Series No 1), Manchester: Equal Opportunities Commission.

Reskin, B. and Hartmann, H. (1986) *Women's Work, Men's Work: Sex Segregation on the Job*, Washington DC: National Academy Press.

Reskin, B. and Roos, P. (1990) *Job Queues, Gender Queues: Explaining Women's Inroads into Male Occupations*, Philadelphia: Temple University Press.

Riska, E. (2001) *Medical Careers and Feminist Agendas: American, Scandinavian, and Russian Women Physicians*, New York: Aldine de Gruyter.

Robinson, C., Taylor, T., Tomaskovic-Devey, D., Zimmer, C. and Irvin, M. (2005) 'Studying race or ethnic sex segregation at the establishment level', *Work and Occupations*, 32 (1): 5–38.

Rossiter, M. (1982) *Women Scientists in America: Struggles and Strategies to 1940*, Baltimore: Johns Hopkins University Press.

Rossiter, M. (1995) *Women Scientists in America: Before Affirmative Action 1940–1972*, Baltimore and London: Johns Hopkins University Press.

Rubery, J. (1992) *The Economics of Equal Value*, Manchester: Equal Opportunities Commission.

Rubery, J., Smith, M., Fagan, C. and Grimshaw, D. (1998) *Women and European Employment*, London: Routledge.

Ryan, M. and Haslam, S. A. (2005) 'The glass cliff: evidence that women are over-represented in precarious leadership positions', *British Journal of Management*, 16 (1): 81–90.

Schultz, U. and Shaw, G. (eds) (2003) *Women in the World's Legal Professions*, Oxford and Portland, OR: Hart Publishing.

Skuratowicz, E. and Hunter, L. (2004) 'Where do women's jobs come from?' *Work and Occupations*, 31 (1): 73–110.

Swedish Institute of Occupational Health (1995) *Women's Work and Health*, Solna: Swedish Institute of Occupational Health.

Tomaskovic-Devey, D. and Skaggs, S. (1999) 'An establishment level test of the statistical discrimination hypothesis', *Work and Occupations*, 26 (4): 422–45.

Tomaskovic-Devey, D., Kalleberg, A. and Marsden, P. (1996) 'Organizational patterns of gender segregation', in A. Kalleberg, D. Knoke, P. Marsden and J. Spaeth (eds) *Organizations in America: Analyzing their Structures and Human Resources*, Thousand Oaks, CA: Sage, 276–301.

TUC (2002) *Black and Underpaid*, London: Trades Union Congress.

Walby, S. (1997) *Gender Transformations*, London: Routledge.

Warrington, M. and Younger, M. (2003) '"We decided to give it a twirl": single-sex teaching in english comprehensive schools', *Gender and Education*, 15 (4): 339–50.

Williams, K. and O'Reilly, C. (1998) 'Demography and diversity in organizations. A review of 40 years of research', *Research in Organizational Behaviour*, 20: 77–140.

Witz, A. (1992) *Professions and Patriarchy*, London: Routledge.

Chapter 3

The gender pay gap

Introduction

Evidence suggests that gendered patterns of participation in the labour market in Britain (and elsewhere) continue to have a substantial effect on the levels of economic security that women and men build up over the life course (Warren 2003; Rubery *et al.* 2005). In particular, women's propensity for part-time, discontinuous work histories leads to lower pension entitlements and personal assets, as well as reducing lifetime earnings. The UK government's Cabinet Office has calculated that on average over the lifetime of a woman with average qualifications, £240,000 is lost (Anderson *et al.* 2001). This is compared with the lifetime earnings of a man with average qualifications.

Low pay is a particular issue for women. In a detailed comparison of Britain, Germany, Luxembourg, Spain and the US, Robson *et al.* (1999) show that low pay was considerably more extensive amongst women than men. In each country, more full-time women workers than men were low paid in every industry with two exceptions: the finance industry in the US and community and personal services in Spain (Robson *et al.* 1999). This makes the existence and generosity of a minimum wage policy particularly important, as we discuss later in this chapter.

The cumulative effect of low pay and less access to other sources of income such as pensions and state benefits leads to a major 'gender income gap' of 48 per cent (2000/01 figures) (EOC 2003). It is therefore unsurprising that women are so much more vulnerable to poverty in old age than men (Ginn *et al.* 2001). A similar picture can be shown for women in the US, where the gender income gap was reported as being 50 per cent in 2001, the same level as it was in 1947 (King 2001). In the Nordic countries, where the welfare regime is not based on labour market participation, there is much less of a gender income gap (Melkas and Anker 1998). Where occupational pensions are a major part of overall pension provision, the occupational segregation of women is important. This is because women tend to be located in small firms and in sectors such as retail that are less likely to offer occupational pension coverage. The coincidence of a high concentration of female workers and low pay has important implications where there is an earnings-related element in the pension system, as in the UK (Ginn *et al.* 2001).

The gender pay gap – the average difference in earnings between women and men (not the issue of equal pay for work of equal value) – is the specific subject of this chapter. The gender pay gap is evident and persistent in all industries and occupations and it is a phenomenon that is found in all industrialized and industrializing countries, including the post-communist countries of Central and Eastern Europe (Grimshaw and Rubery 2001). In the UK, women in full-time work earn on average 82 per cent of the average hourly pay of male full-time employees (Women and Equality Unit 2004). The gender pay gap is also large in the US where in 2001 the equivalent figure was 80 per cent (King 2001). The gap has narrowed in recent years, but King argues that this is at least partly because men's earnings have decreased due to the loss of well paid jobs in manufacturing. In Nordic countries, the gender pay gap is the smallest of all European countries: women in Sweden earn on average 90 per cent of men's pay and in the other Nordic countries slightly less than this (Fransson *et al.* 2001). The gender pay gap has narrowed over the past two to three decades in virtually all OECD countries, but women still earn on average 16 per cent less than men per hour.

This figure disguises the difference between full-time and part-time workers. In the UK, when the hourly pay for women working part-time is compared with the hourly pay for men working full-time, the part-time pay gap is 40 per cent, unchanged since 1975 (EOC 2005). In Europe as a whole, there is evidence that the progressive closing of the gender gap in education and experience has not led to a significant closing of the gender pay gap (Rubery *et al.* 2005). In July 2004 the British government created a Women and Work Commission to examine the problem of the gender pay gap and other issues related to women's employment. We discuss this report, which was published in February 2006, in Chapter 9.

The elimination of the gender pay gap is seen by the European Commission as the responsibility of all social partners – governments, employers and trade unions (European Commission 2005). From a European perspective, the trade union view is that despite the prevalence of equal pay legislation, the gap between men's pay and women's pay remains a major source of inequality (ETUC 2003). Legislation to narrow the pay gap has not been particularly effective (Whitehouse *et al.* 2001).

The gender pay gap is not only a short-term issue, but a long-term one, affecting women throughout their lives and leading to high levels of poverty for older women (Ginn *et al.* 2001). Although it is a particular problem for low-earning women, it exists also among highly skilled and high earning professionals (Rubery 1998). Because there is also a pay gap for women who do not have children, it cannot be 'explained away' by the effect of children on women's labour force participation, although most commentators agree that this is a major factor. In the UK, the gender pay gap for full-time employees is 21 per cent for women with children and 16 per cent for women without children (Women and Equality Unit 2004). In the US, the equivalent figures are 25 per cent and 17 per cent. This is because the careers of women without children more typically mirror male careers (Hardill and Watson 2004). We discuss further below the effect of children on the gender pay gap.

The European Industrial Relations Observatory (EIRO 2002) has concluded that some countries do not prioritize the pay equality issue, focusing instead on measures to increase women's employment participation rate, to combine work and family, or to ease the re-entry of mothers into the labour force following the child rearing phase. The UK employers' perspective is that the best way to close the gender pay gap is to remove barriers to equality of opportunity between men and women in the workplace – for example, improving childcare facilities, promoting flexible working patterns, providing better-quality careers advice and breaking down gender stereotypes (EIRO 2002). EIRO reports that in the 16 European countries that it surveyed, employers' organizations shared the view that existing wage differentials between men and women were not an expression of discrimination against female employees and appeared to see no particular need for action in the field of gender pay policy.

Calculating the gender pay gap

The gender pay gap is typically measured by the difference between the hourly pay of women and men working full-time. Part-time workers are usually excluded from the calculation because their hourly pay is typically lower than that of full-time workers. The emphasis on hourly pay, as opposed to weekly, monthly or annual pay, is designed to exclude the effect of overtime, bonuses and performance pay. Because men get such payments more than women, a pay gap calculated on a weekly, annual or monthly basis will be greater than one calculated on an hourly basis (EOC 1999). Although the calculation based on the hourly pay of women and men working full-time is comparing like with like, it may not show the lived reality of the gender pay gap. This is that many women work part-time and tend not to get overtime and bonuses; thus their take-home pay is usually markedly lower than that of men. To demonstrate this, in the UK, the average weekly earnings of full-time women employees amount to 78 per cent of men's, making a gender pay gap of 22 per cent. The gap reduces to 18 per cent when the calculation is based on an hourly rate (Women and Equality Unit 2004).

Variations in the gender pay gap

A broad-brush calculation of the gender pay gap disguises variations across a number of interconnected and overlapping dimensions including the presence or absence of children, ethnicity, age, occupation and qualifications, and employment sector. Much research on women and employment has focused on the effect of having children on pay, hours of work and career progression. The difference in pay between child-free women and women with children is sometimes referred to as the 'family wage gap' (OECD 2002). Countries with a substantial family wage gap include Austria, the UK and the US. The estimated wage penalty for women in the US is 7 per cent per child (Budig and England 2001). About one-third is explained by the fact that mothers have more employment breaks and part-time employment and therefore accumulate fewer hours of job experience and seniority than non-mothers.

There are clear effects on the gender pay gap of having children and new research suggests that these are not confined to childbirth. In the UK, the two 'risk points' for women's employment prospects, including pay growth, are childbirth and the point at which children go into formal schooling (Brewer and Paull 2006). Perhaps counter-intuitively, analysis of large-scale nationally representative longitudinal data shows that when children go to school, there are negative effects on women's pay and other issues relating to long-term financial security such as security of employment and being in a supervisory role. Brewer and Paull conclude that it is the *accumulation* of periods of low wage growth around the times of birth and school entry that account for the gradual decline in women's pay relative to that of men. Furthermore, the effects of children continue even after children have grown up or left home. This confirms what we say below about women's flatter earnings profile in the middle years (Falkingham and Rake 2001).

Brewer and Paull conclude that these gender differences in the labour market stem from the division of parental duties between mothers and fathers. Whilst this must be at least part of the answer, this conclusion does not shed light on *why* the domestic division of labour is gendered. It is quite possible that women's 'choices' at these crucial points depend not only on the supply of labour but also on the demand for labour, in other words employer behaviour. The effect of different employer practices is borne out by Brewer and Paull's finding that women who work in the public sector have shorter absences from work following birth than those who work in the private sector. Furthermore, the finding that with each successive birth, mothers are less likely to return to the labour market has probably more to do with the cost of childcare. Were childcare to be subsidized by the state as in Nordic countries (as well as being of high quality and quantity), the multiple-child effect could well disappear. The conclusion that it is women's and men's 'choices' about the domestic division of labour at these risk points seems therefore only a partial explanation. Further, Brewer and Paull's conclusion that policy should therefore be directed at women seems questionable.

The presence of children appears to have a strong effect on mothers' pay, but not fathers'. In fact there is a reverse effect – men with dependent children earn about 13 per cent more than those with no dependent children (Women and Equality Unit 2004). Various reasons have been put forward to explain this: mothers are more likely to be working in part-time jobs, where wages tend to be lower; fathers of young children tend to work longer hours than other men; employers may discriminate against mothers on the grounds that they expect them to have a lower commitment to their jobs. However, as shown earlier, the pay gap is evident also for women who are not married and do not have children; therefore it cannot be attributed wholly to the effect of children (Rubery 1998). Brewer and Paull (2006) refer to an anticipatory effect of children, in the sense of women slowing down their approach to employment. This is possible, but evidence is scarce.

Rather, there is evidence that employers anticipate that women will have children, such that they fail to recruit women of childbearing age, or invest less in them as employees (Collinson *et al.* 1990).

With regard to the effect of ethnicity, some minority ethnic women are doing relatively well in terms of pay levels and in terms of the gender pay gap (see Kim 2002 for the US and Modood and Berthoud 1997 for the UK). However, it is important not to generalize about minority ethnic women as some groups are doing better than others. In the UK, Pakistani and Bangladeshi women are the most disadvantaged ethnic group in pay terms. Their average full-time hourly pay is only 67 per cent of that of white men, compared to a figure of 81 per cent in the case of white women. In contrast, black women's average hourly full-time earnings are similar to white women's, while Indian women earn on average more than white, black, Pakistani and Bangladeshi women, their hourly pay being 84 per cent of that of white men (Women and Equality Unit 2004). In the US black women's slightly higher earnings, especially in higher status jobs, is seen to be due to their longer employment history (Sokoloff 1992). They tend to have worked longer hours over a larger number of years and to have had more continuous employment than white women. Similar factors contribute towards gendered pay differentials between ethnic groups in the UK and may also be affected by the tendency for some minority ethnic groups to be located in metropolitan areas, such as London, where wages are higher. Looked at from a different angle, in the UK the pay differentials between black women and black men are smallest, with an earnings ratio of 93 per cent (Women and Equality Unit 2004). This is because black men are doing so poorly in earnings terms compared with white men, pointing to the fact that low pay is not simply a gender issue.

The gender pay gap increases with age. In the UK it is lowest in the 18–21 age range at just 6 per cent when earnings for both sexes are relatively low. It is highest in the 40–49 age range at 23 per cent. However, it decreases in the 50 plus age group to 19 per cent (Women and Equality Unit 2004), when once again average earnings for both sexes start to decrease. In the US the gender pay gap is 9 per cent in the 16–24 age range; 18 per cent in the 25–34; and highest in the 35–44 age range at 29 per cent (UAW 2000). Analysis of the way in which earnings vary between the different age groups reveals that men's earnings profile shows a peak in the middle years, whilst women have a much flatter earnings profile (Falkingham and Rake 2001). This is also the case in the US (US Bureau of Labor Statistics 1998). This suggests that men benefit from a premium in the middle years that may reflect their continuous labour market presence. Bearing in mind the limitations of cross-sectional data, the profile for women could reflect the impact of interrupted employment patterns and labour market segmentation. One optimistic interpretation is that the pay gap is generational in that women in the mid-life age group were forging their careers at a time when women's inequality and sex discrimination were more pronounced. This would suggest that future generations of women will not experience the same level of pay disadvantage. Another, less optimistic, interpretation is that women face increasing pay disadvantage over the life course, caused in part by discontinuous work histories, engaging in part-time work and a combination of gender and age discrimination.

The question of the widening of the gender pay gap as age increases is a crucial one for policy-makers. In order to provide a clear answer, longitudinal data are necessary. In the case of highly qualified women and men, the gender pay gap appears early. Purcell (2002) analysed the occupational outcomes of UK graduates three-and-a-half years after graduation, showing that women graduates can expect to earn 15 per cent less than their male counterparts by the time they reach the age of 24. There appear to be particular areas of employment where gender inequalities in pay are most persistent among graduates: employment in the private sector, generally, and in jobs where law and engineering graduates are employed, in particular. This cannot be explained away by differences between the sexes in occupations and type of degree, argues Purcell: even when women have studied the same subjects and achieved the same class of degree, men earn more than women. This phenomenon is particularly obvious for young graduates in management occupations, where there is a 17 per cent gender pay gap (Purcell 2002). Looking in more detail at management occupations, the pay gap is very clear in the banking, finance and insurance sector (Purcell 2002).

In a subsequent study that tracked these same UK graduates over a seven-year period, an increase in the pay gap with age is confirmed (Purcell and Elias 2004). The gender pay gap for women and men who graduated in 1995 and then entered full-time employment had increased to 19 per cent in 2002/3, having increased from 15 per cent in 1997/8 and 11 per cent in 1995 (the first entry to the labour market). Although some of this gap can be explained by reference to the subject of degree (which is in itself a gendered choice, subject to social constraints) and by the number of hours worked (which may reflect the gendered division of domestic labour) by no means all of the difference can be accounted for in this way. A further point is that the survey revealed that the women had been considerably more likely than the men to have acquired further training, including postgraduate qualifications, during the seven years since graduation. By this stage the gender pay gap in law was 22 per cent.

There are also sectoral and occupational variations in the gender earnings ratio. Women are considerably more likely than men to work in the public sector (Women and Equality Unit 2004) where the overall pay levels are lower than in the private sector, but where the gender pay gap is narrower (Rubery et al. 2005). In Purcell's (2002) study of graduates, there was a concentration of women in education and public services. This form of gender segregation contributes to women's lower earnings overall and thus to the gender pay gap. Perhaps counter-intuitively, in the UK the pay gap is higher for some more qualified and senior level women, demonstrating that being in an occupation that requires high levels of qualification does not guarantee equality in pay. The gender pay gap of managers and senior officials is 26 per cent, compared to only 13 per cent in sales and customer service occupations. However, women in the broad category of professional occupations are relatively high earners compared with men with a ratio of 91 per cent (gender pay gap of just 9 per cent) (Women and Equality Unit 2004). Thus, the picture is not uniform for highly qualified people.

Causes and explanations of the pay gap

According to the European Commission, underlying the gender pay gap are factors including sectoral and occupational segregation, education and training, job classifications and pay systems, lack of awareness and transparency (European Commission 2005). Much of the literature seeks to break down the causes of the gender pay gap into justifiable or explained differences and unjustified or unexplained elements. Rubery *et al.* (2005) argue that this does not take account of the social context within which decisions are made. 'Justifiable' or 'explained' differences in pay usually draw on theories of rational choice and human capital, particularly in relation to education and occupational choice. 'Unjustified' or 'unexplained' elements usually relate to potential discrimination. The belief now reflected in the European Employment Strategy, discussed below, is that even the 'explained' elements of the gender pay gap are likely to reflect discriminatory social norms or indirect discrimination. For example, why do women 'choose' lower paying occupations? Or, why do female undergraduates 'choose' courses that are likely to lead to lower paying occupations?

A high concentration of female workers and the phenomenon of low pay tend to go together. In an important case study in the UK of the British Broadcasting Corporation there was evidence of a link between low pay and occupational sex segregation; the highly female dominated occupations were paid the least and the highly male dominated occupations were paid particularly highly (Browne 2004). However, this is not the same as saying that a high concentration of female workers causes low pay or indeed vice versa, merely that the two appear to be linked.

There does seem to be a strong case that a reduction in the level of occupational segregation is an important factor in achieving pay equality for women across the board (Crompton and Harris 1999). However, this evidence is not clearcut. As Chapter 2 discussed, occupations that are gender-mixed, such as the law and medicine, show particularly large pay gaps, because of their high level of vertical segregation. Walby and Olsen (2002) point out the complexity of the explanations, arguing that the gender pay gap is closely linked to men's and women's different patterns of working, in terms of job 'choices' and also in employment participation history. The latter includes the take-up of flexible and part-time working. The implication here is that past decisions have a lasting effect, as Brewer and Paull (2006) also conclude for the UK and Glass (2004) for the US. Warren (2003) points out the effect of part-time working on overall economic security: an individual with a high hourly wage but who works few hours is likely to accrue in the longer term a smaller financial safety net (pension, savings, etc.) than someone with lower hourly wages, but working much longer hours. Drawing on an analysis of the Family Resources Survey in Britain, Warren (2003) argues that the relative disadvantage of women in managerial and professional jobs is related, in part, to their fewer years in full-time employment.

Women's concentration in part-time work, particularly in the UK, is sometimes given as an explanation for the gender pay gap. As we have seen, women in full-time work in the UK earn on average 82 per cent of the average hourly pay of male full-time employees; women in part-time work earn on average 60 per cent of the hourly male full-time wage (Women and Equality Unit 2004). Even after using statistical procedures that cancel out the effect of qualifications and job characteristics, part-timers earn less than full-timers (Anderson *et al.* 2001). Part-time work is constructed as low-pay low-value work. In both the UK and the US over 50 per cent of part-time women workers are low paid – defined as earnings below two-thirds of median male hourly earnings (Robson *et al.* 1999). There is currently very little opportunity for high-pay, high-value work to be done part-time (Smithson *et al.* 2004). It does not follow, however, that women's full-time working always carries better prospects. In the US, where there is a relative absence of women's part-time working, women's employment prospects in full-time working are no better (Blossfeld 1997). Blossfeld talks about the tendency in the US for married women's full-time jobs that are undemanding, lacking both promotion prospects and responsibility.

One orthodox explanation for the gender pay gap related to gender segregation would be that individuals are rewarded for the skills they take to the labour market – men have more highly prized skills and therefore they earn more. Without doubt patterns of gender segregation are inextricably linked with the skill categorization of jobs and in turn to pay. However, much of the feminist sociological literature draws attention to the social construction of skills (e.g. Collinson *et al.* 1990; Cockburn 1991; Rees 1998). It is considered no coincidence that jobs where there are many (or only) women tend to be poorly paid often because they are considered to be 'women's jobs', and women's skills are undervalued. This is a central factor underpinning unequal pay – (women's) caring skills are often given less value than (male) physical strengths. Generally, skills learned through education and training are more highly valued than 'innate' skills, such as caring (Rees 1998).

It is also important to consider the structures and mechanisms for pay setting and the effect on gendered pay differentials. Wages are determined by institutionalized processes including statutory regulation, collective bargaining, employment contracts and managerial action (Rubery *et al.* 2005). For example, it is clear in the US and UK contexts that union membership and collective bargaining help to raise women's pay in general (Rubery *et al.* 2005; Elvira and Saporta 2001). With reference to the US, women in unions earned an enormous 39 per cent more than their non-union counterparts in 1998 (Elvira and Saporta 2001). Elvira and Saporta cite four main explanations for this. First, unions tend to establish bureaucratic wage-setting procedures that reduce wage dispersion among employees. In this way unionization should reduce the wage gap for women working alongside men in the same organizations and jobs. Second, unions tend to reduce wage differentials within organizations regardless of occupation, which would tend to reduce differences between segregated male and female jobs. Third, management in unionized organizations is more likely to adhere to bureaucratic wage rules, reducing arbitrariness in wage rates and the potential for discrimination. Finally, some unions, especially more recently, have made explicit efforts to achieve gender pay equality. Collective bargaining appears to be beneficial to women. Rubery *et al.* (2005) point out that individualized wage bargaining tends to disadvantage women as they are often unable to supply the factors that attract the highest rewards, such as a commitment to working excessively long hours.

A further explanation is that the 'long hours culture' prevalent in many occupations and industries means that many women are unable to work full-time because of the open-ended nature of the commitment. This relates to the division of paid and unpaid work between women and men, with men prioritizing a 'breadwinner' role and women a 'carer' role. There is evidence that even within 'dual career households' the male career is prioritized and women take on primary responsibility for the home and family (Hardill and Watson 2004). Therefore a traditional division of domestic labour reinforces the gender pay gap. The implication here is that until men work the same amount at home as their wives and partners and/or work fewer hours in their jobs, the pay gap is likely to persist because many women will continue to 'choose' part-time work or to put their career on hold as a coping strategy.

In households where the man earns more than the woman, there is more likely to be a traditional division of household labour (Crompton and Harris 1999) and a longer delay in returning to paid work after childbirth (Brewer and Paull 2006). This underpins the dominant concept of the 'family wage', traditionally held by employers, trade unions and employees. The solution to narrowing the pay gap, according to Crompton and Harris, is a change in the working patterns of both men and women, breaking down the breadwinner/carer dichotomy. The other side of this is that differences between the earnings of men and women can be seen as perpetuating unequal gender divisions of labour within the household and in terms of responsibility for caring activities (Joshi 1998). This is because women's potential or actual earnings are likely to be lower than those of men and thus they are left in a weak bargaining position in terms of the decisions about the allocation of resources (time and money) within households.

Combating the pay gap

Closing the gender pay gap is a major gender equality policy issue within the European Union. The European Employment Strategy (EES) now includes a requirement that member states will take policy action to achieve a substantial reduction in the gender pay gap by 2010 (Rubery *et al.* 2005). Under the EES, EU member states are taking a range of actions to close the pay gap. The Equal Opportunities Commission (EOC 2005) reports that in Germany a review of the public sector grading system and its link to the gender pay gap is underway. In Sweden, the Equal Opportunities Act requires employers to publish wage data by gender and review pay structures and practices on an annual basis. The employer and the employees must cooperate in this area, with the employer required to provide to the trade unions all available information on the gender wage situation in the workplace, in order to draw up an annual plan. Since January 2001, it is explicitly stated in the Act that the main purpose of these mandatory annual plans is to discover, correct and prevent wage discrimination, as well as to estimate the cost of any necessary pay adjustments. Similarly, Danish employers are legally obliged to compile gender-differentiated wage statistics, provided for by a July 2001 amendment to the 1976 Act on Equal Pay for Men and Women (EIRO 2002). In Belgium, union and employers' representatives are being trained on the possible discriminatory effects of job classification systems. In the Netherlands, surveys are being undertaken looking into possible under-payment and gendered differences in remuneration in various business organizations. In the UK, the EOC is promoting voluntary Equal Pay Reviews and the Civil Service is required to undertake pay reviews (EOC 2005). A return to centralized, national-level wage negotiations in Finland has had some unexpected effects for gender equality, as equity supplements were paid to low-wage workers, thereby disproportionately helping women (Rubery *et al.* 2005).

The systematic and long-term gathering of pay statistics is a necessary prerequisite of any strategy to tackle the gender pay gap. There is insufficient space here to go into depth on the issue around the gathering of pay statistics, although we take up the issue in Chapter 9. A particular point is that pay statistics should be as detailed as possible in order to detect 'work of equal value' (EIRO 2002; Fransson *et al.* 2001). European countries have generally adopted legislation of an 'equal pay for work of equal value' type; this can be seen as a 'prohibiting' approach. Its use has turned out to be quite limited, even in those countries where trade unions as well as individuals can mount a legal case (EIRO 2002). In the UK, the limited use of the equal pay legislation has been attributed to its focus on the individual having to make the case against the organization, as well as the complexity and slowness of the procedure and the low success rate (Rees 1998). One recent development in the UK equal pay legislation is the introduction of an 'equal pay questionnaire' enabling individual employees to request specific information from their employers to establish whether they are paid less than a colleague doing the same job, or one thought to be of equal value. Although employers are not legally required to respond to such requests, failure to do so could weaken their defence in any potential employment tribunal case (EIRO 2004).

The UK approach to private sector employers remains one of encouragement towards action, as set out in the Kingsmill Report (2001) commissioned by the Department for Trade and Industry. Browne (2004) sees this as a 'naming and shaming' approach which it was hoped would act as a sufficient incentive. Her conclusion is that pay audits have largely not happened, as the Equal Opportunities Commission confirms (EOC 2006). By early 2006, only one-third of large organizations had completed an equal pay review (EPR). There are also clear differences between the public and private sectors: 61 per cent of public sector organisations have carried out an EPR or have one in progress, compared to only 39 per cent of the private sector. But even where they have occurred Browne argues that they are of limited use, because analysis is generally of poor quality and has little comparative value. This is because the data are not consistent across organizations, despite the production in 2002 by the UK's Equal Opportunities Commission of an 'Equal Pay Review Kit', designed to give employers step-by-step guidance on how to review their pay systems. Browne therefore doubts whether these audits can supply useful information or say much about the impact of equality policies that may be in place within organizations. Similarly, Neathey *et al.*'s (2005) qualitative study of equal pay reviews in 15 organizations found that the process for determining which jobs were of equal value had serious inadequacies in most cases. This meant that deciding where pay gaps between women and men could be justified or needed to be rectified was very difficult. The patchy outcome of Kingsmill's recommendations in relation to pay audit is regrettable. If these reviews were carried out systematically, and using the same methodology, the result would be an important and much-needed comparable data set across employing organizations in the UK labour market. In 2007 in the UK, a 'positive duty' on public bodies to promote equality between women and men will come into force under the Equality Act. All public authorities will have to conduct a systematic institution-wide identification and analysis of potential discriminatory policies, practices and procedures, select priority goals for change and take action to achieve outcomes such as tackling the gender pay gap (as well as examining vertical occupational segregation and the unequal impact of caring commitments). Some public authorities will have specific duties to publish their gender equality goals, monitor progress and publish annual progress reports. Data-gathering issues are obviously relevant, a point that we take up in Chapter 9.

Minimum wage legislation can be seen as another tool in providing a 'floor' to the wage structure (Rubery *et al.* 2005). The UK Equal Opportunities Commission (EOC) supported the introduction of a national minimum wage (NMW) as one means of narrowing the gender pay gap (Labour Research Department 1998). Women benefit disproportionately from a NMW because they are likely to be concentrated in low-paid work and to be in jobs or sectors where there is limited scope for collective bargaining. This reinforces the importance of legal regulation of pay. Nine out of the EU15 countries, including the UK, have a NMW. In the UK 70 per cent of beneficiaries are women, many working part-time (Rubery *et al.* 2005). The NMW impacts more on British women than men because they are more likely to work in low-paid sectors, including retail, hotels and restaurants, health and social work, and small firms. For example, at the time of its introduction in 1999, 66 per cent of women working in hotels and restaurants and an overwhelming 92 per cent in health and social work were earning below the NMW (Labour Research Department 1998). However, although a NMW raises the wages of the most low-paid women, for it to have a major effect on the gender pay gap, the level at which it is set would need to be relatively high, which is not the case.

Job evaluation is another possible tool for closing the gender pay gap (Fransson *et al.* 2001). This involves comparing the relative value of different jobs in terms of the level of demand the work makes on the average worker (ILO 2001). Encouragement of this approach could be argued to represent an example of government seeking to move away from a legislative approach towards getting employers, both in the private and public sectors, to take responsibility voluntarily (Browne 2004). A (re)evaluation of jobs – based on concrete criteria and with a gender perspective – might lead to a favourable valuation of 'typically female' occupations. This is essentially the 'comparable worth' approach and it has the potential to narrow the gender pay gap. The idea is that such systems make it possible to uncover and to rectify past discrimination in relation to the valuation of the work carried out by women.

There are both practical problems with job evaluation and more fundamental ones. One practical problem is the extent to which it is possible to compare jobs across bargaining areas, such as for manual and non-manual workers. There is also the challenge of how to compare very different jobs, often held in different sectors, on the basis of common and objective criteria. A further challenge is the issue of 'market value', which can reflect historical gender-based discrimination. In many countries, men more often work in the private sector; employers can argue that the wages are higher there because of demand-side factors. In Sweden, the 'market value' argument has caused the failure of most of the 'equal value' cases based on job evaluation brought before the Labour Court (EIRO 2002). Further, establishing the characteristics that underpin jobs is quite obviously not straightforward, which throws up more fundamental problems with job evaluation. As Rubery *et al.* (2005) note, organizations' evaluation of jobs may also reflect (gendered) social norms. Job evaluation is an illustration of a process of attaching values to particular jobs that is less than straightforward and indeed may be hedged about with contradictions. The practical problems involved in setting up a high quality and objective 'comparable worth' system for comparing different jobs and occupations are probably considerable.

A case study in the UK of the British Broadcasting Corporation (BBC) illustrates some of these problems (Browne 2004).The Kingsmill Report identified the BBC as a model employer because of its good human resource management, which used the tool of internal audits and reviews (Kingsmill 2001). Diversity objectives were highlighted in the corporate strategy, goals were set and progress towards these goals systematically measured. The tool was an 'objective factor-based job evaluation system'. An independent equality expert worked with a joint management/union group and they evaluated occupations and pay systems in a way that reflected each individual's skills and experience, 'free from gender bias' (Kingsmill 2001: 95). The idea that entirely objective criteria can be constructed in a context where the very concept of skill is infused with gender and gender stereotypes is problematic, if not naïve (see Collinson *et al.* 1990). Initial evaluation is that pay inequality between women and men at the BBC has not been eliminated (Browne 2004). Staff believed that the pay gap would remain because line managers had to meet bottom line budgetary constraints. There was a strong view from the respondents that women were often conceived as an 'inevitable liability'. The respondents also believed that the pay gap would remain until better childcare facilities and paid parental leave were available to both sexes. This implies that voluntary actions have limits, since the greatest chance of getting childcare facilities and paid parental leave is via state intervention.

Challenges for organizations

It has been noted that the significant level of the pay gap between women and men in many European countries acts as a potential disincentive for women to take up work or to remain at work (EIRO 2002). This inevitably impacts on the national economy in terms of loss of tax income and expenditure on welfare systems to combat low incomes, especially in old age (Walby and Olsen 2002). In addition to the gender pay gap being an economic issue for governments, it is also argued to have a significant detrimental effect on employers. The European Trade Union Confederation (2003) argues that pay systems that are simple, transparent and easy to understand send a positive message to the workforce about the value an organization puts on its staff. Therefore paying attention to this issue is about good management. Narrowing the gap increases the organization's morale, efficiency, productivity and competitiveness. In a similar vein, Kingsmill (2001) identifies three types of risks and costs to organizations that do not tackle this issue. The first type is that of 'reputational damage', including loss of investor confidence, loss of shareholder confidence, and loss of consumer base. The second type of risk is that of potential litigation and the third is the risk of not being able to recruit high-calibre employees, due to an organization acquiring a poor reputation as an employer. Thus, Kingsmill establishes a business case for tackling the gender pay gap, arguing that 'the scale and persistence of the gender pay gap in Britain reflects a failure in human capital management that is neither good for the economy nor in the interests of the majority of employers or employees' (2001: 6).

The pool of highly qualified labour is particularly sought after in the knowledge economy. It increasingly contains highly qualified young women, who have a much stronger tendency than less well qualified women to remain in the labour market over their adult lives and to work full-time (Joshi and Paci 2001; Rake 2000). Yet, as Purcell and Elias (2004) show and as we discussed earlier, a gender pay gap persists even at the point of entry into the labour market and grows larger as the cohort gets older. Purcell (2002) argues that the pay gap amongst young women and men graduates is a major challenge for employers. In the private sector particularly, women graduates are less likely than their male counterparts to have accessed high status and high earning jobs. There are clear risks here for organizations' reputation in relation to retention and advancement, as Kingsmill (2001) emphasizes.

Taking a holistic approach to combating the gender pay gap, Kingsmill recommends that organizations gather information on recruitment, career development paths, retention rates and reasons for leaving, comparing women with men, in order to evaluate gendered discrepancies and barriers. This underlines the importance of detailed, consistent and systematic data-gathering. According to Kingsmill, some of the questions that organizations need to ask themselves include: are the talents and aspirations of all staff being used to the greatest benefit of the organizations? Are there hidden pressures to work long or unsocial hours that disadvantage those with family responsibilities? Do pay and promotion structures reward long service in ways that unreasonably disadvantage those with career breaks or who work part-time? (Kingsmill 2001: 8).

Kingsmill clearly believes that there will be more success in tackling the gender pay gap at organizational level if initiatives are undertaken voluntarily and where they support business objectives. Yet, despite the fact that there is now an abundance of advice for employers on tackling the gender pay gap, employer inertia in this area is clear. The European Industrial Relations Observatory gives the example of the way that Sweden used its six-month EU Presidency in 2000 to put the European Commission's 1996 equal pay principle into practice at company and sectoral levels (EIRO 2002). This gives concrete advice and instructions, mainly to employers at company and sectoral levels. However, only seven countries responded, reporting no impact at all of this initiative. The main reason reported is that the code has not been disseminated among employers or promoted to enterprises. The evidence does seem to suggest that voluntary codes of practice have little or no effect.

Conclusions

There is widespread agreement that the gender pay gap (the average difference in earnings between women and men) has serious short-term and long-term effects on women and households. The 'gender income gap' is a wider measure that combines the effects of low pay, the gender pay gap and a range of other kinds of income.

The gender income gap is particularly large in the UK and US, but much less so in the Nordic countries. According to the European Commission, all social partners – governments, employers and trade unions – should be responsible for eliminating the gender pay gap. Yet there is evidence that employers tend to concentrate on other aspects, such as the improvement of childcare provision and promoting flexible working patterns. Employers' organizations in many European countries appear to take the view that existing wage differentials between women and men are not an expression of discrimination against female employees. Trade unions may have growing potential to close the gap; there is evidence that union membership and collective bargaining are having an effect on raising the level of women's pay.

The gender pay gap varies by ethnicity, age, presence/absence of children and by part-time/full-time status. It is particularly large for part-time workers, who constitute a major part of the female workforce in the UK. Although the gap widens as people get older, it is still evident amongst new graduates in the UK, particularly affecting graduates who enter management occupations and the legal professions.

There are many explanations of the pay gap. A particularly recent publication in the UK from the Institute for Fiscal Studies (Brewer and Paull 2006) suggests that it is primarily due to the persistence of a traditional domestic division of labour. Some effect of this is likely, but what underpins the domestic division of labour is a debatable question. Most commentators believe that occupational segregation (see Chapter 2) is the major cause of the pay gap. Another factor is the effect of children, with Brewer and Paull showing that there are two major points that affect pay growth: childbirth and the point at which children go into formal education. It is the accumulation of several periods of low wage growth at these times that makes for the gender pay gap, something which does not recover even when children have left home. Mothers' concentration in part-time working and in non-supervisory roles during this period exacerbates this effect.

Organizations that seek to narrow the gender pay gap increasingly use job evaluations. However, these are also underpinned by social norms and do not necessarily undermine traditional views of what constitutes 'skill'. There is a move in the UK from voluntary pay audits to compulsory ones, although the private sector remains unaffected by any compulsion, unlike in the Nordic countries. We make the point that systematic and consistent data-gathering will be needed if pay audits are to be meaningful and able to be compared over time and between organizations.

References

Anderson, T., Forth, J. and Metcalf, H. (2001) *The Gender Pay Gap, Final Report to the Women and Equality Unit*, London: Cabinet Office.

Blossfeld, H.-P. (1997) 'Women's part-time employment and the family cycle: a cross-national comparison', in H.-P. Blossfeld and C. Hakim (eds) *Between Equalization and Marginalization*, Oxford: Oxford University Press, 315–24.

Brewer, M. and Paull, G. (2006) *Newborns and New Schools: Critical Times in Women's Employment*, London: Institute for Fiscal Studies on behalf of the Department for Work and Pensions.

Browne, J. (2004) 'Resolving gender pay inequality? Rationales, enforcement and policy', *Journal of Social Policy*, 33 (4): 553–72.

Budig, M. and England, P. (2001) 'The wage penalty for mothers', *American Sociological Review*, 66: 204–25.

Cockburn, C. (1991) *In the Way of Women: Men's Resistance to Sex Equality in Organizations*, Basingstoke: Macmillan.

Collinson, D., Knights, D. and Collinson, M. (1990) *Managing to Discriminate*, London: Routledge.

Crompton, R. and Harris, F. (1999) 'Attitudes, women's employment and the changing domestic division of labour: a cross-national analysis', in R. Crompton (ed.)

Restructuring Gender Relations and Employment, Oxford: Oxford University Press, 105–27.

EIRO (2002) *Gender Pay Equity in Europe*, European Industrial Relations Observatory, <http://www.eiro.eurofound.eu.int>.

EIRO (2004) *Gender pay gap examined*, European Industrial Relations Observatory, <http://www.eiro.eurofound.eu.int>.

Elvira, M. and Saporta, I. (2001) 'How does collective bargaining affect the gender pay gap?', *Work and Occupations*, 28 (4): 469–90.

EOC (1999) *Women and Men in Britain: Pay and Income*, Manchester: Equal Opportunities Commission.

EOC (2003) *Women and Men in Britain: Pay and Income*, Manchester: Equal Opportunities Commission.

EOC (2005) *Women: Still Earning Less than Men*, Manchester: Equal Opportunities Commission.

EOC (2006) *Equal Pay Reviews 2005*, Manchester: Equal Opportunities Commission.

ETUC (2003) *Action Programme: Adopted at the ETUC 10th Statutory Congress 2003*, Brussels: European Trade Union Confederation.

European Commission (2005) *Growth and Jobs: Working Together for Europe's Future*, Brussels: European Commission.

Falkingham, J. and Rake, K. (2001) 'Modelling the gender impact of British pension reforms', in J. Ginn, D. Street and S. Arber (eds) *Women, Work and Pensions*, Buckingham: Open University Press, 67–85.

Fransson, S., Johansson, L. and Svenaeus, L. (2001) *Highlighting Pay Differentials Between Women and Men*, Sweden: Ministry for Gender Equality Affairs.

Ginn, J., Street, D. and Arber, S. (eds) (2001) *Women, Work and Pensions*, Buckingham: Open University Press.

Glass, J. (2004) 'Blessing or curse? Work–family policies and mothers' wage growth over time', *Work and Occupations*, 31 (3): 367–94.

Grimshaw, D. and Rubery, J. (2001) *The Gender Pay Gap: A Research Review*, Manchester: Equal Opportunities Commission.

Hardill, I. and Watson, R. (2004) 'Career priorities within dual career households: an analysis of the impact of child rearing upon gender participation rates and earnings', *Industrial Relations Journal*, 35 (1): 19–37.

ILO (2001) *Promoting Gender Equality – a Resource Kit for Trade Unions*, <http://www.ilo.org/public/english/employment/gems/eeo/tu/cha_4.htm#a.%20Equal%20Pay>.

Joshi, H. (1998) 'The opportunity cost of childbearing: more than mother's business', *Journal of Population Economics*, 11 (2): 161–83.

Joshi, H. and Paci, P. (2001) *Unequal Pay for Women and Men: Evidence from the British Birth Cohort Studies*, Boston, MA: MIT Press.

Kim, M. (2002) 'Has the race penalty for black women disappeared in the United States?', *Feminist Economics*, 8 (2): 115–24.

King, M. (ed.) (2001) *Squaring Up: Policy Strategies to Raise Women's Incomes in the US*, Ann Arbor, MI: University of Michigan Press.

Kingsmill, D. (2001) *Kingsmill Review of Women's Pay and Employment*, London: Stationery Office.

Labour Research Department (1998) 'A minimum boost to equality', *Labour Research*, March, 17–18.

Melkas, H. and Anker, R. (1998) *Gender Equality and Occupational Segregation in Nordic Labour Markets*, Geneva: ILO.

Modood, T. and Berthoud, R. (1997) *Ethnic Minorities in Britain: Diversity and Disadvantage*, London: Policy Studies Institute.

Neathey, F., Willison, R., Akroyd, K., Regan, J. and Hill, D. (2005) *Equal Pay Reviews in Practice*, Manchester: Equal Opportunities Commission/Institute for Employment Studies.

OECD (2002) *Employment Outlook*, Paris: OECD.

Purcell, K. (2002) *Qualifications and Careers: Equal Opportunities and Earnings among Graduates*, Manchester: Equal Opportunities Commission.

Purcell, K. and Elias, P. (2004) *Researching Graduate Careers Seven Years On: Higher Education and Gendered Career Development*, Warwick: Institute for Employment Research.

Rake, K. (2000) *Women's Incomes over the Lifetime*, London: The Stationery Office.

Rees, T. (1998) *Mainstreaming Equality in the European Union: Education, Training and Labour Market Policies*, London: Routledge.

Robson, P., Dex, S., Wilkinson, F. and Salido Cortes, O. (1999) 'Low pay, labour market institutions, gender and part-time work: cross-national comparisons', *European Journal of Industrial Relations*, 5 (2): 187–207.

Rubery, J. (ed.) (1998) *Equal Pay in Europe? Closing the Gender Wage Gap*, London: Macmillan.

Rubery, J., Grimshaw, D. and Figueiredo, H. (2005) 'How to close the gender pay gap in Europe: towards the gender mainstreaming of pay policy', *Industrial Relations Journal*, 36 (3): 184–213.

Smithson, J., Lewis, S., Cooper, C. and Dyer, J. (2004) 'Flexible working and the gender pay gap in the accountancy profession', *Work, Employment and Society*, 18 (1): 115–36.

Sokoloff, N. (1992) *Black Women and White Women in the Professions: Occupational Segregation by Race and Gender, 1960–1980*, London: Routledge.

UAW (2000) <http://www.uaw.org/publications/jobs_pay/02/0202/jpe02.html>.

US Bureau of Labor Statistics (1998) *Current Population Survey (Household Survey)*, OECD Corporate Data Environment.

Walby, S. and Olsen, W. (2002) *The Impact of Women's Position in the Labour Market on Pay and Implications for UK Productivity: Report to Women and Equality Unit*, London: Department of Trade and Industry.

Warren, T. (2003) 'A privileged pole? Diversity in women's pay, pensions and wealth in Britain', *Gender, Work and Organization*, 10 (4): 605–28.

Whitehouse, G., Zetlin, D. and Earnshaw, J. (2001) 'Prosecuting pay equity: evolving strategies in Britain and Australia', *Gender, Work and Organization*, 8 (4): 365–86.

Women and Equality Unit (2004) *Interim Update of Key Indicators of Women's Position in Britain*, London: Department of Trade and Industry.

Chapter 4

Women and part-time work

Introduction

It is difficult to make sense of women's employment without specific consideration of women's greater propensity to work part-time when compared with men. Part-time employment is increasingly referred to as flexible or 'atypical' working. Over the past 20 years, alongside women's increasing labour market participation, atypical employment has increased in most OECD countries (Rasmussen *et al.* 2004). Within the European Union part-time work is the dominant form of flexible work and is particularly widespread in areas of employment where women are concentrated (Fagan and Burchell 2002). It is therefore an important aspect of gender segregation in employment.

In most countries there is a strong association between part-time work and low pay. Women employed part-time have the highest risk of being low paid in the US and Europe when compared with women and men who work full-time (Robson *et al.* 1999). However, national policies can have an influence on women's overall levels of employment, particularly part-time work, resulting in cross-national variations in the proportion of women employed part-time. At the same time, it is argued that the 'growth of women's claim to equality, and the right to employment (even when their children are young), is also a more general trend that cuts across national differences' (Crompton *et al.* 2005: 228). Women's part-time work lessens household dependence on the male wage and destabilizes the 'male breadwinner' model of the family, but because earnings are likely to be relatively low, it does not result in a 'dual earner' model. Rather it underpins what has been termed a 'modified male breadwinner' model of the 'one and a half earner' family that has become prevalent in many industrialized countries, including the UK (Crompton *et al.* 2005). Table 1.1 in Chapter 1 illustrates this.

The extent and nature of part-time work

Table 4.1 shows the extent of women's part-time working[1] in selected countries. In all of the countries women are considerably more likely than men to be part-time workers. But there are interesting variations here. For example in Denmark

Table 4.1 Women's part-time employment in 2003, Nordic countries, UK and US

Country	As a proportion (%) of women's total employment	Women's share of part-time employment (%)
Denmark	22	64
Finland	15	64
Norway	33	75
Sweden	21	71
UK	40	77
US	19	69

Source: OECD 2004, extracted from Table E, Statistical Annex, data from European Labour Force Surveys and national labour force data.

and Finland relatively high rates of men are working part-time. In the UK, there are increasing numbers of men working part-time, but this tends to be a transitional labour market state for them, in contrast to a stable one for women (Francesconi and Gosling 2005).

Overall in Europe 41 per cent of employed women and 10 per cent of employed men work part-time (defined as fewer than 35 hours per week) (OECD 2004). Most men who work part-time are either young or approaching retirement. In contrast women often move into part-time work as a way of reconciling work and family life and therefore part-time women workers have a different age profile (Fagan and Burchell 2002). However, a substantial proportion of part-time workers are 'involuntary' (i.e. this is not their desired form of employment). This leads to the conclusion that as presently formulated, part-time working does not always provide an appropriate long-term means of reconciling work and family. According to Fagan and Burchell's study, over one-fifth of part-time women workers would like longer hours. Paradoxically, only half of mothers working part-time reported that their working hours were compatible with their family commitments.

Part-time working in the US is most common amongst young and old (Drobnič and Wittig 1997). In Europe, the overall part-time figure includes 14 per cent of employed women who are in 'marginal' part-time jobs with usual working hours of fewer than 20 per week (Fagan and Burchell 2002). More part-time jobs are organized around marginal hours in the Netherlands and the UK, while longer hours are the norm in Sweden and France.

In addition, 8 per cent of female part-timers hold more than one job. Within Europe there are also cross-national variations in the overall pattern with low levels of part-time work among women in the Mediterranean countries (Greece 2 per cent; Italy 21 per cent; Portugal 12 per cent) and high levels in some northern European countries (Holland 63 per cent; Sweden 36 per cent; UK 42 per cent) (Boisard *et al.* 2002). Fagan and Burchell's (2002) study, based on the European Foundation for the Improvement of Living and Working Conditions survey in

2000 on jobs and working conditions, also reveals gender segregation: part-time women workers account for large proportions of the workforce in feminized areas including service and sales, cleaning, clerical, and health and teaching professions. For example, 23 per cent of Europe's workers in sales, hotels and catering are part-time women; as are 27 per cent in personal services; and 35 per cent in health, social work and education. In contrast, the much smaller proportion of part-time men is dispersed across a wide range of occupations.

Part-time employment – equal or unequal work?

Laufer (1998: 65) argues that, in France at least, part-time work is not an egalitarian practice; it is 'unequal between men and women but also between groups of women'. This statement begs further examination of the nature of part-time work.

The gender pay gap is intricately linked to men's and women's different patterns of working, in terms of choices of job and also in employment participation history, which includes gender differences in the take-up of flexible and part-time working (Walby and Olsen 2002). Because in some countries such large numbers of women work part-time, pay for part-timers is an important gender equality issue. The gender pay gap in part-time work in the UK is 40 per cent, compared with 18 per cent in full-time work (EOC 2004). The gap is greatest when women part-timers are compared with men full-timers as shown in Table 4.2. Table 4.2 also shows that even after controlling for human capital – level of qualifications – women part-timers generally earn less than women full-timers, except at the highest levels of qualification, where the gap is minimal.

The quality of part-time jobs is another important issue from a gender equality perspective. The earnings gap between full-time and part-time women workers is smallest at the highest levels of qualification – see Table 4.2. Therefore, if pay is anything to go by, it looks as though at least in the UK highly qualified women experience high-quality part-time work, although only a minority of such

Table 4.2 Average hourly earnings of employees by qualifications, UK, 2004

Highest qualification achieved	Women full-timers (£)	Women part-timers (£)	Men full-timers (£)
Degree or equivalent	13.63	13.47	17.91
Higher education	10.70	10.42	13.40
GCE 'A' level or equivalent	8.51	7.01	10.88
GCSE grades A–C or equivalent	7.90	6.55	9.54
Other qualifications	7.81	6.44	9.01
No qualifications	6.28	5.67	7.58

Source: extracted from Women and Equality Unit (2004).

women works part-time. However, if we look beyond pay to job content, the picture is not quite so positive. Fagan and Burchell (2002) find that overall part-time jobs offer fewer opportunities for learning, are more monotonous and have fewer strategic responsibilities. Part-timers are the most likely to say that their skills are under-used and they receive less training than full-timers. An Equal Opportunities Commission investigation into part-time and flexible working in Britain found that four in five part-time workers are 'working below their potential', referring to this as a 'hidden brain drain' (EOC 2005). This is even likely to be the case among the minority of part-timers in professional jobs; therefore even being more highly qualified does not insulate against poor conditions and prospects in part-time work. In their analysis of UK data, Hoque and Kirkpatrick (2003) found that part-time professionals are far less likely to discuss their chances of promotion and their training needs with their employer. They are also marginalized in the sense that they are less likely to be asked for their views on future plans for the workplace and changes to work practices. Drawing on interviews within the US legal profession Epstein et al. (1998) argue that one of the biggest barriers to part-time work is the stigma attached to it and the consequences for longer-term career opportunities. They reveal how professionals define themselves, in part, by their commitment to working long hours and therefore professionalism is deemed to be incompatible with part-time work. Similarly, Smithson et al.'s (2004) study of the accountancy profession shows that part-time working damaged women's career and earnings prospects. As we discuss in Chapter 5, the professions may be particularly punitive towards forms of working that deviate from the normative full-time, long-hours, continuous employment pattern. In this way, part-time work reinforces the gender pay gap.

There have been attempts to understand part-time workers by categorizing them into different types, Hakim's being probably the best known (Hakim 1996). We return to this towards the end of the chapter in our discussion of whether part-time working represents a 'choice'. In an analysis which is more particularly related to organizational concerns, Jenkins (2004) identifies three types of part-time working. 'Core' part-time refers to situations where the majority of employees are part-time. 'Peak' part-time refers to the strategic utilization of part-time workers to cover surges in demand across the day and week. 'Ancillary' part-time refers to a situation where part-timers undertake specific tasks outside the 'normal' working hours of the organization. The point of this threefold classification is to highlight the variegated nature of part-time work and the importance of distinguishing between part-time employees based on their role within the organization, rather than simply on the basis of hours worked. From this we can see different employer strategies towards part-time workers that influence the quality of part-time work, although none of the categories emerges unproblematically as high quality. Jenkins found that ancillary part-timers were the most marginalized, being separated from full-time as well as other part-time staff and performing the most routine tasks. Peak part-time work was the most integrated, with part-timers carrying out the same tasks as full-timers. However, even this group did not have access to training and was therefore excluded from progression within the organization. Although the core part-time workforce constituted the majority, Jenkins claims that it was apparent that this group had no opportunity for career development or to work longer hours. None of these categories exemplifies 'quality' part-time working.

Sweden probably equates to the closest example of high-quality part-time working. Sundström (1997) argues that Swedish part-time working has been a prerequisite for Swedish women's relatively high levels of childbearing and also for their gender equality. The argument about fertility is that in the absence of the favourable conditions under which part-time working operates in Sweden, women would have had smaller families. If Sundström is correct, we would expect to see low fertility rates in the US, since it has particularly limited opportunities for part-time working, as we discuss further below. Yet, the US does not have a decreasing birthrate, kicking the trend of the generally decreasing birthrate seen in almost all industrialized countries. The relationship between childbearing and employment patterns is undoubtedly complicated and multifaceted (Windebank 2001). Pfau-Effinger's (2004) study of part-time working in Germany, Finland and the Netherlands emphasizes this complexity. She argues that cross-national differences in levels and function of part-time working need to be explained by a historical study of political, cultural and economic conditions in each country.

The argument about gender equality rests to a large extent on the conditions that part-time working operates under. Generally speaking, the number of hours is a good indicator of good or poor quality. Fagan and Burchell (2002) go so far as to argue that the 'fundamental gender difference in working conditions is the volume of hours worked' (2002: 67). Cousins (1994) shows that where working hours are longer, part-time employment is less strongly linked to low pay, low occupational status and poor long-term prospects. This is also borne out by the Fagan and Burchell study where it was found that women in white-collar managerial jobs work the longest hours among female part-timers. Part-time working in Sweden is relatively high-hours, with over 80 per cent of women part-timers working between 20 and 34 hours per week (Sundström 1997). Their employment rights differ very little from those of full-time workers. Further, part-time workers are often full-time workers who have taken a partial leave of absence, with the guarantee of being able to return to their full-time work; thus, argues Sundström, they are able to move in and out of part-time and full-time working in accordance with the life-cycle stage of their children. Sundström leaves unexamined the normative assumption that it is mothers who vary their employment patterns to fit in with the needs of children. The possibility that part-time working, however temporary, may harm long-term employment prospects is similarly not addressed.

 ## Diversity among women part-time workers

This brings us to a closer examination of who does part-time work. The probability of women with school-age children working part-time is variable in different

European countries (Blossfeld and Hakim 1997; Tijdens 2002). Tijdens shows that in the UK the effect is large, as it is in Sweden. But in Denmark and Finland, it does not affect the likelihood of being part-time. In the UK, a combination of having children under 15, being responsible for domestic work and being what is often termed a 'secondary earner'[2] all have an effect on being part-time. The effect of children is highlighted by the fact that in 2002 over 40 per cent of women who returned to work after childbirth changed from full-time to part-time work, while a quarter continued working full-time and the remainder part-time (Women and Equality Unit 2004). The birth of a second child may now be the trigger pushing women into part-time working (Francesconi and Gosling 2005).

In Denmark, the trend is, however, towards full-time employment, with a lower rate of part-time working in the 30–50 age range; by contrast typically in other European countries the part-time rate for this age group is high, being associated with childbearing and childrearing (Leth-Sørensen and Rohwer 1997). The segmented nature of part-time work (as highlighted by Jenkins' (2004) classification) means that women who switch to part-time work in the childrearing years are often 'thrown off their occupational path' into low-skilled feminized work (Blackwell 2001). Blackwell's longitudinal study of women in the UK over the period 1971–91 revealed that the downward moves involved lower pay, loss of status, poorer conditions of employment and skills atrophy. However, if women switched back to full-time work, there was evidence of some movement upwards and out of female-typed work. This reminds us that it is important to take a life course perspective on women and part-time work because most women do not work part-time for their entire working lives. However, as Brewer and Paull (2006) point out, in the long term women's income does not recover from episodes of part-time working associated with low wage growth. Similarly Francesconi and Gosling (2005) found that even after 15 years, women who had only one year of part-time employment followed by a move to full-time employment earned up to 10 per cent less per hour.

In the UK among the different ethnic groups, Pakistani and Bangladeshi women employees are most likely to work part-time and it is argued that this is explained by lack of formal qualifications combined with heavy family responsibilities (Dale *et al.* 2002). In contrast Indian women and black women are less likely than white women to work part-time (Women and Equality Unit 2004). Many minority ethnic women's earnings may provide a more important source of income than in many white households yet historically part-time jobs have been constructed for white women (Holdsworth and Dale 1997).

Emerging trends in part-time working

In some countries part-time jobs are growing faster and sometimes replacing full-time jobs; they are part of a broader trend towards diverse forms of non-standard or atypical employment (Hakim 1998). Part-time jobs are often presented as meeting both the needs of employers for flexibility and the needs of women for work that fits around family responsibilities (Laufer 1998). Given that it seems unlikely that employers' demand for flexibility will diminish, or that women will cease to take primary responsibility for the home and family, it is equally unlikely that levels of part-time work will decrease. Indeed, Burchell, Dale and Joshi (1997) foresee that there will be little decrease in levels of part-time work in the UK, which will continue to attract many women into low-paid and low-level occupations. Even in France, where part-time working has historically been at a particularly low level, there has been a marked increase in recent years (Laufer 1998).

However, not all countries appear to be moving towards higher levels of part-time working. The US's levels are stable and low, and Denmark's, traditionally high, are decreasing; this is attributed in part to better childcare (Rasmussen *et al.* 2004). A further reason for Denmark's reducing rate of part-time working is a demographic one: decreasing fertility rates. If women are child-free or have only one child, we can surmise that there will be less need for reduced hours. It seems reasonable to expect this trend to continue, as fertility levels drop Europe-wide (OECD 2001).

The growth in part-time working has been fed by a structural shift towards a service economy and a knowledge economy (Rasmussen *et al.* 2004). In all industrialized and industrializing countries, there is an increased diversity of working time; there is a growth in the range of part-time working hours, in unpredictable or irregular working and in unsocial hours (Mutari and Figart 2001). As a result of this, there is a decline in the full-time, standard working week. Nation-specific characteristics need also to be added to this mix. For example, a case study of UK nursing illustrates well the complex context that gives rise to a push toward part-time working (Edwards and Robinson 2004). The 'jigsaw' here is big labour shortages, a planned expansion driven by political response to a public that is persistently anxious about healthcare, and a 24/7 working requirement. Part-time workers may seem the answer, but as we discuss below in further examination of Edwards and Robinson's work, this turns out not to be the case.

Explaining cross-national variations in part-time work

In seeking to explain the varying levels of part-time working in different countries Ellingsæter (1992) emphasizes the complex relations between the market, the state and the family, as well as individual characteristics. It is argued that national 'gender cultures' need to be explained by reference to historical development (Pfau-Effinger 2004). Blossfeld (1997) emphasizes demand-side, supply-side and 'country-context' mechanisms, which include ideology and politics. Fagan and O'Reilly (1998) argue that trends in part-time working are embedded in national structures and cultures; these are then interpreted through particular gender arrangements at household level.

The contrasting cases of the UK and France are instructive and illustrate the impact of state policies on women's employment patterns. The two countries are among those with the highest levels of women's employment in Europe. However, British women are significantly more likely to work part-time (40 per cent) than French women (31 per cent) and this is particularly apparent during the family formation years when French women are more likely to retain continuity of employment and to work full-time (Windebank 2001). The laissez-faire approach to the family of the British state has resulted in high-cost and relatively limited availability of childcare in the UK and this is a significant factor pushing women into local part-time jobs. Government initiatives in the Blair administration have assisted with the costs of childcare and increased the numbers of affordable nursery places. Nevertheless, the cost of childcare remains high in the UK and has increased markedly in recent years, with the average cost being around one-third of the average salary (Daycare Trust 2006). In contrast, France is often seen as a 'halfway house' between the 'woman friendly' states of Scandinavia and the liberal Anglo-Saxon countries (Windebank 2001). Parents in France have few statutory rights to adapt their employment to childcare needs and the labour market does not provide extensive opportunities for part-time work. Windebank argues that the French state compensates for this rigidity by subsidizing and supporting non-home-based childcare for pre-school age children in the form of free nursery education for all three- to six- year-olds and financial assistance to parents using a registered childminder for under-threes.

For many women, caring responsibilities extend beyond raising a family. For example, in the UK, one in five middle-aged women cares for an elderly, sick or disabled relative or friend (ONS 1998). Nor are such (unpaid) caring activities restricted to middle-aged women – ONS figures show that 13 per cent of women aged 30 to 44 have caring responsibilities of this sort. Almost one-third of carers provide help for more than 20 hours per week. In this gender culture, women's expectations of their employment prospects may well be low.

Another aspect of the national policy contexts is the role of trade unions, discussed further in Chapter 8. The impact of trade unions on legitimating and constructing or challenging and breaking down various forms of inequality is hotly debated (e.g. Colling and Dickens 2001). British trade unions can be justifiably criticized for historically neglecting women's interests and for failing to organize and act as a voice for part-time workers. It is certainly the case that countries with highly centralized bargaining structures and high levels of female trade union membership have lower rates of, but better quality part-time working – the Scandinavian countries in particular (Greene and Kirton 2005). The historical construction of part-time work as inferior has arguably not been an issue that trade unions have been overly concerned with in the UK and this neglect could contribute to the jigsaw of explanations for the particular characteristics of UK part-time working. However, more recently the British unions have made a greater effort to 'speak to' part-timers' concerns. Part-time membership, whilst at low levels, has held relatively firm in the years of membership decline (Greene and Kirton 2005). Budd and Mumford (2004) in their examination of the 1998 British Workplace Employee Relations Survey, find that workplaces with recognized unions are more likely to have job-sharing policies (as well as other family-friendly policies) than are similar workplaces with no recognized unions. Job sharing is usually a higher quality type of part-time job, although relatively rare. This is possibly because it appears to be unpopular with employers (Hakim 1998). The implication is that job shares are potentially popular for employees, possibly allowing women to retain more highly skilled jobs, but not for employers who might fear greater costs such as training.

It is not just the extent of part-time working that varies cross-nationally; the quality of part-time working – the degree to which it is associated with low pay, poor conditions and poor employment prospects – also varies (Rasmussen *et al.* 2004). In some cases (the Netherlands and Denmark are cited by Rasmussen *et al.*) part-time working is negotiated between the social partners of government, employers and trade unions, resulting in better quality part-time jobs. In contrast, in other countries where the market is prioritized, part-time working is of a poor quality, and more firmly associated with poor employment conditions and prospects. For example, Table 4.1 shows that women's part-time employment in the US is at a low level, particularly when compared to the UK. As in many other countries, part-time working in the US is generally found in the secondary labour market, where jobs are characterized by low skill requirements, low pay and few prospects for advancement. However, the broader context of part-time work is significantly different from most European countries. Hakim (1998) claims that the US is unlike any EU countries in that American women's high employment rates derive principally from high levels of full-time work. Mothers are often full-time secondary earners; this is a situation where the choice is between full-time jobs and paying for marketized childcare or having no job at all. Most employers pay health insurance for full-time workers, but only a few do so for part-timers – a powerful disincentive to work part-time in the US. Part-time workers tend not to be eligible for sick leave, paid vacations, pensions, or dental and life insurance (Tilly 1996; Drobnic and Wittig 1997). In such a context it is easy to see why women would not choose part-time work as a means of balancing work and family, a theme returned to below.

Making comparisons between countries in terms of the extent and nature of women's part-time working and the institutional and social contexts in which it takes place reminds us that women's work patterns do not necessarily reflect their preferences and choices, as we discuss below.

Do employers demand part-time working?

In the context of a growth in part-time working, there is a debate about whether it is led by employer demand or by employees' preferences and choices. For a multifaceted approach, part-time working can be conceptualized as an interplay between demand and supply factors (Tijdens 2002; Plantenga 2004). As stated earlier, part-time working is the main form of flexible working in the UK and is often seen there as important in terms of competition and as part of a global strategy of deregulation (Standing 1999). This argument positions part-time work as important for the economy and therefore important for employers. Jenkins (2004) cites evidence from Millward *et al.* (2000) that there is a growth in the number of workplaces that are using part-time workers as a 'core' workforce (where most of the employees work part-time). Part-time workers' 'choice' is thus limited by employment policies on flexible restructuring; thus they contest those (for example Hakim 1998, 2000) who argue that the growth of part-time work reflects employee preferences. Millward *et al.*(2000) claim a strong connection between de-skilling and the most marginalized forms of part-time work. As Grant *et al.* (2005) show, managers were often unaware of the skills, talents and aspirations of their part-time workers. Furthermore, they tended to be negative about both part-time workers and the jobs they did.

Writing about the US, Tilly (1991) also places the emphasis on the demand from employers for part-time workers, identifying three broad categories of part-time jobs – short time, secondary and retention part-time jobs – all of which meet different employer needs. Short time jobs are created by employers who are temporarily reducing the number of work hours for economic reasons – as involuntary part-time employment, or even a form of partial unemployment. Secondary part-time jobs are created by employers, argues Tilly, in order to pay low wages and to bring about working time flexibility. Tilly's point is that secondary part-time jobs are characterized by low skill requirements, low pay and fringe benefits, low productivity and high turnover. There is a third category, which is 'retention part-time jobs' – created to retain a company's valued skilled employees, in particular women with young children. It would seem likely that professional and managerial women returning to the same employer following maternity leave fall into this category. As discussed earlier, although the evidence shows that these three categories certainly exist, the most common one is secondary part-time jobs, suggesting that on balance part-time work, as usually constructed, is employer-led.

Nevertheless, some authors have argued that there is a 'mutuality of benefit' in the context of the 'new business case' for part-time working (Edwards and Robinson 2004: 168). For example, the benefits for the employer might include employee retention (benefit to the employer because there are lower recruitment and turnover costs) and more flexible service delivery. For the employee, the benefit is the opportunity to reconcile work with 'non-work' responsibilities, and/or quality of life preferences; the expansion of part-time work can therefore meet a social demand. However, the 'mutuality of benefit' argument ignores the possibility that part-time working can have negative short-term and long-term effects on women's employment conditions and prospects, discussed earlier.

Edwards and Robinson's (2004) study illuminates the particular context of the UK's National Health Service (NHS). Here the business case for part-time working is particularly strong because there are big labour shortages in the context of planned expansion and therefore recruitment and retention of staff is particularly important. For employers, part-time work would be a potential solution in this context, argue Edwards and Robinson, since the health service has to operate 24/7, staffed by a workforce that is almost all women, many of whom have domestic caring commitments. There is also a climate of work intensification in view of government pressure to deal with public dissatisfaction with the health service. However, part-time working was not found to be well established and the potential benefits not realised by either side – employers or employees. Edwards and Robinson question whether the 'new business case' for part-time working is flawed, or whether there are particular factors associated with UK healthcare. One of the factors seems to be that senior managers endorsed the possibilities of part-time working, whereas line managers did not. Thus the principle was accepted at the top level, but the implementation was not popular at operational level. Line managers found that part-time workers were inflexible. They were less willing to work additional hours than full-time workers were, making it difficult for managers to deal with staff shortages. Also their training needs and costs were just as great, although they worked fewer hours. Similarly, the managerial and administrative costs were high, again in relation to fewer hours. Employers said that they could not get the flexibility they needed and therefore they relied on external nursing banks in order to achieve flexibility. Amongst the part-time workers there was little evidence of career opportunities and progression. The full-time staff said that the part-time staff had increased pressure on them. Edwards and Robinson conclude that the NHS management had not adjusted to a new climate where part-timers might have different needs. The part-time nurses themselves were isolated; they did not use their collective industrial strength and did not pressure management. This case study is perhaps indicative of the complex nature of the supply of and demand for part-time working.

Do women choose part-time work?

Much of the debate about women's propensity for part-time work has been sparked by Hakim (1998, 2000) who has argued controversially that the emphasis on the negative effects of part-time working has tended to obscure the positive reasons why women choose to work part-time. Her arguments rest on 'preference theory', as set out in Chapter 1. Hakim's consideration of women and part-time working is a key element of her advancement of this theory. She argues that the explanation of part-time working is a major challenge for social scientists. There is a need to explain why women working part-time apparently express higher levels of satisfaction with their jobs than the reported satisfaction of full-time workers, even though full-time working is objectively higher status, better paid and has better long-term prospects. Her claim is that for many women and some men, part-time work is subordinated to family-centred non-market activities and sometimes to other sorts of activities – political, voluntary, religious, sporting, creative and so forth. Thus, paid work frequently revolves around other sorts of unpaid activities, domestic and non-domestic. Women *choose* this option in preference to full-time jobs and this is a key factor in what she argues is part-time workers' greater job satisfaction. Hakim's assumption is that part-time workers are secondary earners contentedly balancing work and family; thus they will be in two-person households. Missing from the equation, therefore, are single-parent households seeking, and very likely struggling (at least in the UK and US contexts) to combine work and family.

One particular aspect of preference theory relates to part-time working; here the argument is that at least three types of part-time working exist, and that these are linked to different levels of commitment, and to different work orientations. Most part-time working, argues Hakim, is sought by women (i.e. voluntary); only a minority is not sought (i.e. involuntary). The three types are 'marginal jobs' which are up to 10 hours, 'half-time jobs' between 11 and 29 hours weekly and 'reduced-hours jobs', of between 30 and 36 hours a week. This third category is therefore just a few hours short of full-time. Hakim's categorization is considerably more than a mere attempt at dividing up the part-time workforce for analytical purposes, since she links each category to levels of commitment to the labour market – the fewer hours worked the less work commitment a person has.

There is also a reference to women's identity in Hakim's work, since she refers to different work orientations: 'Part-time working ... does not require the same commitment to the employment career as full-time jobs – in time, effort and personal identity' (Hakim 1998: 115).

Marginal jobs do not seriously alter the social status and personal identity of workers (Hakim 1998). Their personal identity and social status derive from their other, full-time activity – as housewife, artist, student and so forth. Such jobs are also referred to as vertical part-time work, because they may only involve one day a week. In practice this type of work is largely taken by students; they account for much of the recent expansion in male as well as female part-time work in countries such as the Netherlands, Denmark and Britain (Plantenga 1995). The highest concentration of part-time jobs is in the 'half-time' category of around 20 hours a week. This is the dominant type in Britain, Germany, France, Belgium, the Netherlands and Luxembourg. Half-time jobs are typically organized by the employer on a permanent long-term basis. They are often constructed as separate jobs from full-time jobs. People are often directly specifically recruited for these types of jobs.

'Reduced hours jobs' are often organized in response to an employee's request; the employer agrees to them in order to retain workers in whom training has been invested or who are otherwise valuable (Tilly (1991) calls these jobs 'retention jobs'). They involve no change of occupation or employer, and can be a temporary arrangement. The worker can return to full-time hours when appropriate. Hakim's argument is that this type of part-time worker is most appropriately classified along with full-time workers and full-time jobs. One example is France, where reduced hours jobs typically consist of standard full-time hours over four days a week, allowing women to stay at home on Wednesdays when schools are closed.

Hakim's ideas are widely criticized for failing to take adequate account of the structural constraints facing many women who want to participate in paid work.

For example, the 'choice' between full-time and part-time work only begins to be a real choice if there is no difference between the two in terms of status and skill levels, hourly pay, conditions and long-term prospects. However, as discussed above, this is not the case in the UK or many other countries. Her assumptions about commitment also appear to be faulty. Crompton and Le Feuvre (1996) looked at female pharmacists and financiers in France and Britain and found that the former were more likely to work part-time because the hours of work in the pharmacy profession were more flexible than in the finance industry. However, the pharmacists were no less committed to their work than the financiers. Nevertheless, it is argued that Hakim's understanding that part-time work equates with less work commitment reflects many employers' perceptions, which explains why there is a reluctance to offer high-skill jobs as part-time (McGlynn 2003; Sommerlad and Sanderson 1998).

 Also not taken into account by 'choice' arguments is the effect of the absence or availability of high quality and affordable childcare provision. Here the cross-national analysis carried out by Bielenski and Wagner (2004) is very relevant; they conclude that the role of part-time work is ambiguous. In countries that offer poor public childcare facilities, part-time work is often the only form of labour market access for women with family responsibilities – that is they only have the choice between part-time work and not participating in paid work. In countries with a well-developed childcare infrastructure, mothers have a more genuine choice about whether and to what extent they engage in paid employment. Bielenski and Wagner (2004) present evidence that women working reduced hours in these countries tend to be doing so because they do not want to work full-time. This strengthens the argument that a more genuine 'choice' is offered by particular social policy contexts.

However, it is equally important to take account of the gendered division of family care and household work. As we show in Chapter 7, the evidence suggests that the husbands/partners of full-time workers share household tasks to a greater extent than those of women who work part-time. Even so, there is little evidence in any industrialized countries of equal partnership arrangements within house-holds and therefore women still tend to carry a 'double burden' of paid and unpaid work (Windebank 2001). This adds to the argument that women's employment choices are constrained.

Challenges for management and organizations

It seems highly unlikely that the prevalence of part-time work in much of Europe will be reversed even if it stabilizes. It is clear from the evidence that most women who work part-time do so in order to reconcile work and family life, but they usu-ally pay a heavy price for making this 'choice'. It is also clear that employers determine the way that part-time work operates in specific organizational con-texts. What then are the prospects for part-time work to offer more genuine choices and a positive means of reconciling work and family life? How can employers be convinced that they can benefit from offering higher quality part-time jobs?

One issue for organizations is to revisit the business case for part-time working. The traditional business case is that labour costs are reduced because of the potential for matching working hours to the needs of the service. This approach is likely to appeal in occupational areas with particular time-limited tasks, such as catering and cleaning. Part-time working is also likely to be attractive to organizations operating on extended hours, such as supermarkets and leisure facilities, thus avoiding expensive overtime premiums incurred from full-time employees. The effect of this kind of cost-minimization approach to part-time work is to produce a segmented and secondary labour force fuelled by a plentiful supply of women, with a lack of collective strength and poor legal and social protection (until recently in the UK).

In order to meet employer needs, does part-time work have to be seen in this rather negative way or is there a 'new business case', to be contrasted with the traditional case? Here the emphasis is more on flexibility as an advantage for employees as well as employers. It can therefore be considered as part of the developing 'diversity climate'. The new business case has a context of legislation throughout Europe that protects those who are unable or do not want to work full-time through age, care responsibilities, disability and so forth. The social and economic context is one of an increasingly diverse workforce, in terms of age, ethnicity and in terms of women being increasingly located in professional employment. One argument might be that the ubiquitous 'long hours culture' of managerial and professional employment could be just as damaging in the longer term for organizations as for employees. Therefore offering more flexible arrangements might enable more women to sustain their careers over the child rearing phase so that their skills and training are not lost to the organization or the wider economy.

A consideration of part-time working inevitably links to the issue of long working hours. In the UK around one-quarter of employees work longer hours than their contracts stipulate and around 20 per cent work more than 48 hours per week on a regular basis (Hogarth et al. 2003). Senior managers, professionals and people in manual occupations are most likely to work long hours over sustained periods of time. A major reason cited by employees in Hogarth et al.'s study for working long hours was a cultural one: custom and practice in that occupation, which resulted in an expectation of 'presenteeism'. One issue in reducing hours is that earnings can relate to hours worked; this is the case in occupations where overtime is the norm. We know that men work overtime considerably more than women (this is the reason for using the hourly calculation of women's and men's pay, rather than a weekly or monthly one, since the inclusion of overtime, carried out disproportionately by men, distorts the pay gap). Thus there may be resistance from employee organizations to reducing hours. Yet, if this is not done, the long hours culture will remain the yardstick against which women are judged. Those who do not match up to this may be disadvantaged in various ways, but particularly in terms of training and promotion opportunities. If long hours are associated with commitment to senior jobs, then many women will be at a disadvantage.

Further, the organizational expectation of long hours has made it less possible for men to share domestic work, leaving this for women and thus creating a vicious circle. Working hours are shaped by gendered social norms that are historically rooted, sometimes over long periods of time (Pfau-Effinger 2004), making them resistant to policy interventions. For example, the EU Working Time Directive was implemented by the UK government in 1998 in the form of Working Time regulations. The basis of these is a maximum 48-hour working week. Following considerable opposition by employer organizations, employees are able to opt out of the regulations, and this has resulted in almost 20 per cent of workers – largely senior managers and manual workers – signing an agreement to opt out of the regulations (Labour Research Department 2004: 25). There is some doubt about whether workers opt out voluntarily: a quarter of those who have signed say they were given no choice. There is some early evidence, however, that the Working Time Regulations may be having some effect on men's working hours, since a slight reduction can be observed in the Labour Force Survey data from 1999–2002 (Hogarth *et al.* 2003).

The UK work–life balance campaign is located in this context, arguably founded on research evidence that all can benefit – a 'mutuality of benefit' (Gottlieb *et al.* 1998: 168). The 'new business case' for high-quality part-time work focuses on employee retention which proves a benefit to the employer because lower recruitment and turnover costs result. The argument is that a skilled part-time workforce will be able to increase its time commitment in the long term and this provides sound argument for building 'quality' part-time working (Bruegel and Perrons 1995). For the employee, the opportunity is to reconcile work with 'non-work' responsibilities, and/or accommodate quality of life preferences (Dex and Scheibl 1999). Yet, a study of women part-timers and their managers in the UK has shown that many women had 'demoted' themselves to low-grade part-time jobs because of the intensity of work in senior level, full-time jobs and because of the absence of work–life balance policies (Grant *et al.* 2005). Once in a low-paid part-time job, they tended to lose confidence in their abilities.

The 'new business case' set out by Bruegel and Perrons (1995) will, however, come at a cost. The creation of 'quality' part-time working would involve a longer-term strategy, being focused less on cost-minimization than on improving the quality of working life within the organization, as well as building opportunities for progression and promotion. Part-time working would need to be available across all types and levels of work (Grant *et al.* 2005). Yet Edwards and Robinson (2004) found in their study of part-time workers in the UK's National Health Service (discussed above) that employers reported additional labour costs and took the view that these were not necessarily outweighed by enhanced recruitment and retention. It seems unlikely that all organizations will go down the 'new business case' road or that the terms and conditions implied by it would be evenly applied to all types of part-time workers. Most likely to benefit from such an approach are highly qualified and professional women, leaving lower skilled part-time workers just as vulnerable and marginalized as at present.

Conclusions

Part-time working is a major component of women's employment in the UK, although in the US this is not the case. In some countries (e.g. France) it is increasing and in others decreasing, perhaps associated with the development of one-child families. Because of its prevalence in the UK, its consequences in terms of women's economic wellbeing are particularly important. Although some part-time jobs, particularly long-hours ones, are 'quality' jobs, most commentators believe that part-time working is a major factor in women's economic insecurity, because much of it is poorly paid, has short hours and lacks prospects. Even being highly qualified does not insulate against negative consequences; working part-time can be seen as a symbol of lack of commitment. The overall quality of part-time jobs in Europe and the US is then quite poor, but analysis of other countries shows the influence of labour laws and welfare policies. In the Nordic countries, part-time working carries fewer penalties; this leads to the possibility that some types of approach to welfare may yield more of a genuine choice for women. But even in this context, it is possible that part-time working has negative long-term effects; this is because it is perhaps inevitably compared to the normative yardstick of the full-time long-hours model of male employment.

We have discussed the debate, particularly focusing on Hakim's work, about whether part-time working is undertaken because many women freely choose it – or whether it is more a function of constraints. Regardless of the outcome of this academic debate, the everyday reality for women is that if part-time jobs are low paid and have little training or lack long-term opportunities, then there will be negative short-term and long-term effects. These will impinge on individuals' economic wellbeing, obviously, but they also have an effect on governments with a commitment to maintain income for older people. The unanswered question is whether organizations see it as their responsibility to upgrade the quality of part-time working. Evidence from cross-national research indicates that this is more likely to be achieved as the result of negotiation between government, employers and trade unions. We return to the issues for organizations in the concluding chapter.

Notes

1 The definition of part-time work that is used by most international data-gathering organizations such as OECD is fewer than 30 hours per week. However, some surveys such as the UK *Labour Force Surveys* also ask for a self-definition.
2 A secondary earner is defined as 'someone who relies on another person as the primary earner and contributes partial or secondary income to the collective pot' (Hakim 1998: 115).

References

Bielenski, H. and Wagner, A. (2004) 'Employment options of men and women in Europe', in J. Giele and E. Holst (eds) *Changing Life Patterns in Western Industrial Societies*, Oxford: Elsevier, 137–61.

Blackwell, L. (2001) 'Occupational sex segregation and part-time work in modern Britain', *Gender, Work and Organization*, 8: 146–63.

Blossfeld, H.-P. (1997) 'Women's part-time employment and the family cycle: a cross-national comparison', in H.-P. Blossfeld and C. Hakim (eds) *Between Equalization and Marginalization*, Oxford: Oxford University Press, 315–24.

Blossfeld, H-P. and Hakim, C. (1997) *Between Equalization and Marginalization: Working Part-time in Europe and the United States of America*, Oxford: Oxford University Press.

Boisard, P., Cartron, D., Gollac, M. and Valeyre, A. (2002) *Temps et travail: la durée du travail*, Dublin: European Foundation for the Improvement of Living and Working Conditions.

Brewer, M. and Paull, G. (2006) *Newborns and New Schools: Critical Times in Women's Employment*, London: Institute for Fiscal Studies on behalf of the Department for Work and Pensions.

Bruegel, I. and Perrons, D. (1995) 'Where do the costs of unequal treatment for women fall? An analysis of the incidence of the costs of unequal pay and sex discrimination in the UK', *Gender, Work and Organization*, 2 (3): 113–24.

Budd, J. and Mumford, K. (2004) 'Trade unions and family-friendly policies in Britain', *Industrial and Labor Relations Review*, 57 (2): 204–22.

Burchell, B., Dale, A. and Joshi, H. (1997) 'Part-time work among British women', in H.-P. Blossfeld and C. Hakim (eds) *Between Equalization and Marginalization*, Oxford: Oxford University Press, 210–46.

Colling, T. and Dickens, L. (2001) 'Gender equality and trade unions: a new basis for mobilization?', in M. Noon and E. Ogbonna (eds) *Equality, Diversity and Disadvantage in Employment*, Basingstoke: Palgrave.

Cousins, C. (1994) 'A comparison of the labour market position of women in Spain and the UK with reference to the "flexible" labour debate', *Work, Employment and Society*, 8 (1): 45–67.

Crompton, R. and Le Feuvre, N. (1996) 'Paid employment and the changing system of gender relations: a cross-national perspective' *Sociology*, 30 (3): 427–45.

Crompton, R., Brockman, M. and Lyonette, C. (2005) 'Attitudes, women's employment and the domestic division of labour: a cross-national analysis in two waves', *Work, Employment and Society*, 19 (2): 213–33.

Dale, A., Shaheen, N., Fieldhouse, E. and Kalra, V. (2002) 'The labour market prospects for Pakistani and Bangladeshi women', *Work, Employment and Society*, 16 (1): 5–25.

Daycare Trust (2006) *2006 Childcare Costs Survey*, London: Daycare Trust, <www.day-caretrust.org.uk>.

Dex, S. and Scheibl, F. (1999) 'Business performance and family-friendly policies', *Journal of General Management*, 24 (4): 33–37.

Drobnič, S. and Wittig, I. (1997) 'Part-time work in the United States of America', in H.-P. Blossfeld and C. Hakim (eds) *Between Equalization and Marginalization*, Oxford: Oxford University Press, 289–314.

Edwards, C. and Robinson, O. (2004) 'Evaluating the business case for part-time working amongst qualified nurses', *British Journal of Industrial Relations*, 42 (1): 167–183.

Ellingsæter, A. (1992) *Part-time Work in European Welfare States: Denmark, Germany, Norway and the United Kingdom Compared*, Oslo: ISF.

EOC (2004) *Facts about Women and Men in Great Britain*, Manchester: Equal Opportunities Commission.

EOC (2005) *Part-time is No Crime: So Why the Penalty?* Manchester: Equal Opportunities Commission.

Epstein, C. F., Seron, C., Oglensky, B. and Saute, R. (1998) *The Part-time Paradox: Time Norms, Professional Lives, Family, and Gender*, London: Routledge.

Fagan, C. and O'Reilly, J. (1998) 'Conceptualising part-time work: the value of an integrated comparative perspective', in J. O'Reilly and C. Fagan (eds) *Part-time Prospects*, London: Routledge.

Fagan, C. and Burchell, B. (2002) *Gender, Jobs and Working Conditions in the European Union*, European Foundation for the Improvement of Living and Working Conditions: Dublin.

Francesconi, M. and Gosling, A. (2005) *Career Paths of Part-time Workers*, Manchester: Equal Opportunities Commission.

Gottlieb, B., Kellaway, E. and Barham, E. (1998) *Flexible Work Arrangements*, Chichester: John Wiley.

Grant, L., Yeandle, S. and Buckner, L. (2005) *Working Below Potential: Women and Part-time Work*, Manchester: Equal Opportunities Commission.

Greene, A. M. and Kirton, G. (2005) 'Trade unions and equality and diversity', in A. Konrad, P. Prasad and J. Pringle (eds) *Handbook of Workplace Diversity*, London: Sage, 489–510.

Hakim, C. (1996) *Key Issues in Women's Work*, London: Athlone Press.

Hakim, C. (1998) *Social Change and Innovation in the Labour Market*, Oxford: Oxford University Press.

Hakim, C. (2000) *Work–Lifestyle Choices in the 21st Century*, Oxford: Oxford University Press.

Hogarth, T., Daniel, W., Dickerson, A., Campbell, D., Wintherbotham, M. and Vivian, D. (2003) *The Business Context to Long Hours Working*, London: Department for Trade and Industry.

Holdsworth, C. and Dale, A. (1997) 'Ethnic group differences in women's employment', *Work, Employment and Society*, 11 (3): 435–57.

Hoque, K. and Kirkpatrick, I. (2003) 'Non-standard employment in the management and professional workforce: training, consultation and gender implications', *Work, Employment and Society*, 17 (4): 667–89.

Jenkins, S. (2004) 'Restructuring flexibility: case studies of part-time female workers in six workplaces', *Gender, Work and Organization*, 11 (3): 306–33.

Labour Research Department (2004) 'Proposals on working time disappoint unions', *Labour Research*, December.

Laufer, J. (1998) 'Equal opportunity between men and women: the case of France'. *Feminist Economics*, 4 (1): 53–69.

Leth-Sørensen, S. and Rohwer, G. (1997) 'Women's employment and part-time work in Denmark', in H.-P. Blossfeld and C. Hakim (eds) *Between Equalization and Marginalization*, Oxford: Oxford University Press, 247–66.

McGlynn, C. (2003) 'The status of women lawyers in the United Kingdom', in U. Schultz and G. Shaw (eds) *Women in the World's Legal Professions*, Oxford and Portland, OR: Hart Publishing, 139–56.

Millward, N., Bryson, A. and Forth, J. (2000) *All Change at Work? British Employment Relations 1980–1998*, London: Routledge.

Mutari, E. and Figart, D. (2001) 'Europe at the crossroads: harmonisation, liberalisation and the gender of work time', *Social Politics*, 8 (1): 36–64.

OECD (2001) *Employment Outlook*, Paris: OECD.

OECD (2004) *Employment Outlook*, Paris: OECD.

ONS (Office for National Statistics) (1998) *Social Focus on Men and Women*, London: Stationery Office.

Pfau-Effinger, B. (2004) *Development of Culture, Welfare States and Women's Employment in Europe*, Aldershot: Ashgate.

Plantenga, J. (1995) 'Part-time work and equal opportunities: the case of the Netherlands', in J. Humphries and J. Rubery (eds) *The Economics of Equal Opportunities*, Manchester: EOC, 277–90.

Plantenga, J. (2004) 'Changing work and life patterns: examples of new working-time arrangements in the European member states', in J. Giele and E. Holst (eds) *Changing Life Patterns in Western Industrial Societies*, Oxford: Elsevier, 119–35.

Rasmussen, E., Lind, J. and Visser, J. (2004) 'Divergences in part-time work in New Zealand, the Netherlands and Denmark', *British Journal of Industrial Relations*, 42: 637–58.

Robson, P., Dex, S., Wilkinson, F. and Salido Cortes, O. (1999) 'Low pay, labour market institutions, gender and part-time work: cross-national comparisons' *European Journal of Industrial Relations*, 5 (2): 187–207.

Smithson, J., Lewis, S., Cooper, C. and Dyer, J. (2004) 'Flexible working and the gender pay gap in the accountancy profession', *Work, Employment and Society*, 18 (1): 115–36.

Sommerlad, H. and Sanderson, P. (1998) *Gender, Choice and Commitment: Women Solicitors in England and Wales and the Struggle for Equal Status*, Aldershot: Ashgate.

Standing, G. (1999) *Global Labour Flexibility*, Basingstoke: Macmillan.

Sundström, M. (1997) 'Managing work and children: part-time work and the family cycle of Swedish women', in H.-P. Blossfeld and C. Hakim (eds) *Between Equalization and Marginalization*, Oxford: Oxford University Press, 272–88.

Tijdens, K. (2002) 'Gender roles and labor use strategies: women's part-time work in the European Union', *Feminist Economics*, 8 (1): 71–99.

Tilly, C. (1991) 'Reasons for the continuing growth of part-time employment', *Monthly Labor Review*, 114 (1): 10–18.

Tilly, C. (1996) *Half a Job: Bad and Good Part-time Jobs in a Changing Economy*, Philadelphia: Temple University Press.

Walby, S. and Olsen, W. (2002) *The Impact of Women's Position in the Labour Market on Pay and Implications for UK Productivity: Report to Women and Equality Unit*, London: Department of Trade and Industry.

Windebank, J. (2001) 'Dual-earner couples in Britain and France: gender division of domestic labour and parenting work in different welfare states', *Work, Employment and Society*, 15 (2): 269–90.

Women and Equality Unit (2004) *Interim Update of Key Indicators of Women's Position in Britain*, Department of Trade and Industry.

Chapter 5

Women in the professions and management

Introduction

In this chapter we take up many of the issues covered in earlier chapters and apply them to highly qualified women. We focus on the traditional professions of law, medicine and the natural sciences, and in a separate section we examine the position of women in management. In our concluding section, we touch on some 'new professions'. The development of the professions is unique to different countries and in this chapter we largely focus on the UK, although we make reference to US literature where appropriate.

Women's increasing acquisition of higher level qualifications has been hailed as the 'success story' for women in the 1990s (Walby 1997: 43). There continues to be a decline in the proportion of women with no qualifications and an increase in the number with degree level qualifications. The proportion of British women with a degree level qualification has increased from 10 per cent in 1997 to 16 per cent in 2004. Men's educational attainment has also increased from 14 per cent with a degree in 1997 to 18 per cent in 2004, but the gender gap has narrowed (WEU 2004). This development is important because higher levels of education are strongly associated with improved employment prospects. However, as we show, the acquisition of qualifications has gendered outcomes.

Our consideration of highly qualified women could be criticized on the basis that these are privileged women whose 'problems', in comparison with other women in low-wage sectors, could be seen to be minor. We would argue that an examination of women in the professions and management is instructive for the debate about women and employment as a whole, but it should not be regarded as *the* key issue for gender equality. Women who have acquired qualifications are interesting for a number of reasons. Crucially, they are more likely than less qualified women to have the material assets that allow them to 'contract out' caring activities, leaving them with a greater range of 'choices' about how to balance work and family. The acquisition by women of this human and economic capital is often seen by policy-makers as the solution to problems of gender inequality in employment. Major employers and government have backed campaigns to increase women's representation in the professions and management, for example Opportunity Now (www.opportunitynow.org.uk/), which works with employers 'to realise the economic potential and business benefits that women at all levels contribute to the workforce'.

However, as we will show, equivalently qualified women and men who are working in professional and management fields do not have equivalent occupational outcomes. Thus, in the manner of a test case, this suggests that much more profound cultural and structural issues relating to gender are at play. Indeed, Hakim (1996) argues that highly qualified women may confront considerably more discrimination than other women; they compete on apparently equal terms with men because of their equivalent qualifications but are often treated as uncommitted secondary earners. This creates considerable tensions for those charged with managing their employment. It also poses challenges for professional bodies: if they ignore the unequal outcomes of equivalently qualified women and men, they could be criticized for safeguarding professional credentials only at the beginning of their members' careers.

Sommerlad and Sanderson (1998) argue that informal exclusionary practices within the workplace that impact on professional women may be more difficult to overcome than the formal exclusions of the early twentieth century. If this is the case, there are considerable challenges for those who manage such workplaces, including small 'family' firms, the growing number of large corporate law firms, major organizations such as national healthcare systems and higher education employment.

Women in the professions

The term profession is contested, but is traditionally used to cover occupations that control entry, typically through a professional body that oversees the acquisition of a high level of qualification, usually of university level. To varying degrees it can also control occupational activities via a moral code of practice. The classic 'elite professions' are law and medicine, while occupations such as teaching and nursing have been characterized as 'semi- or quasi-professions', that is ones that are dominated by the state (Etzioni 1969). It should also be noted that the latter are also 'professions' that are historically female dominated and often exist in a subordinate relationship with male dominated professions, indicating the gendered nature of constructions of the classification of professions. The natural sciences are also seen as professions, although their process of professionalization took place somewhat later than the law and medicine (see Glover 2000). Advantages of the professions include a job ladder; access to specialist knowledge; a degree of autonomy and financial rewards; and planning, managing and monitoring the work of non-professional workers (Sokoloff 1992). Professionals can be employed either in the private sector or in the public sector, especially higher education and health.

Crompton (1999: 181) argues that attempts to identify a universal definition of 'professions' have been abandoned and that there has been a shift towards an analysis of professional restructuring from which many different types of professional occupations have emerged. Reflecting this, new professions have developed through the course of the twentieth century, reflecting aspects of industrialization. For example, the occupation of 'Information and Communication Technology (ICT) Professional' did not appear in the UK government's classification of occupations until 2000 (ONS 2000). Thus the expansion of occupations classified as professions is indicative of changing conceptions of the term 'profession'; it is clear that new professions do not control entry in the same way as the 'classic' professions, although membership bodies may issue codes of practice. There has then been a blurring of the boundary between professional and managerial work, although Crompton (1999: 123) distinguishes the two by arguing that professional knowledge and expertise are regulated by an external standard, whereas managerial expertise is directly evaluated by the employing organization. The distinction between the two is underlined in the government's official categorization of occupations, the Standard Occupational Classification (ONS 2000), where professional and managerial occupations are classified in separate major groups.

Over the course of the past hundred years, women have been increasingly able to enter the professions due to their qualifications. But once in, the 'qualifications lever' (Crompton and Sanderson 1990) appears insufficient to allow them to move on in the same way as men. In all professions, regardless of whether women are well or poorly represented in numerical terms, patterns of internal segregation can be found. Women and men appear to take different routes through the professions for which they are qualified. There is considerable evidence of women being concentrated in particular 'niches'. For example, in the natural sciences Rossiter (1982, 1995) uses the concept of 'territorial segregation' to describe the way that US women scientists' employment over the twentieth century has been concentrated in specific fields of science. She argues that these patterns have left their mark to this day. Many women scientists remain concentrated in 'behind-the-scenes' employment, often supporting the work of their more visible male colleagues (Glover 2000). This is an example of women entering the professions because they are qualified to do so, but tending to be located in low-status, low-paid segments, a phenomenon that could be described as 'contained inclusion'. In itself internal segregation is not automatically a problem, but for the fact that these segments tend to be poorly paid, relative to others in the same professional area. They are typically low status, and sometimes locally based; for example in the UK in the legal profession there is a concentration of women as local magistrates (McGlynn 2003) and in the medical profession as community-based general practitioners (Riska 2001; EOC 2001). We discuss further below the phenomenon of internal segregation.

Historical aspects

Witz (1992) has pointed to the gendered nature of controlled entry or 'closure' practices that served to ensure women were under-represented in most professions. At the beginning of the twentieth century, women were largely absent from the professions. In the UK, the 1919 Sex Disqualification (Removal) Act in theory allowed women to become members of professional bodies and thus to practise as professionals; the reality was that a few single, middle-class women managed to do this. Monitoring and enforcing mechanisms did not develop until the mid-1970s in the UK with the Sex Discrimination Act and the establishment of the Equal Opportunities Commission. There was no means of monitoring the effect of the early legislation, nor any means of enforcing it. As the Earl of Selbourne said in the 1917 Lords Debate on the Solicitors (Qualification of Women) Bill: 'This is not a Bill to compel you to employ women as solicitors. Nobody need employ a woman even after she is qualified' (quoted in Sommerlad and Sanderson 1998: 255).

At the beginning of the twentieth century, the possibility of women entering the traditional professions provoked strong resistance from the men in the professions. This was particularly obvious in medicine, where women were barred from medical courses in universities and thus unable to become qualified in medicine (Witz 1992). In the case of the law, barriers to getting law degrees were less formal, with a few women obtaining these qualifications from the end of the nineteenth century onwards (McGlynn 2003). There was no sudden movement of qualified women into the legal profession, however, since the Law Society resisted this until 1922. The 'marriage bar' was furthermore used to exclude married women from many professions. As well as this structural barrier, there were many social obstacles to women's entry into the professions. Dyhouse (1995) presents evidence to show that despite holding appropriate qualifications, women were told that they were not employable because of their potential for marriage and childbearing.

In the first part of the twentieth century until the 1960s in industrialized countries, the presence of women in the traditional professions was very limited. In medicine and the law, a dramatic growth in the number of women took place in the 1970s in the UK. At the beginning of the twenty-first century major changes for law and medicine can be observed: women account for over 50 per cent of medical and law students (Crompton 1999; McGlynn 2003). This growth is a common feature of industrialized countries (Riska 2001). For law, the 1970s was the decade of change. McGlynn suggests that one of the reasons for this in the UK is the growth in polytechnics during the 1970s (which became the 'new universities' in the 1990s); these less traditional universities may have been more open to 'outsiders'.

This marked growth in numbers has not been seen in science, engineering and technology, however (Glover 2000). Women's presence has increased in some fields, but in others, such as physics, there are few women. In the relatively new field of ICT there is evidence of a decrease in the representation of women; this is the case in the US as well as Britain (Fountain 2000; Shifrin 2005). Recent evidence suggests that women make up just 17 per cent of British software professionals (EOC 2005).

In the UK, women hold about 40 per cent of professional occupations overall,[1] with a small increase over the previous five years or so (ILO 2004: Figure 2.2). Norway and Denmark show similar figures. In Sweden the figure is 50 per cent, with a small decrease. Clear comparisons cannot be made here with the US, since the ISCO international classification is not used there. However, calculations from the ILO, using an earlier classification, show that in the US women's share of professional jobs at the beginning of the twenty-first century was 55 per cent (ILO 2004: Figure 6.1).

Women in the medical professions

Although the majority of those with medical degrees in the UK are women, the hourly pay gap for full-time health professionals in 2000 was 23 per cent (EOC 2001: 4). In the US, women physicians earned only 63 per cent of the salary of their male colleagues (Weinberg 2004). One explanation is that women and men doctors work in different niches which attract different pay and in addition the profession is marked by internal vertical segregation. Taking an example from the UK, of all hospital consultants (the highest grade), 79 per cent are men (thus 21 per cent are women). Within this grade, 95 per cent of consultant surgeons (the most prestigious job) are men (EOC 2001: 5). Statistics both in Europe and in the United States confirm that women work mainly in niches of the healthcare system that are characterized by relatively low earnings or prestige (Riska 2001). Thus, internal segregation is likely to explain some of the gender pay gap referred to above. However, even within grades, a gender pay gap can be shown for women physicians in the US (Laine and Turner 2004). One factor here is that women appear to start off with lower salaries and do not make up the difference over time (a phenomenon that is sometimes referred to as the 'sticky floor', discussed later in this chapter).

Notably, in the UK there has been an increase in female general medical practitioners (GPs) from 25 per cent in 1989 to 34 per cent in 1999 (EOC 2001). It is claimed that this is a consequence of part-time work and job sharing becoming more established in the medical profession. By 1999 41 per cent of female GPs were working part-time or job sharing (EOC 2001). The structure of general practice lends itself to the reconciliation of paid work and domestic work, but whether this leads to women being located in spheres of influence may be doubtful. Pringle (1998) has a different perspective on the tendency for women doctors to work part-time and for low pay. She argues that, in Australia, medical women's organizations are beginning to call for more flexible employment, such that both men and women could contribute their full potential without sacrificing their personal lives. Her perspective is that the profession is potentially threatened by women doctors being prepared to work part-time and in jobs that are not well paid. If this happens in large enough numbers, this could lower the status of the profession as a whole. But it could also change the nature of the profession in positive ways, at least for patients, since women appear to be less concerned with power and income, less likely to stand on ceremony, and more willing to cooperate with a range of healthcare practitioners. Thus, argues Pringle, this presents a new light on the common assumption that when women move into an occupation, status falls. From this perspective, the profession's status could rise, at least in the eyes of its clients.

In a cross-national comparative study of Britain, France and Norway, Crompton and Harris (1999) show that women doctors were concentrated in areas/specialisms where they could control their hours. This is clear evidence of a constrained or situated choice. Many women doctors are 'practitioners', not 'careerists' (see Crompton and Sanderson 1990). The areas in which they are concentrated are relatively low status – but it is unclear whether they have become low status because they are highly feminized, or whether they were low status before the women joined them. Women are concentrated in the lower paid specialisms such as paediatrics and psychiatry – although why these specialisms should be lower paid must be questioned.

Women in the legal professions

Women working and studying in the law tend to be 'under-represented, underpaid and marginalized' (McGlynn 2003: 56). There is clear evidence of vertical segregation. For example, only around 9 per cent of members of the senior judiciary, high court judges and above are women (EOC 2006). In higher education employment, women are well represented in law departments, but there is vertical segregation. Women account for 40 per cent of all academic staff, but only 14 per cent of law professors are women, while 49 per cent of lecturer grade staff are women (McGlynn 2003: Table 5).

In the US, women lawyers earn 73 per cent of their male counterparts' salaries (Chao and Utgoff 2005). Internal segregation is undoubtedly a major factor in a gender pay gap of 15 per cent (EOC 2001: 5) for legal professionals in the UK. Nevertheless, it cannot be the only reason, since within grades, there is evidence of a gender pay gap (McGlynn 2003, citing Law Society data). Even in first jobs, women are earning less than men. The difference between the earnings of comparable samples of men and women at the beginning of their careers has been shown to be widest for law graduates (Purcell 2002). A study of women in the legal profession in Scotland (MacMillan et al. 2005) found that a steadily increasing gender pay gap began to emerge after the first five years in practice and had reached its highest level at between 21 and 25 years after entry with a gap of £36,000 in favour of men.

Women in scientific professions

In the scientific professions, growth in the number of women has been much slower, with women still very much a minority in many scientific fields, both in education and employment. This is the case in all industrialized countries (European Commission 2000). Even when qualified women scientists do enter scientific employment, retaining them in the labour force is a challenge. At any one time there are 50,000 qualified women scientists who are not in the labour force (DTI 2002). And in higher education there is considerable evidence of vertical segregation.[2] Even when women are employed in relatively large numbers in particular fields such as chemistry and biology, they are concentrated in low level positions (see Appendix 5.1 for more details).

Choices and constraints in women's professional careers

Internal segregation (the concentration of women and men in different niches within professional fields) is undoubtedly a major factor in explaining the male/female salary differential. We noted above (Purcell 2002) that the gender pay gap exists even for women and men at the beginning of their professional careers. How can this be explained? Do young women and men as agents gravitate towards differently paid sectors out of choice? Or, are there barriers in the way of women? Sommerlad and Sanderson (1998) argue that in the legal profession women are not free to make choices in the labour market as currently constructed. They argue that particular professions have cultural and structural aspects and these have an effect on individual agency. This argument focuses firmly on constraints or at least constrained choice, thus taking issue with 'preference theory' (see introductory chapter). What might be the structures within occupational fields that lead to gendered choices? In the legal profession, Sommerlad and Sanderson emphasize that 'personalist networks' underpin decision-making; they argue that these reinforce the 'fraternal contract' of the legal profession. Employers, they argue, assume that women will be less committed. The culture of both science and law is a professional model that is based on a clear and visible exclusion of other commitments (Ellis 2003; Sommerlad and Sanderson 1998). Sommerlad and Sanderson's research on employers of legal professionals in the UK shows that the concept of commitment was the principal selection criterion for both recruitment and advancement. It was widely assumed amongst employers that women would have a lack of commitment. Interestingly, those firms that had employed women did not mention women's lack of commitment, only those who had not. Sommerlad and Sanderson argue that the (unmeasurable) concept of commitment is in practice a way of assessing conformity to the traditions of the organization; it demonstrates availability and is a test for loyalty.

In higher education employment it is argued that, as gendered institutions, universities' assumptions about competence and success have led to practices and norms constructed around the life experiences of men (Bailyn 2003). For example, attributes such as assertiveness, assuming the autonomous expert role and giving top priority to one's work are associated with masculinity and are taken for granted as necessary for a successful academic career, but they can be regarded as gendered social constructions that privilege men. This type of explanation of women's employment outcomes in the professions is very far from human capital explanations that focus on life events associated with women exercising a free choice to privilege childbirth and child rearing over career.

Furthermore, many professional fields are 'unfriendly' towards women's career patterns, particularly in relation to family responsibilities. For example, in the legal profession there is evidence that there are very limited opportunities for combining part-time work and senior level positions (McGlynn 2003). In addition, career breaks act as a barrier to career progression within the profession (MacMillan et al. 2005) and it is suggested that professionals working on 'non-standard' contracts are likely to be marginalized and treated unequally (Hoque and Kirkpatrick 2003).

Suitably qualified yet faced with obvious inequality, there is a question about why women appear not to resist (Witz 1992). Sommerlad and Sanderson (1998) argue that people with legal training believe that the labour market is based on the classical liberal ideas of free contracts entered into in rational ways. Both law and science are predicated on notions of neutrality and rationality and this ideology is the basis of professionals' training. Thus, were women to cite discriminatory employment practices, they could be seen as questioning the rational bases of the profession. Sommerlad and Sanderson argue that women's subscription to the 'legal ideology of neutrality and universality precluded them from mounting an effective, separatist challenge' (Sommerlad and Sanderson 1998: 76). Similarly, Glover (2000) suggests that women scientists' socialization into the principle of universalism may have precluded resistance. Universalism is the requirement that 'information presented to the scientific community be assessed independently of the personal characteristics of the source of the information' (Mulkay 1977: 98).

Furthermore, both science and law professionals need to develop reputational capital in order to succeed (Hagan and Kay 1995; King 1994). They need to fall in with the expectations of their colleagues; recognition is dependent upon conformity. In this context, resistance seems unlikely. Following this, the conventional wisdom is that the professionalization process might weaken affiliation to trade unionism associated with organized resistance (Healy and Kirton 2002). However, levels of unionization are high among professionals. In the UK around half of professional workers are union members, compared with an overall average of 29 per cent (Grainger 2006). As shown in Chapter 8 trade union leaders are typically male and unions have been criticized for not taking up the issues of most concern to women. Nevertheless, there is some evidence that female professional workers are prepared to use their unions as a vehicle for articulating challenges to unequal terms and conditions and for resistance to managerialist undermining of professional values and autonomy (Healy and Kirton 2002).

Women in management

In 1973 American academic Victoria Schein famously coined the phrase 'think manager, think male' (Schein 1973). This reflected not only the *fact* of women's under-representation in management, but captured a growing belief that the characteristics associated with management were very similar to those associated with men. Similarly, Kanter in her classic study of women and men managers in corporate America, *Men and Women of the Corporation*, spells out the effect of a masculinist construction of management:

A 'masculine ethic' can be identified as part of the early image of managers. This 'masculine ethic' elevates the traits assumed to belong to some men to necessities for effective management: a tough-minded approach to problems;

analytic abilities to abstract and plan; a capacity to set aside personal, emotional considerations in the interests of task accomplishment; and a cognitive superiority in problem-solving and decision-making. These characteristics supposedly belonged to men; but then, practically all managers were men from the beginning. However, when women tried to enter management jobs, the 'masculine ethic' was invoked as an exclusionary principle.

(Kanter 1997: 22)

Both Schein's and Kanter's studies found that this had implications for the selection of managers and for women themselves who might find it difficult to think of themselves as management material. Although in today's era of declarative gender equality, some of these ideas might seem old-fashioned, women remain significantly under-represented in management, although the situation has improved in many industrialized countries (ILO 2004). Generally women are less well represented in management when compared to the professions, although as with women's representation in the professions, women's share of management jobs has increased. Overall women hold about 33 per cent of management positions in the UK (EOC 2005), compared with a markedly low 2 per cent in 1974 (EOC 2006). There are variations according to occupational/employment sector as Table 5.1 reveals.

Just as in the professions, women managers are found in greater numbers in lower-paying sectors. At junior management levels women are usually found in functions regarded as 'non-strategic', such as human resources and administration, rather than areas with clear paths to higher levels (ILO 2004). Some of the management areas where women are well or over-represented might be feminized niches such as equality and diversity managers (Kirton *et al.* 2005). Such feminized niches are often cul-de-sacs and this then impacts on women's representation in senior management.

As a rule, the higher the management level, the less likely women are to be found, although this too is changing over time. For example, only 14 per cent of directors in the UK are women (compared with 1 per cent in 1974) (EOC 2006). On the positive side, research shows that a record 78 FTSE 100 companies now have women directors and women make up 10.5 per cent of all directorships in the FTSE 100 – up from 5.8 per cent in 2000 (Singh and Vinnicombe 2005).

Table 5.1 Women as a percentage of managers in the UK

Office managers	67%
Retail and wholesale managers	35%
Marketing and sales managers	26%
ICT managers	18%
Production, works and maintenance managers	9%

Source: adapted from EOC (2005).

However, the picture is less positive for minority ethnic women. While 121 direc- torships in FTSE 100 companies are held by women, only four are held by minority ethnic women (EOC 2006).

As suggested earlier, even if women were proportionally represented on the main boards of companies, this would not mean that gender equality had been achieved. Only a tiny minority of the workforce can expect to reach such senior levels and arguably the gender equality project should be more concerned with the majority of women. However, the presence of women at the highest level of the organizational hierarchy is of symbolic significance.

Choices and constraints in women's management careers

How can women's under-representation in management be explained? From the perspective of human capital theory it might be argued that women's historic and current under-representation in management simply reflects a historically lower volume of human capital. As women are now just as likely as men to be highly qualified, in time they will climb organizational hierarchies in equal proportion with men and in future alter the gender composition of management. This is the 'trickle up' perspective (see McGlynn 2003). One argument has been that women have invested less in relevant (vocational) education. However, it is now the case that women are equally represented in business studies degrees, so again we might expect to see greater numbers of women managers in future, armed with their relevant degrees and able to compete with male graduates. Purcell (2002) asks whether business studies graduates under 30 are a 'suitable case for equal- ity'. Her study of early career graduates found that female business studies graduates were employed primarily in a narrow range of occupations, particularly business services and distribution, retail and catering. In addition, as we have seen earlier, the women were earning less than their male counterparts. While improv- ing women's educational attainment is a key element involved in increasing their representation in management, it is not the whole story.

Other authors have focused on women's orientations to work, suggesting that women do not have the necessary commitment to pursue high-level management careers. For example, Hakim (2000) claims that higher education does not alter the basic pattern of sex-role preferences, with there being a minority of career-oriented and work-committed women, a minority of home-centred and family-oriented women and a larger group hoping to combine work and family roles. The latter group will not commit wholeheartedly to their career, but instead will seek trade- offs, such as fewer development and promotion opportunities in return for more flexible working arrangements. Hakim (1996) argues that part-time working (the most common form of flexible working) represents a qualitative difference in terms of commitment, as well as a quantitative difference in terms of hours. Hakim does not deal with the more thorny question of where sex-role preferences come from and we are left with the impression that because it is typical it is therefore natural for women to 'choose' to combine work and family. This perspective is reflected in the popular concept of 'career woman', defined in the Collins dictionary (1998) as 'a woman with a career who is interested in working and progressing in her job, rather than staying at home doing housework and looking after children'. (There is of course no entry for 'career man'.)

This either/or situation – concentrating on career *or* family – does not of course reflect the reality of most women's lives in the twenty-first century. As discussed in Chapter 7, women, including those in professional and managerial roles, continue to take primary responsibility for the home and family and continue to face the very practical problems of how to reconcile work and family. For women, this is not simply an intellectual exercise involving thinking about which career to privilege in the long term, but a practical one concerned with a range of tasks such as who will pick up the children from nursery or school. There is also a management aspect to these caring activities – even if other people are paid to do them, their quality and reliability needs to be monitored.

It must be emphasized, also as discussed in Chapter 7, that gender roles reflect structural constraints as well as an element of choice about which life activities to prioritize. Because management careers are tied to organizational hierarchies and usually involve working long hours, they are generally even less 'family friendly' than professional careers where there is more likely to be the possibility for part-time employment (as in some areas of the teaching and medical professions), self-employment (as in some areas of accountancy and the law) and other more autonomous, self-managing forms of work. Many women managers experience considerable work–family conflict and as research has shown, there can be no doubt that holding down a demanding management level job and having a young family is bound to be difficult (e.g. Houston and Marks 2005). However, some of the contemporary policies that are meant to ease this conflict – work–life balance – do not always seem to have the desired effect. As we discuss in Chapter 7, research shows that women who choose to take advantage of flexible work arrangements tend to pay a price in that they are likely to experience reduced opportunities for training and development and exclusion from decision-making processes, which in turn has longer term implications for career progression (Hoque and Kirkpatrick 2003). As Liff and Ward (2001) note, women managers who show an interest in flexible working risk being seen by superiors as not a career person. This is similar to Sommerlad and Sanderson's (1998) conclusion about employers' assumption of professional women's 'commitment deficit', discussed above.

Against a background of women's encroachment into the traditionally male territory of management, Liff and Ward (2001: 32) have argued that a newer image of the manager has emerged, replacing the one reflected in Schein's (1973) phrase cited above, captured by the phrase 'think female manager, think childless superwoman'. It is relatively common for senior women managers to be partner-free and child-free and for male managers to be married with children (Alvesson and Billing 1997). Indeed this is popularly seen as the 'natural' and 'right' state of affairs as evidenced by the media frenzy whenever a so-called 'have-it-all' woman (i.e. a senior level manager with dependent children) gives up her job to spend more time with her family. This points vividly to a context of gendered constraint and reminds us that we must question the extent to which women's career trajectories are freely chosen.

As the discussion of work and family suggests, placing the emphasis on human capital explanations or sex-role preferences has not had much purchase in the women and management literature. Here there is a greater emphasis on the barriers and constraints at both societal and organizational levels that prevent women from forging management careers. With regard to the organizational context faced by women managers, it is widely accepted that management careers are gendered (Liff and Ward 2001). Largely for reasons related to the traditional domestic division of labour (see Chapter 7), women face greater challenges in satisfying organizational demands from the need to work long hours, be geographically mobile, travel extensively or simply to demonstrate the 'right' characteristics and behaviours.

The 'glass ceiling' is a term coined in the 1970s in the US to describe the invisible, artificial barriers created by institutional attitudes and processes that block women from senior management positions. Some authors (e.g. ILO 2004) have also begun to talk about 'glass walls' that keep women managers in traditional feminized sectors or ghettos with fewer opportunities for upward progression and higher pay. Meyerson and Fletcher (2000: 231) characterize gender inequality today as 'the problem with no name', highlighting how blatant cases of sex discrimination, at least in the corporate world, are now rare, but yet discrimination against women 'lingers in a plethora of work practices and cultural norms that only appear unbiased'. These ideas point to the gendered nature of organizations, which for Acker (1991: 52) means that 'advantage and disadvantage, exploitation and control, action and emotion, meaning and identity, are patterned through and in terms of a distinction between male and female, masculine and feminine'.

One institutional attitude that continues to act as a barrier to women's management careers is that conceptions and images of leadership remain largely masculine and sex-role stereotyping remains prevalent. This makes it difficult for a female manager to strike a balance between being seen as a competent manager and as sufficiently feminine not to be regarded as defying gender norms (Alvesson and Billing 1997). Related to this, it is argued that women have problems establishing themselves as plausible candidates for promotion because the stereotype of the successful manager remains strongly male (Liff and Ward 2001). Collinson and Hearn (1994) identify five discourses and practices of masculinity that they believe are pervasive and dominant in organizations: authoritarianism, paternalism, entrepreneurialism, informalism and careerism. These are interrelated with different management styles and serve to reinforce the managerial domain as a male one. However, the possible solution for women of adopting stereotypical masculine traits appears also to be doomed: with reference to women employed in the finance sector, McDowell (1998) argues that women who 'perform' outside of their expected gender roles will not be successful.

In terms of breaking through the glass ceiling, women are often cut off from both formal and informal networks that are necessary for advancement within organizations. There is now a belief that mentoring relationships are one of the formal ways in which women's management careers can be developed. It is argued that mentors provide legitimacy to their female 'protégés' because they challenge gender-based stereotypes, offer reflected power and share information that is generally only gained by being on the inside of a particular (informal) network; many senior women managers report having benefited from these relationships (Blake-Beard 2001). However, black and minority ethnic women seem to be less likely to be mentored and where they are it is often by a white man, simply because of white men's domination of senior management positions (Fine 1995). Writing from a US perspective, Blake-Beard (2001) argues that there are many unacknowledged complexities and challenges inherent in cross-gender and interracial mentoring relationships that need to be recognized and addressed if minority ethnic women are to benefit from this practice. The metaphor of the 'glass ceiling' is inadequate to describe the obstacles to progression experienced by black women managers for whom sexism is entwined with racism (Bell and Nkomo 2001). Instead, they suggest, we must conceive of a two-dimensional structure – a concrete wall topped by a glass ceiling. The concrete wall facing black women manifests itself through experiences such as daily exposure to racism, being held by senior managers to a higher standard, being invisible to senior management, being excluded from informal networks, and receiving challenges to authority from subordinates.

Furthermore, research indicates that once women reach leadership positions, their performance is often placed under close scrutiny and they are not always positively evaluated. In addition, women managers are often disliked and distrusted by subordinates (Ryan and Haslam 2005). All of this makes for a hostile environment in which women must constantly prove themselves. Ryan and Haslam's study (2005) of FTSE 100 companies reveals that women are particularly likely to be placed in positions of leadership in circumstances of general financial downturn and downturn in company performance. This leaves them dangerously exposed, vulnerable to criticism and likely to be blamed for negative outcomes that were more a function of contextual factors than leadership behaviour. Ryan and Haslam refer to this as women leaders being placed on top of a 'glass cliff', a precarious position that might end up promoting 'the very inequality that women's advancement is intended to address' (2005: 88). A further concept of 'sticky floor' has been developed (Booth et al. 2003). Here it has been shown that when women are promoted, they tend to be put on lower pay within grades, as compared with their male counterparts in the same grade.

Conclusions

So, is the outlook bleak or positive for highly qualified women? It is clear from the above discussion that while women have become better represented in the professions and management, the picture of change is both complex and multifaceted. With regard to the professions, in both the legal and scientific fields, a key change has been the change in the size of employing organizations. In the legal profession the growth of corporate law has been a driver in the increasing amount of employment of women. There is a move towards very large firms employing many more women than was the case in the small, more traditional firms (Sommerlad and Sanderson 1998). The multinational firms of the pharmaceutical industry are a major destination for women scientists both in Europe and the US (European Commission 2003; Marasco 2003). The changing legislative context and the emphasis on the public face of corporate social responsibility means that large firms that are often household names have to show a commitment to equal opportunities, showing for example openness in terms of policy and practice in recruitment and promotion. This bureaucratic rationality might provide the context for women to make more progress than in former times. Furthermore, such organizations are much more likely than small traditional firms to offer possibilities for flexible working. However, Sommerlad and Sanderson (1998) conclude that down-shifting is the consequence of the take-up of these policies, since it reinforces the collective label of 'commitment deficit'. Consequently women – the main users of flexible working – get locked into a secondary market, sometimes in associate professional jobs (for which high-level qualifications are not typically required). Their conclusion is that until these sorts of arrangements are taken up if not by all, then at least evenly by women and men employees and thus lose their accompanying stigmas and penalties, the male standard in the workplace remains in place. Furthermore, they argue that in large legal firms, a culture persists of acting in a particularly aggressive and assertive 'macho' way, as well as a 'work all hours' practice. Personal bonds – the ability to build up relational and cultural capital – appear to remain central (McGlynn 2003). McGlynn concludes that women remain outsiders, despite their individual human capital. The weakness is the reliance on the business case as the basis for policy change, and the downplaying of the moral arguments of equal opportunities. McGlynn argues for strategies where equality is the principal aim and not just a by-product of the wish to improve productivity.

With regard to professional and managerial women, one question is whether the presence of a critical mass of women changes the culture of the occupation/organization so that women are more able to forge successful careers. Kanter (1977: 248–9) argued that people whose 'type' (for example, women) is represented in very small proportions would tend to feel more visible, feel more pressure to conform and make fewer mistakes, find it harder to gain credibility, be more isolated and peripheral and to have a range of other negative perceptions and experiences. On the other hand those whose 'type' (for example, men) is represented in very high proportions tend to have positive experiences and perceptions of the organization. For example, they are more likely to perceive the organization to be supportive of their careers. Kanter also argued that a critical mass (defined as at least 30 per cent) of women is necessary to shift the culture towards one that is more positive for women. From this perspective, efforts to increase the proportions of women represented in particular professions and organizations would pave the way for greater gender equality. However, a note of caution is necessary. The cases of the legal and medical professions, where women are well represented, suggests that the critical mass perspective does not explain why in some fields where there are large numbers of qualified women they do not advance in the same way as men. In those scientific fields where women are well represented, advancement is no more likely than in those fields where they are not well represented (Glover 2000). This highlights the complexity involved in destabilizing gender segregation for highly qualified women specifically, but also for women generally. It also underlines the need to look beyond policies that seek to boost the recruitment of women; issues of retention in employment and advancement tend to be neglected, as Glover (2000) has argued in relation to women scientists.

Can the trickle-up perspective be relied upon? In other words, will time sort out the problem of women's under-representation in the professions and management as more highly qualified women trickle up through the hierarchy? There is some evidence of change as a consequence of women's increased human capital, but the pace is on the whole slow. It is highly improbable that women's greater investment in education and training will alone solve the problem of their under-representation in the professions and management. It should therefore not be an excuse for failing to investigate the problem or for failing to develop a broader range of policies at the level of individual organizations and specific professions.

The newer professional occupations – for example, ICT, media, management – might provide clues as to the likelihood of future change. Available evidence is not wholly optimistic as it suggests both that these remain numerically dominated by men (unlike medicine and the law which have both moved beyond this stage) and that women are disadvantaged in terms of advancement (Betzelt and Gottschall 2004; Fountain 2000.) Women managers face what has been termed a 'glass ceiling' which acts as a kind of informal, gendered social closure mechanism that might be more difficult to break down than the formal social closure associated with the 'classic' professions. They may also face 'sticky floors', 'concrete walls' and 'glass cliffs'. Management occupations appear to favour the working conditions that men are more likely to be able to meet, including long and unpredictable hours. In addition, perhaps the IT profession needs to be seen in the light of what we know about the traditional science, engineering and technology jobs – that is that the organizational culture appears unappealing to women (Glover 2000).

In the new professions and certainly in management, the entry requirements may be more blurred and less prescriptive; the boundaries are not patrolled in the same way that they are in the legal and medical professions. However, in some ways this means that there is less transparency about how to enter and what it takes to be successful; therefore whether this allows a greater diversity of social groups to enter these areas more easily is questionable. The 'job queues' argument (Reskin and Roos 1990) posits that only when these occupations become less appealing do they become more available to those lower down the occupational hierarchy and therefore possibly feminized. Relating this to the ICT industry, there is likely to be an increase in its economic importance in industrialized and industrializing economies; therefore these jobs do not appear likely to lose their appeal to men. If

Reskin and Roos are correct, this sector will not open its doors to women in the near future. However, against this argument is the reality that global ICT firms are actively seeking to increase their recruitment of women. Fountain (2000) argues that the human capital requirements of the knowledge economy require women to participate as experts, owners and designers of information technologies; stronger representation by women in technical roles would change and increase the range of technological applications, products, standards and practices.

This also ties in with the now widely promulgated idea, discussed in more detail in Chapter 6, that a diverse workforce can be beneficial to organizations seeking to reach new markets and appeal to broader customer bases. However, the evidence in support of this is insubstantial, indicating that the demands of markets alone will not properly address gender inequalities in employment and organizations. Neither, as we have shown, will women acquiring increased human capital resolve the issue quickly. The Equal Opportunities Commission (EOC 2006) has calculated that at the current rate of change it will take 20 years to achieve gender equality in Civil Service top management, 40 years to achieve an equal number of female directors of FTSE 100 companies and 40 years to achieve an equal number of senior women in the judiciary. It is clear that the complexity of the profound structural, institutional and cultural barriers standing in the way of women in the professions and management will need to be confronted if the gendered outcomes of qualifications are to change. It is in the interests of the economy, organizations and professional bodies, as well as women themselves, to find the means to do this.

Notes

1 These figures are based on the ISCO-88 (ILO 1990) classification.
2 There is a focus here on higher education employment; private sector statistics are particularly scarce.

Appendix 5.1: Vertical segregation amongst women scientists employed in the UK higher education sector

Table 5.2 shows a hierarchy of posts in UK higher education employment, from professor to researchers. A distinction has been made between those researchers who are employees of universities and the much more common position of researchers who are funded on external grants. Although some working conditions have improved because of the Fixed Term Employees Regulations 2002, externally funded researcher posts are notoriously insecure and poorly paid (DTI 2003). They are therefore located at the bottom of the hierarchy of science-based employment in higher education.

Table 5.2 UK women scientists employed in higher education in four scientific fields, as a percentage of each job category, 2002/3, 1994/5 figures in brackets

Job category	Biosciences %		Chemistry %		ICT %		Physics %	
Professor	9	(5)	4	(0)	12	(7)	3	(1)
Senior Lecturer	18	(9)	10	(3)	25	(12)	7	(2)
Lecturer	32	(24)	17	(11)	30	(20)	10	(9)
Researcher (university funded)	43	(36)	24	(17)	27	(21)	17	(11)
Researcher (externally funded)	48	(41)	27	(21)	26	(15)	15	(12)
All	37	(30)	20	(14)	27	(22)	12	(9)
N	9885	(6974)	3300	(3082)	1790	(4206)	3440	(3069)

Source: Higher Education Statistics Agency, data extracted from http://setwomenresource.org.uk/.

References

Acker, J. (1991) 'Hierarchies, jobs, bodies: a theory of gendered organizations', in R. Ely, E. Foldy and M. Scully (eds) (2003) *Reader in Gender, Work and Organization*, Malden, MA: Blackwell, 49–61.

Alvesson, M. and Billing, D. B. (1997) *Understanding Gender and Organizations*, London: Sage.

Bailyn, L. (2003) 'Academic careers and gender equity: lessons learned from MIT' *Gender, Work and Organization*, 10 (2): 137–53.

Bell, E. and Nkomo, S. (2001) 'Our separate ways: barriers to advancement', in R. Ely, E. Foldy and M. Scully, (eds) (2003) *Reader in Gender, Work and Organization*, Malden, MA: Blackwell, 343–361.

Betzelt, S. and Gottschall, K. (2004) 'Publishing and the new media professions as forerunners of pioneer work and life patterns', in J. Giele and E. Holst (eds) *Changing Life Patterns in Western Industrial Societies*, Oxford: Elsevier, 257–280.

Blake-Beard, S. (2001) *Mentoring Relationships through the Lens of Race and Gender*, Boston, MA: School of Management Center in Gender and Organizations, CGO Publications.

Booth, A., Francesconi, M. and Frank, J. (2003) 'A sticky floors model of promotion pay and gender', *European Economic Review*, 47 (2): 295–322.

Brook, K. (2002) 'Trade union membership: an analysis of data from the autumn 2001 LFS', *Labour Market Trends*, July, 343–54.

Chao, E. and Utgoff, K. (2005) *Women in the Labor Force: A Databook*, Washington: Department of Labor.

Collinson, D. and Hearn, J. (1994) 'Naming men as men: implications for work, organization and management', *Gender, Work and Organization*, 1 (1): 2–22.

Crompton, R. (1999) *Restructuring Gender Relations and Employment*, Oxford: Oxford University Press.

Crompton, R. and Sanderson, K. (1990) *Gendered Jobs and Social Change*, London: Unwin Hyman.

Crompton, R. and Harris, F. (1999) 'Attitudes, women's employment and the changing domestic division of labour: a cross-national analysis', in R. Crompton (ed.) *Restructuring Gender Relations and Employment*, Oxford: Oxford University Press, 105–27.

DTI (2002) *Maximising Returns to Science, Engineering and Technology Careers*, London: Department of Trade and Industry.

DTI (2003) *The Research Careers Initiative: Final Report 1997–2002*, London: Department of Trade and Industry.

Dyhouse, C. (1995) *No Distinction of Sex? Women in British Universities 1870–1939*, London: UCL Press.

Ellis, P. (2003) 'Persistence and progression for women in science-based employment', unpublished PhD submitted to the University of Surrey.

EOC (2001) *Women and Men in Britain: Professional Occupations*, Manchester: Equal Opportunities Commission.

EOC (2005) *Response to DTI, Advancing Equality for Men and Women: Government Proposals to Introduce a Public Sector Duty to Promote Gender Equality*, Manchester: Equal Opportunities Commission.

EOC (2006) *Sex and Power: Who Runs Britain? 2006*, Manchester: Equal Opportunities Commission.

Etzioni, A. (1969) *The Semi-professions and their Organizations*, New York: The Free Press.

European Commission (2000) *Science Policies in the European Union: Promoting Excellence through Mainstreaming Gender Equality. A Report from the ETAN Expert Working Group on Women and Science* (EUR 19319), Luxembourg: Office for Official Publications of the European Communities.

European Commission (2003) *Women in Industrial Research: A Wake Up Call for European Industry*, Brussels: DG Research.

Fine, M. (1995) 'Building successful multicultural organizations: challenges and opportunities', in R. Ely, E. Foldy and M. Scully (eds) (2003) *Reader in Gender, Work and Organization*, Malden, MA: Blackwell, 308–18.

Fountain, J. (2000) 'Constructing the information society: women, information technology, and design' *Technology In Society*, 22 (1): 45–62.

Glover, J. (2000) *Women and Scientific Employment*, Basingstoke: Macmillan.

Grainger, H. (2006) *Trade Union Membership 2005*, London: DTI.

Hagan, J. and Kay, F. (1995) *Gender in Practice: A Study of Lawyers' Lives*, New York: Oxford University Press.

Hakim, C. (1996) *Key Issues in Women's Work*, London: Athlone Press.

Hakim, C. (2000) *Work–Lifestyle Choices in the 21st Century: Preference Theory*, Oxford: Oxford University Press.

Healy, G. and Kirton, G. (2002) 'Professional and highly qualified women in two contrasting trade unions', in F. Colgan and S. Ledwith (eds) *Gender, Diversity and Trade Unions: International Perspectives*, London: Routledge, 186–204.

Hoque, K. and Kirkpatrick, I. (2003) 'Non-standard employment in the management and professional workforce: training, consultation and gender implications', *Work, Employment and Society*, 17 (4): 667–89.

Houston, D. and Marks, G. (2005) 'Working, caring and sharing: work–life dilemmas in early motherhood', in D. Houston (ed.) *Work–Life Balance in the 21st Century*, Basingstoke: Palgrave Macmillan, 80–105.

ILO (International Labour Organization) (1990) *ISCO–88: The International Standard Classification of Occupations 1988*, Geneva: ILO.

ILO (International Labour Organization) (2004) *Breaking through the Glass Ceiling: Women in Management*, Geneva: ILO.

Kanter, R. M. (1977) *Men and Women of the Corporation*, New York: Basic Books.

King, M. (1994) 'Women's career in academic science: achievement and recognition', in J. Evetts (ed.) *Women and Career: Themes and Issues in Industrialized Societies*, Harlow: Longman.

Kirton, G., Greene, A. M. and Dean, D. (2005) *British Diversity Champions as Change Agents – Radicals, Tempered Radicals or Liberal Reformers?* Paper presented to Gender, Work and Organization Conference, Keele University.

Laine, C. and Turner, B. (2004) 'Unequal pay for equal work: the gender gap in academic medicine', *Annals of International Medicine*, 141 (3): 238–40.

Liff, S. and Ward, K. (2001) 'Distorted views through the glass ceiling: the construction of women's understandings of promotion and senior management positions', *Gender, Work and Organization*, 8 (1): 19–36.

McDowell, L. (1998) *Capital Culture: Gender at Work in the City*, London: Blackwell.

McGlynn, C. (2003) 'The status of women lawyers in the United Kingdom', in U. Schultz and G. Shaw (eds) *Women in the World's Legal Professions*, Oxford and Portland, OR: Hart Publishing.

MacMillan, M., McKerrell, N. and McFadyen, A. (2005) *Women in the Legal Profession in Scotland*, Glasgow: Equal Opportunities Commission.

Marasco, C. (2003). 'Déjà vu for women in industry', *Chemical and Engineering News* (American Chemical Society), 81 (41): 51–4.

Meyerson, D. and Fletcher, J. (2000) 'A modest manifesto for shattering the glass ceiling', in R. Ely, E. Foldy and M. Scully (eds) (2003) *Reader in Gender, Work and Organization*, Malden, MA: Blackwell, 230–41.

Mulkay, M. (1977). 'Sociology of the Scientific Research Community', in I. Spiegel-Rösing, and D. de Solla Price (eds) *Science, Technology and Society*, London: Sage, 92–148.

ONS (Office for National Statistics) (2000) *SOC2000*, London: ONS.

Pringle, R. (1998) *Sex and Medicine: Gender, Power and Authority in the Medical Profession*, Cambridge: Cambridge University Press.

Purcell, K. (2002) *Qualifications and Careers: Equal Opportunities and Earnings among Graduates*, Manchester: Equal Opportunities Commission.

Reskin, B. and Roos, P. (1990) *Job Queues, Gender Queues: Explaining Women's Inroads into Male Occupations*, Philadelphia: Temple University Press.

Riska, E. (2001) *Medical Careers and Feminist Agendas: American, Scandinavian, and Russian Women Physicians*, New Jersey: Aldine Transaction.

Rossiter, M. (1982) *Women Scientists in America: Struggles and Strategies to 1940*, Baltimore: Johns Hopkins University Press.

Rossiter, M. (1995) *Women Scientists in America: Before Affirmative Action 1940–1972*, Baltimore and London: Johns Hopkins University Press.

Ryan, M. and Haslam, A. (2005) 'The glass cliff: evidence that women are over-represented in precarious leadership positions', *British Journal of Management*, 16 (2): 81–90.

Schein, V. (1973) 'The relationship between sex role stereotypes and requisite management characteristics', *Journal of Applied Psychology*, 57 (2): 95–100.

Shifrin, T. (2005). 'Bridge gender gap to avert skills crisis, warn top IT women', *Computer Weekly.com.*

Singh, V. and Vinnicombe, S. (2005) *The Female FTSE Index 2005*, Centre for Developing Business Leaders, Cranfield School of Management.

Sokoloff, N. (1992) *Black Women and White Women in the Professions: Occupational Segregation by Race and Gender, 1960–1980*, London: Routledge.

Sommerlad, H. and Sanderson, P. (1998) *Gender, Choice and Commitment: Women Solicitors in England and Wales and the Struggle for Equal Status,* Aldershot: Ashgate.

Walby, S. (1997) *Gender Transformations*, London: Routledge.

Weinberg, D. (2004) *Evidence from Census 2000 about Earnings by Detailed Occupation for Men and Women*, Washington, DC: US Census Bureau.

WEU (2004) *Interim Update of Key Indicators of Women's Position in Britain*, London: Women and Equality Unit, Department of Trade and Industry.

Witz, A. (1992) *Professions and Patriarchy*, London: Routledge.

Chapter 6

From equal opportunities to diversity management

Introduction

In the UK the pursuit of gender equality has been one of the central features of equal opportunities policies for the past 25 years or so, underpinned by the Sex Discrimination Act (1975). However, just as in many other countries (see Humphries and Grice (1995) on New Zealand; de los Reyes (2000) on Sweden; Cox (1994) on the US; Blommaert and Verschueren (1998) on various European countries), in the UK the traditional equal opportunities agenda has now given way to the concept and language of diversity in much organizational policy and practice. Indeed, diversity has become a popular concept in the UK management and practitioner literature, where organizations are urged to celebrate diversity in order to achieve success (e.g. Kandola and Fullerton 1994; EOR 2001). Because different countries have their own specific history of women's and civil rights and different legal frameworks that shape public and employer policy on gender equality, the discussion contained in this chapter focuses on the UK experience of the shift from equal opportunities to diversity management. However, the discussion has considerable salience beyond the UK, particularly as the newer discourse of diversity is potentially a global one (Humphries and Grice 1995).

Equal opportunities – the traditional approach to tackling sex discrimination

During the late 1970s and 1980s, following the introduction of the Sex Discrimination Act (SDA) (1975) and the Race Relations Act (1976), increasing numbers of British organizations in the public and private sectors began to declare that they were equal opportunities (EO) employers (Cockburn 1989). The SDA covers discrimination against women, men, married persons and since 1996 transsexual people. The legislation does not really seek to promote equality or deal with the social problems facing women; rather it concentrates on providing redress for individual victims of discrimination. For this reason it is widely regarded as minimalist and a weak instrument for combating gender inequalities (Johnson and Johnstone 2005).

However, the SDA has underpinned the dominant organizational approach to gender equality policy-making in the UK. Many larger employers developed EO policies in order to give effect to the legislation and by the mid 1980s a formula, containing a set of prescriptions, had emerged to eliminate (sex and race) discrimination from employment decisions (Webb 1997). This was backed by 'codes of practice' issued by the Equal Opportunities Commission (on sex discrimination) and the Commission for Racial Equality (on race discrimination), bodies set up by the British government to enforce and advise on the legislation and development of employer policies aimed at legal compliance. EO policies typically involved the use of procedures to formalize employment decisions, particularly at the recruitment and selection stage. The idea was quite simple: that if women and men were treated equally (i.e. the same), decisions would be perceived as fair and the ultimate result would be more equal and fairer outcomes. Managers and other recruiters were issued with strict guidelines on how to conduct interviews and other tests, including what questions to ask, how to evaluate candidates objectively, how to record the decisions made, etc. Many organizations also paid attention to the wording of job adverts (e.g. rooting out gendered images and language) and to where jobs were advertised in order to encourage a wider pool of applicants. However, by the late 1980s trade unions, academics, equality activists and other commentators had begun to critique EO on grounds that managers were able to ignore or subvert policy prescriptions, that the exercise of subjectivity and discretion had not been fully eliminated by the procedural approach, and that fairer outcomes did not necessarily flow from EO policies (Collinson *et al.* 1990; Cockburn 1991; Webb 1997).

Theoretical approaches

To understand the substance of the critique, it is useful to turn to the theoretical and philosophical underpinning of EO. Particularly influential have been the ideas of Jewson and Mason (1986). Jewson and Mason argued that participants in the EO policy-making process were using terms and concepts in a confused, arbitrary and contradictory manner. This meant that it was often unclear what the aims of policies were and the long-term effect was to generate disappointment and distrust of EO. In response they developed a twofold typology of EO policies, which they called the liberal and radical conceptions. The liberal and radical approaches each contain different underlying principles, methods of implementation, measures of effectiveness and perceptions about what needs to be done.

Jewson and Mason's (1986) liberal and radical conceptions of equality are now summarized. Central to the *principles* underpinning the liberal conception is the belief that 'equal opportunity exists when all individuals are enabled freely and equally to compete for social rewards' (1986: 307). The removal of collective barriers to the expression of individual talent will enable the best person to win and allow all individuals to make the best of themselves. Notions of individual ability and merit, rooted in theories of classical liberalism, feature strongly within the liberal conception. It is also important to note that the moral arguments of fairness are at the heart of the principles of EO within both the liberal and radical conceptions, although what counts as fairness is contestable, as discussed below.

The role of the policy-maker within the liberal conception is to develop procedures to allow individual ability and merit to shine through; in other words to ensure that the rules of the competition do not discriminate and that they are fairly applied to all participants. Therefore, the liberal conception is concerned with equality of treatment. *Implementation* of the EO policy is achieved through bureaucratization of decision-making so that custom, tradition and personal patronage play no role. One example of the liberal policy approach is standardized recruitment and selection methods, as opposed to informal, word-of-mouth methods, which should broaden the pool of applicants. Put simply, candidates are selected on the basis of what they can do, rather than who they know (Kirton and Greene 2005).

For its *effectiveness,* the liberal conception also depends on positive action. Positive action must not be confused with positive discrimination (what Americans call 'affirmative action' and discussed below), as the two are conceptually distinct. The aim of positive action is to promote 'free and equal competition among individuals'. For a gender equality policy, this might include a workplace crèche, childcare vouchers, flexible work arrangements and a host of other family-friendly initiatives aimed at making it easier for women to balance work with caring responsibilities. A stronger example of positive action is special management training courses for women that some organizations offer. These positive action measures might be viewed as levelling the playing field to enable women to compete for jobs equally and freely with men and do not tamper with the decision-making process itself (Kirton and Greene 2005).

Perceptions of EO policies within the liberal conception are concerned with whether justice is seen to be done. Therefore there might be various kinds of publicity and usage of different communication channels to convey the supposed strengths and effectiveness of the policy in order to generate the approval and quell the suspicion of the workforce that, for example, women are being promoted because they are women and beyond their capabilities. The aim is to eliminate the stigma that can be attached to some EO initiatives (Cockburn 1991).

The *principle* underlying the radical conception, as defined by Jewson and Mason (1986), is that it is the *outcomes* of EO policy that matter; the aim is to achieve a fair distribution of rewards among employees. Here, discrimination affects individuals, but it can only be identified at the level of the group and 'since it is manifestly the case on *a priori* grounds that women and black people are the equals of men and whites, the actual distribution of occupational rewards *should be made* to reflect this fact' (Jewson and Mason 1986: 222, emphasis added). In addition, the radical conception regards talent and ability as socially defined by those in positions of power so that the very terms contain and conceal a series of value judgements. Accordingly, radicals question whether the skills and educational qualifications demanded of certain jobs are in fact necessary or whether they are used as screening devices aimed at preserving the best jobs for more powerful groups (men, the middle class, etc.).

As can be seen from the principles, the radical conception is concerned with equality of outcome. Therefore, EO policy *implementation* within the radical perspective is concerned with engineering decisions that advance the sectional interests of under-represented or oppressed groups. Radicals are impatient with the procedural (liberal) approach, such as that enshrined in (UK) legislation, and believe it can have only a limited impact. Therefore, bureaucratization is not necessarily involved in the radical conception and radicals might reject it in favour of a strategy of politicization of organizational life, where all decision-making is based on a consideration of the implications for women or black people and a number of other social groups. If this position were adopted, the implication is that outcomes would be monitored. This in turn implies the systematic gathering by organizations of high-quality longitudinal data that are disaggregated by a number of social groups. The information would then be used to inform the basis for special or even preferential treatment of under-represented groups.

Positive discrimination (or in the US 'affirmative action') would be the main policy tool to achieve effectiveness, with policy-makers and managers aiding, advancing or even favouring members of disadvantaged groups wherever possible. This could be done informally by individuals or groups acting together or formally using specific policy initiatives such as monitoring data. The use of quotas in jobs or layers of the hierarchy where women are under-represented would be one formal example of a positive discrimination policy initiative. However, it needs to be noted that quotas are not permitted under UK law; therefore in practice the radical conception is more or less inoperable. In the US, since the 1991 amendment to the Civil Rights Act of 1964, employers can give preference to 'protected classes' (including African Americans, Asian Americans and women), but quotas are no longer allowed (Mor Barak 2005).

The aim within the radical approach is to manipulate *perceptions* of EO policies, to expose the inadequacies of the procedural (liberal) conception in order to raise consciousness of disadvantage and discrimination so that collective awareness and solidarity might be increased, thus promoting employee resistance to inequalities and demands for more radical interventions.

Critiques of traditional EO

There are a number of ambiguities, contradictions, tensions and areas of confusion within the traditional approach to EO that the distinction between liberal and radical conceptions exposes.

One area of ambiguity concerns what the terms 'fair' and 'equal' actually mean. The debate centres on whether treating people equally involves treating them the same or differently. For example, will women's equality be achieved if women are treated the same as men? Surely the gender equality project involves recognizing, if not women's biological difference, their different social roles? Does it make sense to treat all women the same, when clearly women are a diverse group differentiated by race, ethnicity, sexuality, etc.? Further, 'sameness' and 'difference' are both relative concepts. Deciding whether to treat women the same as or differently from men involves setting standards and norms against which such treatment can be judged. In this way the male experience and masculine characteristics usually become the norm (Liff and Wajcman 1996). Put simply, women have to compete with men on men's terms. The dominant (liberal) approach to EO has tended to minimize differences between women and men and has thus simplified the gender equality project. For example, policy attention has focused on applying the same recruitment and selection criteria and procedures to women and men. But this approach has failed to deal with the fact that women typically have different career trajectories that are closely bound up with their role as primary carers in the family, meaning that women have a greater need for access to flexible work arrangements and childcare. In summary, critics, particularly feminists, have argued that gender equality will not be achieved by treating women the same as men.

However, another tension is that this does not mean that there is widespread support for treating women differently from men as a basis for EO policy; indeed positive discrimination has proved highly controversial (Mor Barak 2005). In her research Cockburn (1989) did not find much support for the radical conception of EO (involving special treatment and positive discrimination) even among those who might benefit from it. Members of disadvantaged groups, including women, were opposed to the idea of favouritism and of violating the merit principle. Even in the trade union context where 'special measures' have been widely used to promote gender equality, this has provoked controversy (see Chapter 8). The major contradiction of the radical EO approach seems to be 'that it seeks to put right old wrongs by means that themselves are felt to be wrong' (Cockburn 1989: 217). So, giving women preferential treatment over men proves unpopular in most contexts.

Cockburn suggested that in place of a liberal/radical dichotomy another way of thinking about EO policy was to conceptualize an EO agenda of shorter or longer length. A short EO agenda would involve measures to minimize bias in procedures such as recruitment and promotion, while the long agenda would be a project of organizational transformation that would look for 'change in the nature of power, in the control ordinary people of diverse kinds have over institutions, a melting away of the white male monoculture' (1989: 218). The concept of short and long EO agendas is an alternative way of thinking about the goals of policy enabling EO to be conceptualized as a journey, which Cockburn believes would engage a larger constituency than approaches that pursue the vested interests of minority groups. Here, Cockburn identifies another of the tensions within the traditional approach to EO (especially more radical measures) – the likelihood of it generating a backlash from majority groups (especially white men).

In practice, Cockburn (1989) found the liberal/radical dichotomy a straitjacket that did not adequately reflect the multiplicity in the experience both of management and of disadvantage in employment and consequently in the range of EO responses. Drawing on her case study research Cockburn argued that some managers identify a business case for equality; others are worried about legal claims of discrimination; others are genuinely committed to social justice. These multiple management perspectives mean, according to Cockburn, that no single organization can be deemed to have a unified and uniform interpretation of, or approach to, EO. Cockburn (1989: 216) also argued that it was just as difficult to conceive of disadvantaged groups of employees as opposing management with a 'one-dimensional radical version of EO'. For example, the needs of women and black and minority ethnic employees might differ and each group itself is not a unitary category, with for example, professional women having different EO concerns to lower-skilled women, as is evident from an examination of the case of professional and managerial women in Chapter 5. Also, given the costs involved in developing and implementing EO initiatives, advancing the interests of one group might be at the expense of another. For example, white middle-class women benefit more from 'work–life balance' and flexible working policies than black and working-class women (see Chapter 7).

Turning to policy implementation, one area of confusion that Jewson and Mason (1986: 227) discuss is whether espoused policy principles actually reflect the values and goals of policy-makers. For example, they claim that radicals sometimes 'disguise themselves in liberal clothing' in order to get around the constraints of the law (which in the UK context is characterized as liberal and prohibits positive discrimination). This might mean that they covertly pursue a policy of positive discrimination (preferential treatment of women, for example) under the guise of positive action or procedural reform. Similarly, liberals might seek to justify potentially costly procedural reform by claiming that it will have radical outcomes (for example, new performance appraisal procedures will see more women break through the 'glass ceiling'). The consequence of this kind of obfuscation of the principles and aims is to make it difficult to evaluate the success or otherwise of EO policy initiatives – if it is unclear what an organization is trying to achieve, how can we know if it has succeeded? This then opens the door for critics to claim that EO has failed (EOR 1995).

Thus one major contradiction and confusion arising from the procedural (liberal) approach to EO was that it seemingly failed to deliver equality of outcome. As stated above, most British organizations formulated their EO policies of the 1980s based on the necessity to comply with anti-discrimination law which itself was essentially liberal in nature, requiring very little of employers (Dickens 1994). The UK legislation emphasized formal, procedural equality and was concerned with avoiding discrimination and equality of treatment (as per the liberal conception), rather than with promoting equality and delivering equality of outcome (as per the radical conception). In particular the UK legislation (unlike the US) prohibited positive discrimination, although it did (and still does) allow for some forms of positive action (such as women-only training for particular occupations where women are under-represented). The point is, though, that employers were not *required* to promote women's equality in this way. With legal compulsion lacking, most organizational policies went no further than 'cleaning up' recruitment and selection procedures to ensure that women were not actively discriminated against or excluded from applying for particular jobs (Cockburn 1991). In this policy context, gender inequalities in employment continued into the 1980s and 1990s as evidenced by the gender pay gap and the under-representation of women in senior positions (Cockburn 1991).

One question that has been widely debated in the British context is *why* organizations seemed to be lacking in the will to take steps to move beyond the minimal requirements of the law and reflect the spirit of EO contained in the anti-discrimination legislation. Many commentators, activists and policy-makers began to ask, what have organizations to gain from EO? (This question clearly has salience beyond the British context.) As Jewson and Mason (1986) make clear, whether an EO policy is liberal or radical in nature, it is fairness or social justice that is the ultimate goal. In her conception of short and long agendas, Cockburn (1989) seems to believe that many people in many organizations have good intentions and believe that equality is worth pursuing for its own sake.

Nevertheless, British equality activists began increasingly in the late 1980s/early 1990s to construct a 'business case' for EO in the belief that it would prove more persuasive with employers than pleas to move beyond minimal legal compliance based on social justice arguments or the morality of EO. The argument was that once employers appreciated that they stood to gain from EO initiatives, they would begin to pay more than mere lip service and make real efforts to deliver equality outcomes (Dickens 1994). One of the main business-case arguments of the period in the UK concerned the so-called 'demographic time bomb'. Falling numbers of young people available for full-time employment meant that labour shortages were predicted and employers were encouraged by the UK government to think of ways of attracting more women (especially married mothers) into employment. This involved among other things addressing women's need for part-time, flexible jobs and there was a considerable amount of employer activity in these areas. However, critics claimed that the business case was contingent and limited in both scope and depth, related as it is to employer need rather than to notions of fairness or social justice (Dickens 1994; McGlynn 2003).

To summarize, traditional conceptions of and approaches to EO have been found wanting both by advocates of equality and by critics in the policy-making and academic arenas (Kirton and Greene 2005). On the one hand, conceptual flaws and weaknesses have been identified that mean that it is inevitable that there will be disappointment in the slow pace and superficial nature of the changes. From another perspective many people and organizations have been left suspicious of EO and wondering what they have to gain. Against this, new conceptual and policy developments began to occur in the mid 1990s.

Changing social and economic context

The notion of a business case for equality and other developments in concepts of equality and in EO policy need first to be situated within the changing social and economic context facing much of the industrialized world during the 1990 presently. Structural economic change, in particular the decline of the manufacturing base and growth of the service sector, has fundamentally altered the business and employment context with different skill sets required compared to a generation ago. Labour and skill shortages have occurred in some areas, partly caused by the decline in the birth rate over the past couple of decades. Added to this, it is argued that within a context of globalization the business environment has become more competitive. Within the 'new economy' customer expectations have changed and there is now a strong demand for access to goods and services 24 hours a day; increasingly this means that organizations must operate outside of the traditional nine-to-five hours (Houston 2005). As a consequence of the emergence of this 'new economy', it is argued that employers in industrialized countries are now competing with each other for the 'best' (meaning most talented, skilled and qualified) workers and can no longer afford to ignore previously under-utilized groups such as women (Kandola and Fullerton 1994).

Changing workforce demography has then become an issue for employers. In the US, the now widely discussed *Workforce 2000* report (Johnston and Packer 1987) projected that by 2000 85 per cent of new entrants to the workplace would be women, people of colour, and immigrants. One of the most fundamental social changes of the last 30 or 40 years in industrialized societies has been the increase in women's employment, especially mothers of young children. The gap in the employment rates of women and men has declined. In the UK just over half of women (52 per cent) with pre-school children (under five) are in paid work, while 70 per cent of women with children aged five to ten are employed (EOC 2005a). As we discussed in Chapter 1, decreasing numbers of families (in the US and Europe) now display the traditional model of the 'male breadwinner household' where fathers are in paid work and mothers remain at home to care for the family. However, as we showed in Chapter 1 (Table 1.1) the majority of British women in two-adult households where there are children below 11 work part-time, demonstrating the now typical British female pattern of combining paid work and family care. Nevertheless, not all women conform to this employment pattern. What have been termed 'dual career households' (Hardill and Watson 2004) in which both partners, often highly qualified, are pursuing full-time employment, form a growing minority of households, between 10 and 20 per cent of all couples in Britain, the US and Canada. Women now perform a broader range of jobs than 30 or 40 years ago and in particular the proportion of women in professional and managerial work has increased significantly (Hardill and Watson 2004).

What is interesting about these patterns for the purposes of this chapter's discussion is that women are now the primary source of labour for many occupations including the traditional ones such as general office work, but also for some areas of management and the professions, and for many employers in many sectors of the economy, especially private services, for example retail and finance. To a large extent then there appears to be a prima facie business case for organizations to develop policy initiatives to attract and retain women. But does this mean that employers must strive towards gender equality by developing special measures for women or does it mean that women are simply stepping into the breach to fulfil employer need? For example, despite women's apparent need to fit paid work around unpaid caring activities, most British women do not have access to the kind of flexible arrangements that would allow them to do so. Only 12 per cent of women work on 'flexitime', only 8 per cent are on term-time only contracts and only 2 per cent job share (EOC 2005a). The evidence indicates that it is women who must fit family life around work patterns established by employers, rather than organizations offering work that fits around women's needs. This usually means that British women 'choose' part-time work – 43 per cent of British women overall work part-time, but this rises to 65 per cent of women with children under five and 64 per cent with children under 11 (WEU 2004). From an equality perspective the problem is that most part-time jobs are low skill, low paid and offer few prospects. It is only good quality part-time jobs that promote gender equality (Bleijenbergh *et al.* 2004), as we discussed in Chapter 4. Furthermore, we argue in Chapter 7 that flexible working arrangements that have developed as part of the 'work–life balance agenda' may not be in women's long-term financial interest.

Changing political and public discourses of equality

There can be no doubt that the 'equal opportunities revolution' has changed the gender structure of employment and opened up many more opportunities for the present generation of employed women compared to earlier ones. However, it is also clear that gender inequalities persist in terms of lifetime income, domestic labour, working patterns, access to transport and technology etc. (e.g. Howard and Tibballs 2003). It is also clear that policy-makers' and the general public's views on what, if anything, should be done to tackle gender inequalities have changed over time and that in turn changing political and public discourses of equality shape state and organizational policy in the area. This is particularly relevant to the emergence of the diversity discourse.

Cockburn (1991: 35) argued that the British equality legislation was the product of the era of welfare capitalism and that this ended with the election of a Conservative government in 1979. The so-called 'rolling back of the state' in the period (at least up until the change of government in 1997) served to place the emphasis on the individual and on people taking responsibility for their own lives. Such an emphasis does not of course sit easily with the concept of collective barriers to equal opportunity, or with notions of equal rights and social injustice embedded in the traditional approach to equal opportunities. From this perspective, employment regulation of any kind interferes with the forces of a free market economy. The election of the Labour government in 1997 brought about renewed effort to tackle gender inequalities as demonstrated by the establishment of the Women and Equality Unit (WEU) and Ministers for Women. The WEU highlights the gender pay gap, women's under-representation in the boardroom and increased rights for parents of young children as significant policy areas requiring attention. The Ministers for Women are responsible for '*promoting and realising the benefits of diversity in the economy and more widely*' (emphasis added) (WEU 2006). In context of the discussion about the shift from equal opportunities to diversity management, it is of course significant that the British government is emphasizing the business case for *diversity*.

It is likely that this new state policy orientation both reflects and shapes the wider public's perspective on equality issues. In Britain the Equal Opportunities Commission (EOC) commissioned research to learn more about how people understand and talk about gender equality issues (Howard and Tibballs 2003). The authors found that although people are aware that social inequality and discrimination are still widespread in Britain today and believe that society should be fairer, they are also sceptical about measures such as positive discrimination that seek to achieve equal outcomes. With regard to gender equality, most women could see that women generally have less well paid jobs and do more household work than men, but they saw these experiences as a function of *individual* choices and natural gender differences, rather than as inequalities (2003: 9). Following from this, gender inequality was not seen as a major or priority issue and there was some resistance to group claims (i.e. that all women experience inequality), with a strong sense that people should take personal responsibility (2003: 35).

One of the central themes emerging from Howard and Tibballs' research is what they see as a difference between professional (equality specialist/academic researcher) and public views of gender inequality, summarized in Table 6.1. On the one hand, those professionally involved in the area of equality continue to identify significant gender inequalities and the professional analysis of the causes highlights the gendered nature of society and organizations. Initiatives targeted at the group level are still widely believed to be necessary as can be seen from many organizational equality and diversity policies (see Johnstone 2002). On the other hand, from Howard and Tibballs' research, it appears that ordinary citizens take a more liberal view that leans towards essentialist explanations for gendered employment patterns and outcomes.

It would, however, be incorrect to suggest that professional perspectives on equality have not changed at all, although the changes might seem more subtle

Table 6.1 Differing professional and public perspectives on equality

Citizen perspective	Professional perspective
Pay gap does not exist	Persistence of pay gap
Women have equal opportunities	Gendered work/care
Individual responsible	Collective action vital
Nature makes difference	Social construction matters
Society gender neutral	Gender bias ingrained

Source: Howard and Tibballs (2003: 44).

and a question of emphasis, rather than fundamental (see for example Kirton *et al.* 2005). The changing professional perspective is reflected in the description of the role of the Ministers for Women and in the activities of the WEU and EOC, with the greater emphasis on the business case for equality/diversity and on the multiplicity and intersecting nature of various forms of discrimination and disadvantage.

Part of the explanation for changing citizen and professional perspectives on equality probably lies in the decline of political ideologies, such as feminism and class politics, that promote specific group allegiance. The 'equal opportunities revolution' owes much to the feminist movement of the late 1960s/early 1970s, which formulated demands such as an end to sex discrimination, increased legal rights, and financial independence for women (Cockburn 1991). Although there are different types of feminism, the following definition captures the central tenets. Feminists:

> (a) recognize the validity of women's own interpretations of their lived experiences and needs and acknowledge the values women claim publicly as their own (as distinct from an aesthetic ideal of womanhood invented by men) in assessing their status in society relative to men; (b) they exhibit consciousness of, discomfort at or even anger over institutionalized injustice (or inequity) towards women as a group by men as a group; and (c) they advocate the elimination of that injustice by challenging, through efforts to alter prevailing ideas and/or social institutions and practices, the coercive power, force or authority that upholds male prerogatives.
>
> (Offen 1992)

The ideas of feminism now provoke controversy and fewer women are prepared to self-identify as feminists. Feminists have been depicted in the media as aggressive man-haters and the phrase 'I'm not a feminist but ...' has become a familiar one that reflects the views of women who still believe in gender equality, but who do not want to be associated with the negative imagery of feminism (Webb 1997). In addition, the media has extensively covered the stories of so-called 'have-it-all' women (with high-flying careers) who have discovered that they cannot 'have it all' when their marriages fall apart, their families 'suffer' or they discover they are unable to have children having left it 'too late'. This has all provoked a backlash against feminism and the achievements of equal opportunities initiatives that are underpinned by feminist demands and ideas, based in collectivism and reflected in some trade union thinking.

Classic feminist thought has also been subjected to a substantial academic critique. Barrett and Phillips (1992) argue that in the 1970s feminists were united in the importance they attached to the causes of women's inequality (as reflected in Offen's definition above), but that that consensus has since broken up. They attribute the decline in the appeal of feminist theories to (i) black women's critique of the racist and ethno-centric assumptions of 'white' feminism, (ii) the fact that sexual difference came to be viewed as more intransigent, but also more positive than most 1970s feminists had allowed, and (iii) the development by feminists of post-modernist ideas (1992: 5). With regard to the latter point, there is now greater interest in the multifaceted nature of social identity and a 'politics of difference', which contends that women are positioned in relation to class, race, educational background and many other factors, as well as gender. From this perspective women's subjective experiences are heterogeneous and therefore no single policy response will be a gain for all women (Pringle and Watson 1992). This makes it more difficult, although not impossible, to conceive of collective positions or actions on gender equality in the way that 1970s-style feminism had done.

Diversity management

The changing social and economic context and changing political and public discourses of equality paved the way for the emergence and ascendance of a 'new' way of thinking about equality policy – diversity management. The term 'diversity' was first heard in the US in 1987 when Johnston and Packer (1987) published their highly influential report showing how the population of America was going to change over the next decade and the impact that this would have on the labour market. The report served as a warning to US firms relying on a homogeneous pool of labour (white men) that they needed to start developing policies to recruit and retain a more diverse workforce. The diversity debate in the US and in some European countries (e.g. Sweden, Denmark) (de los Reyes 2000; Wrench 2005) has centred on race and ethnicity. The concept of diversity arrived in the UK in the early 1990s and has now become firmly established in organizational policy and in academic literature and generally covers a broader range of diversity dimensions, including gender.

The central tenets of diversity management have been summarized as: (i) internally driven, not externally imposed – that is the concern is with business or organizational need, rather than with minimal legal compliance; (ii) focused on individuals, not groups – diversity claims to benefit everyone and not simply disadvantaged groups; (iii) concerned with diversity not equality – recognizing difference rather than trying to achieve sameness; (iv) addressing the total culture, not just the systems – moving the policy focus away from rules and procedures towards culture change initiatives; (v) the responsibility of all, not just personnel – the role of line-managers is played up (Ross and Schneider 1992). These ideas are reflected in the diversity statements of many British organizations (see Johnstone 2002). In addition, diversity management refers to 'the systematic and planned commitment on the part of organizations to recruit and retain employees with diverse backgrounds and abilities' (Bassett-Jones 2005).

Diversity management has been portrayed by some as an evolutionary step from equality (Kandola and Fullerton 1994); a sophistication of the equality approach (Overell 1996); a repackaging of equality (Ford 1996); a sanitized, market-oriented notion (Webb 1997) and a 'comfort zone' (Ouseley in Overell 1996).

Some of the differences between EO and diversity management have provoked controversy among key actors in the employment relationship, including employers and trade unions (Kirton and Greene forthcoming). This is discussed further below.

Theoretical approaches

It is difficult to produce actual evidence of the supposed benefits of diversity because diversity management seems to suffer from the same problems of conceptual confusion as equal opportunities. While the central tenets, described earlier, appear to be agreed upon, at present there is very little literature detailing and discussing precisely what measures and initiatives comprise 'systematic and planned commitment' (Bassett-Jones 2005) to diversity management within British organizations. Liff's (1997) typology of four diversity management approaches is useful as it differentiates between the underlying principles and aims of policy and therefore reflects the multidimensional nature of many organizational policies. Using this typology enables us to see more clearly the relationship between diversity management and equal opportunities and also what type of initiatives we are likely to see within diversity management.

The first approach Liff (1997) identifies – *dissolving differences* – involves a series of initiatives that stress individualism. Differences between people are not seen as based on gender (or any other social group membership), but are individually based. For example, in their definition Kandola and Fullerton (1994: 8) state that 'diversity consists of visible and non-visible differences which will include factors such as sex, age, background, race, disability, personality and workstyle'. It follows that initiatives would seek to respond to individual needs, for example individual performance reviews and training plans, rather than to group claims of inequality. This approach has echoes of Jewson and Mason's (1986) *liberal* approach to EO that conceives of talent and ability as individual attributes. However, the liberal approach believes that *collective* barriers to the expression of individual talent must be dismantled, for example the barriers that women experience; whereas the 'dissolving differences' approach ignores the systemic and structural nature of inequality. It requires little of employers beyond ensuring that women are not actively discriminated against. It is concerned mainly with organizational efficiency, rather than fairness.

Diversity signals that equality is not simply about sameness, but about celebrating difference and this is reflected in the second approach – *valuing differences.* In this respect diversity responds to another of the criticisms of EO – that women's differences are suppressed and downplayed in order to make the claim for equality seem more legitimate. In 'valuing differences' Liff (1997) refers to social group-based differences and the recognition of the way in which these contribute to inequality; thus difference is a moral concern. Initiatives would include provision of training for employees from under-represented groups (e.g. management training for women) to help overcome past disadvantage.

According to Liff's conception, this approach also has strong echoes of the *liberal* model of EO in so far as there is a concern to dismantle *collective* barriers. However, the intention of the *liberal* approach is to minimize rather than value differences. In practice it appears that some organizations in both the private and public sectors in Britain (Johnstone 2002) understand *valuing differences* as to do with individual, rather than group-based differences, so whether or not a *valuing differences* approach can address gender inequalities is not clear.

The third approach is *accommodating differences*, which is broadly similar to traditional liberal EO where there is a commitment to creating policies that open up opportunities (rather than providing special measures) to under-represented groups. This approach might be found where the most compelling business case for diversity relates to the changing demographic composition of the labour market, particularly women's increased employment. Examples of policy initiatives might include flexible work arrangements and other 'family-friendly' measures. The central concern is again for organizational efficiency.

The final approach Liff identifies is *utilizing differences*, where social group-based differences are recognized and provide the basis for different treatment rather than the focus of equality policies. Therefore this approach is not concerned with social justice, rather these differences will be put to use for the benefit of the organization, but whether or not equality goals will inadvertently be met depends very much on the organization's motives for utilizing difference.

Benefits of diversity

From Liff's typology we can see that it is only the 'valuing differences' approach that might have a moral basis. Thus, diversity management claims to respond to one of the major perceived weaknesses of traditional equal opportunities (with its emphasis on fairness and social justice) in that it is argued that there is a strong business case for diversity. The UK government has promoted this belief:

> A diverse workforce can be more creative than one which has been recruited in the image of a particular manager. It may be able to establish new clients for the business, and help to reach a wider market.
>
> (Cabinet Office 2001)

This removes the emphasis from what organizations have to do by law and onto what organizations can or should do to benefit from diversity. This argument appeals to critics of EO who have claimed that the moral case of equality has little purchase in the competitive world of business. Four main advantages to organizations are usually emphasized: (i) taking advantage of diversity in the labour market; (ii) maximizing employee potential; (iii) managing across borders and cultures; (iv) creating business opportunities and enhancing creativity (Cornelius *et al.* 2001). Even in the public sector, where the emphasis has traditionally been placed on being a 'model employer', organizational and managerial reforms introduced from the early 1980s onwards have brought organizations closer to the market and in so doing have created new pressures to make a business case for equality initiatives (Carter 2000; Cunningham 2000).

The first advantage pinpointed by Cornelius *et al.* (2000) – taking advantage of diversity in the labour market – highlights the changing demographic composition of the workforce such as the increased employment participation of women, the ageing workforce and larger numbers of minority ethnic workers. This argument is founded on the belief that only organizations that attract and retain a diversity of employees will be successful, particularly in tight labour markets. British organizations seem to be particularly persuaded by this argument.

The second advantage – maximizing employee potential – argues that the harnessing of human capital possessed by diverse groups will improve organizational performance. Conversely, unfair and discriminatory treatment creates low morale and disaffection, leading to poor performance. Therefore organizations need to actively manage diversity in order to extract the highest levels of performance from employees. This resonates with the 'special contribution' argument – the idea that because of their different life experiences women can offer something 'essential' or special to organizations. From this perspective women might be taken to be more people-oriented, to have a more democratic leadership style and to be more caring and nurturing (Alvesson and Billing 1997: 161). It is argued that in the new economy these 'feminine' skills are what are needed for business success. Whether they lead towards women's advancement in employment is another matter.

The third advantage – managing across borders and cultures – mainly concerns the globalization of world markets and the international labour market that many organizations draw on. Here the argument is that a diverse workforce can enhance an organization's ability to reach and satisfy a broader customer base. While this might seem to apply more to commercial business organizations operating at a multinational level, it is also possible to situate this argument within the public sector, for example the UK's National Health Service and its active recruitment of overseas nurses might spring to mind. It might be argued that this strategy enables hospitals to meet the needs of a diversity of patients.

The fourth advantage – creating business opportunities and enhancing creativity – is about tapping the supposedly culturally specific experiences and insights that a diverse workforce possesses in order to move the organization forward. For example, it might be argued that women understand other women's purchasing habits and needs; therefore it is useful to have women employed in, say, the marketing or product development departments. This could however perpetuate the concentration of women in particular niches, something that could contribute to vertical segregation and the negative consequences that arise from this (see Chapter 2).

Diversity management and the gender equality project

It is clear from Liff's (1997) multidimensional model that there are some parallels between diversity management and equal opportunities approaches, but the over-arching emphasis of diversity management is on organizational efficiency, rather than delivering (gender) equality. A link between EO and diversity management is to be expected given the impossibility of a complete break from past approaches, especially in view of the existing gender equality legislation in industrialized countries. However, despite being widely represented as a way forward, whether diversity management will advance or hold back the gender equality project is highly debatable.

The first main area of concern is diversity management's heavy reliance on the business case. This has the effect of privatizing equality and turning it into an internal matter for the individual organization, rather than a societal level issue. There is evidence that some British organizations have constructed a business case for gender equality/diversity (see for example the membership list and case studies of the campaign organization Opportunity Now (Business in the Community 2006)). There are suggestions that diversity management can deliver organizational benefits if initiatives are formulated in ways that are sensitive to the existing culture and practices and if some of the potential dilemmas and chal-lenges are dealt with (Cornelius *et al.* 2000; Sinclair 2000; Maxwell *et al.* 2001).

However, as discussed, critics have argued that the business case for equality (and diversity) is an insecure foundation for advancing the gender equality project (e.g. Dickens 1994; Colling and Dickens 2001). One of the strands of critique of diversity management concerns the scant evidence to support the claim that in prac-tice all organizations can benefit equally from diversity. A similar discussion has taken place on whether equality is good for business. It has been argued that the business case for *equality* is 'partial and contingent' and does not have universal purchase (Dickens 1994). For example, some organizations compete on the basis of low cost; therefore diversity measures, such as work–life balance policies, might not be cost-effective. In addition, some organizations might benefit from an absence of equality in so far as discriminatory practices can contribute to the bottom line – organizations can benefit from, for example, the utilization but under-valuing of women's labour (Dickens 1994). After all, the gender pay gap means that women are cheaper to employ. Therefore it is possible for organizations to benefit from hav-ing and utilizing a diverse workforce, but whether or not there will be benefits from *valuing* diversity depends very much on the type of organization and its business and employee relations strategies. An organization with a cost-minimization strat-egy might regard its low-paid female workers as entirely dispensable and replaceable and be unwilling to invest in potentially costly diversity initiatives.

Advocates of the business case for diversity (e.g. Ross and Schneider 1992; Kandola and Fullerton 1994; EOR 2001) have tended to gloss over these issues, making broad-brush statements about the benefits of diversity that lack a contex-tualized analysis. There is no solid evidence that diversity management policies are any less partial and contingent than traditional EO; they might even be more so (Kirton and Greene 2005).

The second area of concern is the strong strand of individualism contained in diversity management when compared with traditional equal opportunities (Liff 1997). Difference is viewed through an individual lens and there seems less potential to identify common causes among women (Webb 1997) in the way that traditional EO with its links to feminist ideas does. The individual difference lens might be of benefit to middle-class highly qualified women where there is likely to be a stronger business case for their retention and therefore whose individual needs are more likely to be accommodated through policies such as career break schemes (see Chapter 7). However, diversity management does not provide a strong rationale for the kinds of positive action initiatives (such as management training courses specifically for women) that have helped to increase women's representation in higher level jobs (Cockburn 1991).

In contrast, in traditional EO the social difference lens has been used to highlight and address discrimination and disadvantage as experienced by a greater diversity of women (Merrill-Sands et al. 2000). The individualism of diversity management could lead to less emphasis on standardized procedures to eliminate discrimination (such as job evaluation to determine pay, which is shown to benefit women) and more on individualized management-controlled techniques such as performance appraisal and performance pay (where women are often disadvantaged). The lesser emphasis on formal procedures that are based in legislation could also lead to greater managerial discretion in decision-making. Collinson et al.'s (1990) and Cockburn's (1991) in-depth case studies are a perfect example of the gendered dynamics of social relations and practices in organizations that allow managers to act in ways that reinforce the traditional patterns of female disadvantage.

The third area of concern is the fact that diversity management is positioned as a top-down management activity; something that is 'done' to employees, rather than something they actively construct and participate in (Lorbiecki and Jack 2000; Kirton and Greene forthcoming). In Kandola and Fullerton's (1994: 8) widely used definition, the words 'harnessing differences' reveal how it is expected that diversity can be controlled and put to such use as the organization sees fit. This stands in contrast to traditional EO where 'bottom-up' pressure from employees, often applied through trade unions (as discussed in Chapter 8), has been just as important as management commitment in setting the equality agenda (Colling and Dickens 2001). Trade unions have traditionally played a role in promoting and advancing gender equality in UK workplaces and there is evidence that workplaces with recognized trade unions are more likely to have developed formal equality policies than non-unionized firms (Noon and Hoque 2001). Even with their imperfections it is clear that formal EO policies provide women with some protection against discrimination.

Conclusions

Many large organizations employ an equality and diversity specialist to provide advice on and develop policy initiatives. It is clear from the discussion in this chapter that the role is bound to be a challenging one that may provoke resentment, hostility and criticism from various quarters. Lorbiecki (2001) positions what she calls 'diversity vanguards' as 'outsiders-within' – people who feel compelled to speak out against discrimination and yet also have to uphold the organization's business objectives. Research in various countries has found a dissonance between diversity specialists' beliefs about what needs to be done and the more business-focused objectives of organizations (Jones *et al.* 2000; Lawrence 2000; Sinclair 2000; Litvin 2002). In addition, discovering the strong business case that it is argued that 'good diversity management' should seek (Cornelius *et al.* 2000) is no easy task in view of the partial and contingent nature of the business case. However, it is also possible that diversity management could provide a fresh look and impetus for the equality agenda (Sinclair 2000) and that the central tenets of EO and diversity management as reflected in policy and practice need not always be mutually exclusive. For example, some private sector organizations have begun to see diversity management as part of their broader 'corporate social responsibility' agenda that is reflective of the greater concern for ethical business practice (Johnstone 2002). The business-led women's equality campaign organization Opportunity Now has seen its membership rise from 61 on its launch in 1991 to 360 in 2006, suggesting a growing concern with equality and diversity issues. In the public sector in the UK, although promoting the business case for diversity has become commonplace, there remains a policy concern about gender inequalities. The government is shortly to introduce a legal duty to promote gender equality, which will require public bodies to actively consider gender equality when setting their priorities and to ensure that they take reasonable steps to deliver it. This will involve a specific duty to produce gender equality goals and schemes and to tackle equal pay. The Equal Opportunities Commission sees this as the most important change to sex discrimination law for 30 years (EOC 2005b). However, against all this activity on gender equality, we must remember that very strong indicators of women's inequality that are discussed in the various chapters of this book remain in place.

References

Alvesson, M. and Billing, Y. (1997) *Understanding Gender and Organisations*, London: Sage.

Barrett, M. and Phillips, A. (1992) *Destabilising Theory*, Cambridge: Polity Press.

Bassett-Jones, N. (2005) 'The paradox of diversity management, creativity and innovation', *Creativity and Innovation Management*, 14 (2): 169–75.

Bleijenbergh, I., de Bruijn, J. and Bussemaker, J. (2004) 'European social citizenship and gender: the part-time work directive', *European Journal of Industrial Relations*, 10 (3): 309–28.

Blommaert, J. and Verschueren, J. (1998) *Debating Diversity*, London, Routledge.

Business in the Community (2006) 'Opportunity Now', http://www.bitc.org.uk/ programmes/programme_directory/opportunity_now/index.html, accessed May 2006.

Cabinet Office (2001) *Equality and Diversity: The Way Ahead*, London: Cabinet Office.

Carter, J. (2000) 'New public management and equal opportunities in the NHS', *Critical Social Policy*, 20 (1): 61–83.

Cockburn, C. (1989) 'Equal opportunities: the short and the long agenda', *Industrial Relations Journal*, 20 (3): 213–25.

Cockburn, C. (1991) *In the Way of Women*, Basingstoke: Macmillan.

Colling, T. and Dickens, L (2001) 'Gender equality and trade unions: a new basis for mobilisation?' in M. Noon and E. Ogbonna (eds) *Equality, Diversity and Disadvantage in Employment*, Basingstoke: Palgrave, 136–55.

Collinson, D., Knights, D. and Collinson, M. (1990) *Managing to Discriminate*, London: Routledge.

Cornelius, N., Gooch, L. and Todd, S. (2000) 'Managers leading diversity for business excellence', *Journal of General Management*, 25 (3): 67–78.

Cornelius, N., Gooch, L. and Todd, S. (2001) 'Managing difference fairly: an integrated "partnership" approach', in M. Noon and E. Ogbonna (eds) *Equality, Diversity and Disadvantage in Employment*, Basingstoke: Palgrave, 32–50.

Cox, T. (1994) 'A comment on the language of diversity', *Organization*, 1 (1): 51–58.

Cunningham, R. (2000). 'From great expectations to hard times? Managing equal opportunities under new public management', *Public Administration*, 78 (3): 699–714.

de los Reyes, P. (2000) 'Diversity at work: paradoxes, possibilities and problems in the Swedish discourse on diversity', *Economic and Industrial Democracy*, 21: 253–66.

Dickens, L. (1994) 'Wasted Resources?' in K Sissons (ed.) *Equal Opportunities in Employment: Personnel Management*, Oxford: Blackwell, 253–95.

EOC (2005a) *Facts about Women and Men in Great Britain*, Manchester: Equal Opportunities Commission.

EOC (2005b). *Response to DTI, Advancing Equality for Men and Women: Government Proposals to Introduce a Public Sector Duty to Promote Gender Equality*, Manchester: Equal Opportunities Commission.

EOR (1995) 'Managing diversity: succeeding where equal opportunities has failed', *Equal Opportunities Review*, 59 (January/February): 31–6.

EOR (2001) 'Diversity now the ultimate test of management capacity', *Equal Opportunities Review*, 96 (March/April): 11–17.

Ford, V. (1996) 'Partnership is the secret of progress: equality policy and diversity programs', *People Management*, 8 February, 2 (3): 34–6.

Hardill, I. and Watson, R. (2004) 'Career priorities within dual career households: an analysis of the impact of child rearing upon gender participation rates and earnings', *Industrial Relations Journal*, 35 (1): 19–37.

Houston, D. (2005) 'Work–Life balance in the 21st century', in D. Houston (ed.) *Work–Life Balance in the 21st Century*, Basingstoke: Palgrave Macmillan, 1–10.

Howard, M. and Tibballs, S. (2003) *Talking Equality: What Men and Women Think About Equality in Britain Today*, London: Future Foundation.

Humphries, M. and Grice, S. (1995). 'Equal employment opportunity and the management of diversity', *Journal of Organizational Change Management*, 8 (5): 17–32.

Jewson, N. and Mason, D. (1986) 'The theory and practice of equal opportunities policies: liberal and radical approaches', *Sociological Review*, 34 (2): 307–34.

Johnson, L. and Johnstone, S. (2005) 'The legal framework for diversity', in G. Kirton and A. M. Greene (eds) *The Dynamics of Managing Diversity*, Oxford: Elsevier Butterworth-Heinemann, 143–71.

Johnston, W. and Packer, A. (1987) *Workforce 2000: Work and Workers for the 21st Century*, New York: The Hudson Institute.

Johnstone, S. (2002) *Managing Diversity in the Workplace*, London: IRS.

Jones, D., Pringle, J. and Shepherd, D. (2000) '"Managing diversity"' meets Aotearoa/New Zealand' *Personnel Review*, 29 (3): 364–80.

Kandola, R. and Fullerton J. (1994) *Managing the Mosaic: Diversity in Action*, London: Institute of Personnel and Development.

Kirton, G. and Greene, A. M. (2005) *The Dynamics of Managing Diversity*, Oxford: Butterworth Heinemann.

Kirton, G. and Greene, A. M. (forthcoming) 'The discourse of diversity in unionized contexts: views from trade union equality officers', *Personnel Review*.

Kirton, G., Greene, A. M. and Dean, D. (2005) *British Diversity Champions as Change Agents – Radicals, Tempered Radicals or Liberal Reformers?* Paper presented to Gender, Work and Organization Conference, Keele University, UK.

Lawrence, E. (2000) 'Equal opportunities officers and managing equality changes', *Personnel Review*, 29 (3): 381–401.

Liff, S. (1997) 'Two routes to managing diversity: individual differences or social group characteristics?' *Employee Relations*, 19 (1): 11–26.

Liff, S. and Wajcman, J. (1996) '"Sameness" and "Difference" revisited: which way forward for equal opportunity initiatives?' *Journal of Management Studies*, 33 (1): 79–94.

Litvin, D. (2002) 'The business case for diversity and the "Iron Cage"', in B. Czarniawska and H. Hopfl (eds) *Casting the Other*, London: Routledge, 160–84.

Lorbiecki, A. (2001) *Openings and Burdens for Women and Minority Ethnics Being Diversity Vanguards in Britain*, paper presented to Gender, Work and Organization Conference, Keele University, UK.

Lorbiecki, A. and Jack, G. (2000). 'Critical turns in the evolution of diversity management', *British Journal of Management*, 11 (Special Issue): S17–S31.

McGlynn, C. (2003) 'The status of women lawyers in the United Kingdom', in U. Schultz and G. Shaw (eds) *Women in the World's Legal Professions*, Oxford and Portland, OR: Hart Publishing, 139–56.

Maxwell, G., Blair, S. and McDougall, M. (2001) 'Edging towards managing diversity in practice', *Employee Relations*, 23 (5): 468–82.

Merrill-Sands, D., Holvino, E. and Cumming, J. (2000) 'Working with diversity: a focus on global organizations', in R. Ely, E. Foldy and M. Scully (eds) *Reader in Gender, Work, and Organization*, Malden, MA: Blackwell, 327–42.

Mor Barak, M. (2005) *Managing Diversity: Toward a Globally Inclusive Workplace*, California: Sage.

Noon, M. and Hoque, K. (2001) 'Ethnic minorities and equal treatment: the impact of gender, equal opportunities policies and trade unions', *National Institute Economic Review*, 176 (April): 105–16.

Offen, K. (1992) 'Defining feminism: a comparative historical approach', in G. Bock and S. James (eds) *Beyond Equality and Difference*, London: Routledge, 69–88.

Overell, S. (1996) 'Ouseley in assault on diversity', *People Management*, 2 (9): 7–9.

Pringle, R. and Watson, S. (1992) 'Women's Interests and the Post-structuralist State', in M. Barrett and A. Phillips (eds) *Destabilising Theory*, Cambridge: Polity Press.

Ross, R. and Schneider, R. (1992) *From Equality to Diversity*, London: Pitman.

Sinclair, A. (2000) 'Women within diversity: risks and possibilities', *Women in Management Review*, 15 (5/6): 237–45.

Webb, J. (1997) 'The politics of equal opportunity', *Gender, Work and Organization*, 4 (3): 159–69.

WEU (2004) *Interim Update of Key Indicators of Women's Position in Britain*, London: Women and Equality Unit, Department of Trade and Industry.

WEU (2006) 'About the Women and Equality Unit', http://www.womenandequalityunit.gov.uk/about/index.htm, accessed May 2006.

Wrench, J. (2005) 'Diversity management can be bad for you', *Race and Class*, 46 (3): 73–84.

Chapter 7

Work–life balance

Flexible working?

Introduction

The concept of 'work–life balance' is seemingly ubiquitous in discussions about employment in the twenty-first century in the UK. In the context of an associated decline of the full-time standard working week, flexible employment, working time and the reconciliation of work and family life have become central issues of current policy and academic debate in the UK (Cousins and Tang 2004). Kingsmill (2001) argues that up until relatively recently employers have tended to see their employees as either 'breadwinners' or 'homemakers'. This way of seeing the world has meant that employers have typically faced little pressure to address the needs of those who wish to combine both of these in some form or another. However, the 'war for talent' has refocused their attention (Croner Consulting 2004a). Whether the so-called 'business case' for work–life balance policies is a sufficiently solid base is arguable, and this is discussed below. Whether work–life balance policies are wholly advantageous for women is also the subject of argument, again discussed below. It appears likely that such policies may be beneficial for employers in terms of recruitment and retention, but there is growing evidence that they may be negative for employees in terms of their progression (Crompton *et al.* 2003). In four contrasted organizations studied by Crompton *et al.*, high-level 'career' jobs demanded full-time working, with long hours, not the profile that may be the result of taking advantage of flexible working policies. It may therefore be possible to argue, in the context of more women than men taking up these measures, that these forms of working actually reinforce gender inequalities.

Industrialized countries show a growth in unpredictable or irregular working and in unsocial hours (Mutari and Figart 2001). Work–life balance may be a particular issue for the UK, but it is also a policy area affecting other countries. In the US, work–life balance policies (inasmuch as they exist) are realistically only taken up by high-income families since they can afford to do so (Blair-Loy and Wharton 2002; Parcel and Cornfield 2000). The Family and Medical Leave Act acknowledges citizens' right to paid work and the right to care, but employers have some freedom in implementation (Lambert and Haley-Lock 2004). The legislation allows for parental leave, but the data on its implementation and usage show that only 11 per cent of private sector workplaces and only 55 per cent of workers are covered.

An earlier concept of 'work–family balance' has changed to 'work–life balance', signalling a political sensitivity that parents are not the only ones to want to put more emphasis on non-work time. This can be seen as an attempt by government and employers to ward off a backlash against a perceived favouring of employees with caring commitments, especially women. Lambert and Hayley-Lock (2004) cite the refocusing in the US of the concept of 'work–family balance' to a wider concept of 'work–life balance', linking this to the concept of the 'good employer'. Employer guides emphasize the need for the good employer to see the concept in a wider way, beyond the statutory requirements (Croner Consulting 2004a). In the UK, the Department for Trade and Industry encourages employers to become examples of 'good practice' by widening the idea of work–life balance so that it reaches all employees; it publishes 'good practice case studies'.

In the context of a European employment strategy that promotes flexible employment and the reconciliation of work and family life, the EU's directives relating to working time, parental leave and part-time workers' rights have filtered down to member states. For countries such as the UK, with until recently little tradition of such policies, their adoption represents a major shift. Such changes are much less obvious in Scandinavian countries, since many of these measures have long been in place, underpinned by ideologies of egalitarianism. The Nordic countries have a long history of rights for all parents; thus, specific work–life balance policies are probably unnecessary in this context. The UK has a patchy record of policies that would lead to better work–life balance, with a mixture of individualism (the solution being left up to the family) and a slow growth of state policies.[1] In a comparison of the US with ten European countries in terms of work–life policies, Gornick and Meyers (2004) classify countries on a gender equality scale – whether they offer any paid paternity leave, the nature of parental leave rights, whether benefits are wage related and at what level of wage replacement. The Nordic countries come out top and the liberal countries bottom, with the US standing out as exceptionally low.

Britain also lags behind other European countries. In 1999 Britain was the last EU member state to make parental leave a legal entitlement, 25 years after it was first introduced in Sweden. The 2007 legislation (at the time of writing its status is the Work and Families Bill) extends paternity leave. If the mother returns to paid work after six months of maternity leave, the remaining six months can be transferred to the father. This will be paid at the same rate as statutory maternity pay (in 2005 this was £106 per week). *The Guardian* (20 October 2005) reports that whilst campaigners welcome the extension of paternity leave and pay, the low level of payment is unlikely to offer a genuine choice to fathers. When parental leave can be taken by either parent, fathers have tended to take comparatively little of it (OECD 2001). This point links to the gender pay gap. In the average household, the man's pay will be higher than the woman's; thus a decision that the man forgoes his income during the leave will have a greater impact on the household finances than if the woman forgoes her income. Power relations within the household are relevant here too, as bargaining theory suggests (Persson and Jonung 1997). A policy of non-transferable leave, set at a generous level, may be the only way to avoid a replication of gender imbalance.

The political context that gave rise to the work–life balance concept in the UK can probably be traced to a wish to devise an approach that does two things: it allows individuals to perform caring activities that are not provided by the state and it allows these same individuals to be economically productive. There is a generalized fear that the quality of home and community life is deteriorating, but at the same time the economic drivers related to the demographic 'time bomb' of a declining workforce require that women are in the labour market (Guest 2002). From a labour market perspective, it is important to direct policies towards women with small children; otherwise there is a danger of loss of contact with the labour market and thus a decline in human capital (OECD 2001).

A further element is the continuing debate in the UK about the possible short-term and/or long-term harm of institutionalized childcare (DTI 2005b). In this respect, therefore, work–life balance policies that involve a reduction of working hours are the logical outcome. This could be seen as another example of a Blairite 'third way' since it seeks to provide a middle route that encompasses both labour market participation and parenting. 'Over-work' in 'unyielding' jobs has led to a crisis of care, not only in industrialized countries but also in countries that are seeking to be globally competitive (Rapoport and Bailyn 2002). Figures for the UK in 2000 show that one in six people aged 16 or over cared for a sick, disabled or elderly person and one in five households contained a carer (DTI 2005b). An estimated 5.3 million carers are of working age. Approximately 3.5 million of these are working either full- or part-time. Were this unpaid labour to be costed in terms of paid work, very large sums of taxpayer money would be involved. Time-flexible working is the form of working that could address a need both for paid labour and for unpaid caring work. Everyone wins, argues the Home Office: a balance between 'work and home' is advantageous for carers, those receiving care, employers, the economy and society as a whole (Home Office 1998). This 'win–win' list, however, does not mention employees. There is a growing amount of evidence, discussed in this chapter, that work–life balance policies can have a downside for many employees. Furthermore, carers are often referred to in gender-neutral terms; yet the reality is that in a context where the division of domestic labour is relatively unchanging, carers are particularly likely to be women. We discuss below the apparent stasis in 'who does what' in the home.

In this multifaceted context, work–life balance, as an ideology that is operationalized into a set of policies, is logical. Thus a flexible approach to work hours is the solution: the way that work is arranged has a major effect on employees' ability to work and care (Bailyn and Harrington 2004). If they do not have flexibility, then there will be negative effects for employers in terms of productivity, because there will be high turnover and high absenteeism.

Defining 'work–life balance'

'Work–life balance' (WLB) is a notoriously slippery concept, meaning different things to different people. One way is to define it as a menu of policies, all of which have the potential to change work hours in one way or another (Moss and Deven 1999). Another is to see it as an ideology that emphasizes quality of life in a context of individualism, personal choice and control (Jones 2004). Alternatively, in the context of the European Union's stated bid to bring about the 'reconciliation' of paid and unpaid domestic work, it can be seen as a process of debate, review, negotiation and conflict (Moss and Deven 1999). Moss and Deven's emphasis on conflict seems far removed from the 'menu of policies' approach that can be found on UK government websites that proselytize 'WLB'.

As well as focusing on formal policies that ease the paid/unpaid work relationship, the WLB rhetoric invariably uses, often unproblematically, the concept of flexible working. The term 'flexibility' is clearly presently used in different ways both in the academic literature and by policy-makers. In this chapter, we use the term 'flexible working' to describe the range of forms of working that may affect the way that individuals spend their time in both paid work and other spheres. Thus, our definition focuses on time flexibility, as opposed to other types, such as functional or numerical. We underline the fact that part-time working is the most common form of flexible working for women (DTI 2005a). Eighty-one per cent of employers that received funding from the UK Government's Work–Life Balance Challenge Fund to implement family-friendly measures report financial savings (DTI 2005a), although it is unclear where these savings come from. A perhaps cynical viewpoint is that a part-time worker is cheaper than a full-time one.

The issue for women's employment is whether this seemingly new concept heralds anything different from the employment patterns that became institutionalized after the Second World War – i.e. part-time working. As Chapter 4 showed, part-time working has been argued to have negative short-term and long-term effects for women. The challenge for the crusaders of work–life balance policies will be to show that these negative effects have been overcome. Relating this point to part-time working, the challenge is to show that quality short-hours working is possible.

As mentioned in Chapter 1, the concept of 'greedy organizations' that seek undivided loyalty from employees (Coser 1974) has been taken up by Epstein *et al.* (1998) to develop the concept of 'greedy jobs'. Perhaps the main 'greediness' is in relation to time, in terms of both unpredictability and expectations of long hours, taken to be a sign of commitment, as discussed in Chapter 4. From the perspective of the UK's trade union movement, the Trades Union Congress (TUC) talks of a time-squeeze that should be a bargaining point between unions and employers, alongside more traditional debates around pay and conditions (TUC 2005a).

In the run-up to the 2005 general election in the UK, *The Times* newspaper developed a concept of 'do-it-all woman', thus:

To clinch a third term, the Government reckons that it needs to win over a key voter, a hard-working, capable individual who is invariably exhausted and who craves much more than money or status – the precious commodity of time. Step forward do-it-all woman ...

(The Times, T2, 3 February 2005)

Setting aside the possibility that work–life balance policies have been supported by the second Blair administration for political gain, this quotation leads to the consideration of the 'time squeeze'.

How many roles?

If we consider the unpaid roles that women typically take on in addition to paid work, we can start to think about several 'greedy institutions' that have the potential to be in conflict with one another. The analysis of women's work has a long tradition of seeking to establish the number of roles that women carry out, the way that these roles interact and how policy can reconcile these roles so that they articulate smoothly. The concept of 'reconciliation' of the two spheres of work and home remains popular in the work–life balance rhetoric, with the implication that policy can resolve their articulation.

There is a 'daily juggling of obligations: to employers, children, husbands, parents, friends and so on' (Himmelweit 2002: 243). A 'third burden' arises from the 'functional incompatibility' of the two broad spheres of paid and unpaid work; women exhaust themselves through trying to do both (Sichtermann 1988). The coterminous nature of the roles of paid and unpaid work and their management causes stress and a further layer of role management, conceptualized by the French sociologist Haicault as the *charge mentale* (Haicault 1984, 1994). Haicault argues that the continual movement between possible conflicting demands of time and space places weighty psychological demands on women. This mental to-ing and fro-ing implies that unpaid domestic activities are not distinct from paid work, but rather they are embedded in one another. For example, it is possible to imagine that a paid work activity (standing at a production line, sitting at a computer, participating in a meeting) is accompanied by wondering/worrying about the smooth running of one or other of the unpaid activities (Glover 2002). The sphere of unpaid domestic work contains interacting sub-spheres, relating broadly to a series of roles (Glover 2002). A non-exhaustive list would include domestic worker, household manager, daughter, mother and wife/partner. Further, Beck (1992) has argued that the domains of experts have partly moved to the citizen; this would imply extra items on the list, such as medical and educational roles in relation to children.

The more general role of household manager is often overlooked in time use surveys (Haicault 1994). These surveys typically ask only who does what – not who sees what needs to be done, coordinates efforts, shares out tasks, initiates meetings to discuss who does what, does future planning and so on, all managerial activities that are highly valued in the labour market (Sullivan 2000). There is another level of complexity involved in the coordination of travel between various places of care and education (Skinner 2005). Skinner argues that 'coordination complexity' represents a considerable amount of time and effort, and therefore presents a major barrier to women being involved fully in the labour market. Many of the women in her study reported that the level of complexity around caring arrangements for their children had led them to alter their working patterns in order to reduce this level of stress, reflecting Haicault's '*charge mentale*'.

Hochschild (1989) suggests three spheres: 'job, children and housework'. Leisure is absent from this list and indeed there is little suggestion in the dual/triple roles literature that leisure is allocated any time. Sullivan argues that the complex coordination required in coordinating time schedules in households, as well as doing most of the domestic labour, results in a fragmentation of any leisure time that the woman does have (Sullivan 2000). This suggests the gender-blindness of the concept of a 'mosaic society' and the associated notion of the 'boundaryless career' (Guest 2002) in which the boundaries between work and leisure are becoming increasingly blurred. Related to these ideas, 'border theory' conceptualizes people as daily border-crossers, moving between the spheres of home and paid work (Clark 2000). Although Clark does not develop gender aspects, it seems likely that women and men experience border-crossing in different ways. Whether these multiple roles imply conflict and stress – or not – depends on a harmonious division of domestic labour (Kossek *et al.* 2001).

The division of domestic labour

Individuals' use of time is clearly linked to household decision-making. This approach to understanding economic behaviour and decision-making is a departure from the traditional neoclassical approach in economics of treating the labour market as composed of atomized individuals, whose location in the household and family is ignored (Rubery *et al.* 1998). The way that time is spent in the household – the division of domestic labour – has fundamental consequences for the time that is left for paid work outside the household. From a human rights perspective and using Sen's concept of 'capabilities' (being able to take on a range of identities and carry out certain actions) Robeyns (2003) argues that people have the right to time autonomy. Focusing on the division of domestic labour and the division of time and responsibilities for market work, non-market work and leisure, her argument is that the current gender division of labour is unjust and generally to women's disadvantage. Even in dual career households, where the expectation might be that the division of domestic labour is equalized, there is substantial evidence of women facing more time pressure than their partners.

In its WLB rhetoric, the UK government's punctilious reference to genderless parents as sources of paid and unpaid work may be disingenuous. This is because there is ample evidence of the gendering of the division of domestic labour. In very broad terms, it is clear from comparisons of women in full-time paid work and men (most of whom will presumably be in full-time paid work) that women still spend considerably more time in childcare activities and in other domestic activities (OECD 2001 citing the work of Fisher and Layte 2002; Anderson *et al.* 1994; Spain and Bianchi 1996). In the United States, Sweden and the UK (especially the UK) women and men spend markedly different amounts of time on such activities, even when both are in full-time paid work (Blumberg 1991; Lewis 1997). On average, full-time working mothers spend about twice as much time on unpaid work as fathers; housewives spend around two-and-a-half times as much. This tells us a lot about the time-poor situation that many women working full-time find themselves in. However, the number of hours spent in full-time working is very different for women and men (OECD 2001). For example in the UK, men are spending almost twice as much time on full-time paid work as women, similarly defined as being in full-time paid work. This illustrates the long work-hours culture in the UK, something that affects many men and which constitutes the yardstick of 'commitment' against which women are measured.

Gender cultures appear to be persistent. In a study of the occupational outcomes of UK graduates three-and-a-half years after graduation, Purcell (2002: 28) notes that 'young women still accept the cultural mandate that has allocated the primary parenting responsibility to females'. Twenty-seven per cent of a nationally representative sample of women graduates from UK universities aged under 30 at the time of Purcell's survey agreed strongly that they expected to take career breaks for family reasons, and a further 38 per cent agreed somewhat. The equivalent figures for men were 2 per cent and 10 per cent. Only 17 per cent of the women said that they would expect their partner to take career breaks for family reasons, whilst 41 per cent of the men expected that their partner would do so. Further, mothers are consistently more likely to be aware of their right to ask for flexible working than are fathers (DTI 2005a).

The long-lasting nature of these gendered cultural norms is emphasized by Pfau-Effinger (2004). However, some small differences between countries and social regimes are detectable. Crompton and Harris (1999) compared the effect of different types of gender role attitudes on the division of domestic labour in two countries of relevance to this book: Norway and Britain. The conclusion is that where there are less traditional gender role attitudes, there is also a less traditional division of domestic labour. In both of these countries there is a generational effect: the younger people are, the less likely they are to have a non-traditional division of household labour. This coincides with the conclusion of Anderson *et al.* (1994) that although change in the division of domestic labour in the UK is slow, there are signs of changes amongst younger men. Crompton and Harris (1999) found that where the man earns more than the woman in a partnership, a traditional division of household labour was more likely. This is because women who have actual or potentially lower earnings are thought to be in a weaker bargaining position in terms of who does what in the household and family (Persson and Jonung 1997). As Guest (2002) says, an understanding of work–life balance requires an exploration of the detail of family life. Although Crompton and Harris

(1999) do not extend their conclusion cross-nationally, there is the implication that in countries where the gender pay gap is narrow, then the division of domestic labour is more likely to be non-traditional. In terms of the division of domestic labour, men in Sweden contribute more, including time given to childcare, than men in the United States and in the United Kingdom (OECD 2001).

Flexibility and Policy

In the UK, the Flexible Work Regulations contained in the Employment Act 2002 allow parents of children under six years old to ask for flexibility of employment. This right will be extended to carers of sick and disabled adults by 2007, in its current (2006) form, the Work and Families Bill. It is an important point that this legislation does not give the right to have flexibility of employment, just the right to ask for it and to be given a reason should it be refused. The legislation allows parents to request to work from home for all or part of the time, to change their start and finish times and the days on which they work. Parents can ask for a variety of patterns, including compressed, term time, seasonal, staggered, as well as a reduction of hours. They have to show how their request will fit in with the employer's business. Thus there is a clear favouring of measures to keep parents in the labour force, backed up by measures to improve maternity and paternity pay and leave. The UK government has claimed that in the first year since the new right was introduced, almost a quarter of parents of children under six asked to change to a more flexible working pattern and that over three-quarters of these requests were fully accepted and another 9 per cent were partly accepted or a compromise was reached (DTI 2005b). However, these figures are contested. The TUC claims that more than half a million people who have asked for a shorter working week have had their requests turned down and that over three-quarters of UK employees have no element of flexibility in their employment contracts (TUC 2005b). Based on an analysis of *Labour Force Survey* data the TUC also shows a decrease in the percentage of employees working on a 'flexitime' arrangement (from 14.9 per cent in 1995 to 11.5 per cent in 2005) and a small reduction in the level of job sharing and compressed week arrangements.

Caring policy

If the achievement of full employment is seen as key to the UK's economic growth, with women as a relatively untapped pool, then a logical conclusion is the state funding of childcare and eldercare. However, the reality for the UK is that the historical neglect of this issue would imply major resourcing. It would also imply the embracing of a very different ideological approach to the role of the state in what has hitherto been seen as the private sphere of the family in order to approach the levels of many European countries.

Starting from a very low base, some development in relation to childcare has occurred in this respect at the end of the twentieth and beginning of the twenty-first centuries, during the Blair administration. Under the National Childcare Strategy (DfEE 1998) state provision is targeted towards the economically disadvantaged, with the requirements of other parents being left to the private sector. Childcare provision in the US is almost entirely market-led (Brayfield 1995; Gornick and Meyers 2004). For many parents in the UK and in the US, affordable childcare of a good quality is not a reality (Daycare Trust 2006).[1]

A consideration of self-regulation and state regulation raises the issue of whose responsibility it is to put in place policies that would bring about work–life balance. Guest (2002) asks whether this falls to the individual, the family, the employer, the community or the state. In a strongly liberal regime, such as that of the US, it seems reasonable to conclude that this is an issue for the individual, who has responsibility for her or his career self-management. This is borne out by the absence of national policies of paid maternity leave, something that Gornick and Meyers (2004) identify as exceptional in industrialized countries. The UK has taken a middle road here, with the state taking responsibility for some measures. State provision of childcare is growing slowly, but is typically targeted at the poorest families. The principal childcare programme of the Blair government, Sure Start, does not have as its aim the encouragement of all women's employment. It is based on a 'welfare to work' approach that seeks to change the employment behaviour of poorly qualified women who would otherwise be out of the labour market. Thus child poverty can be alleviated, through the efforts of both the state and of individual parents. It also has an educational aspect, in that parenting skills are taught. State-financed childcare does not exist for the children of economically advantaged parents. As we noted earlier, the cost of marketized childcare can be very steep. Other policies that would lead to work–life balance, such as the ability to work shorter hours or flexible hours, are in existence, but the final word rests with the employer. Some extension of rights relating to maternity, paternity and parental leave has come about, but the basis for these may be just as much about children's wellbeing as about women's employment.

A cross-national comparison of early childhood education and care shows major differences between industrialized countries (Gornick and Meyers 2004). The highest providers are Sweden and Denmark where one-half to three-quarters of children aged one and two were in public care and about 80 to 90 per cent of children aged three and older. By contrast, in the UK and the US, publicly supported childcare for one- and two-year-olds is very restricted, being largely available for low-income parents. Only just over half of three- to five-year-olds are in publicly subsidized care in the US and most of these are part-day programmes.

The business case for WLB

There is a distinction to be made here between the traditional business case for work–life balance policies and the so-called new case. The traditional case focused on part-time working (Edwards and Robinson 2004). Labour costs were lower; working hours could be matched to employer needs; part-time workers were deemed suited to particular time-limited tasks, such as catering and cleaning; they were suitable to cover a long-hours economy, thus avoiding expensive overtime incurred from full-time employees. The 'new business case' seeks to move beyond a focus on part-time working towards a range of employment forms that represent a 'mutuality of benefit' (Edwards and Robinson 2004: 168; Houston and Waumsley 2003; Dex and Scheibl 2002). For the employee, the opportunity is to reconcile work with 'non-work' responsibilities, and/or quality of life preferences. For the employer, the benefit is lower recruitment and turnover costs (Gottlieb *et al.* 1998). This mutual benefit argument is echoed by the UK government:

> flexible working is: good for children, enabling families to spend time with their children, as well as work and contribute to the family income; good for parents, helping them to find working hours to match their caring responsibilities; and, good for businesses, enabling them to draw on a wider pool of skills and talents in the workforce, improve recruitment and retention rates and increase staff morale and productivity.
>
> (DTI 2005b: 8)

In the context of the 'war for talent', three broad elements to the traditional business case argument can be identified: employee morale, employee retention and the avoidance of litigation (McGlynn 2003). The Confederation of British Industry (CBI) states that implementation and effective enforcement of equal opportunities policies by a firm will improve employee morale and thus have a positive effect on the productivity of the firm (CBI 1996). The 'new business case' also focuses on employee retention (Yeandle *et al.* 2003 Dex and Scheibl 2002). An initial outlay will bring about better retention rates and thus increased efficiency. To get a good return on investment in for example training, employers should make best use of the enhanced human capital. Furthermore, it is more expensive to incur extra recruitment expenses than to provide policies and programmes that will help retention.

Guest (2002) argues that the new business case, based on a shortage of knowledge and professional workers, is forcing companies to take initiatives to retain workers. Measures to increase flexibility and thus improve work–life balance are a key part of their strategies. Hochschild (1997) argues that employers use work–life balance policies to enhance commitment to the organization. However, this implies that WLB policies are only directed towards employees whose skills are in short supply or who have firm-specific knowledge and skills that are highly valued; we discuss below the possibility that such policies are more available for some employees than others.

Third, the availability of work–life balance policies can avoid expensive sex-discrimination claims, since these can often centre on flexibility issues. McGlynn (2003) concedes that although compensation awards are typically very low, adverse publicity from high-profile cases can follow, as well as management time being used in managing and defending such actions. Requests for flexible working turned down by employers or an absence of flexible arrangements that would allow activities relating to children to be carried out (e.g. dropping children at school) could be construed as indirect sex discrimination, since more women have need for such arrangements than men (Croner Consulting 2004b).

McGlynn (2003) argues that the ideological basis for these rationales is based solely or mainly on the 'bottom line' argument. It is only weakly related to the moral arguments of fairness, and thus there is the risk that such policies would not persist in adverse economic conditions (McGlynn 2003). Unemployment at the beginning of the twenty-first century is low and there is a demand for labour. This raises the question of whether there would be the same enthusiasm for such policies if unemployment was high. What would happen if there was less demand? Would the arguments for work–life balance appear less attractive to employers? McGlynn puts the case that the business case on its own cannot be effective unless it is underpinned by moral arguments about equality; similarly the moral arguments are unlikely to be effective unless there is support from employers.

Negative effects of take-up of WLB policies

There is a growing body of evidence that the take-up of WLB policies can have a negative effect on various aspects of employees' working lives, with a particular emphasis on the trade-off between possible short-term gain and long-term consequences (Blair-Loy and Wharton 2002; Glass 2004). Short-term gain can be that the quality of life is better. The '*charge mentale*' associated with coordinating several roles (Haicault 1984, 1994, see above) could be less onerous. However, against this, there is evidence, as discussed above, that spending fewer hours in paid work increases the number of hours spent in unpaid work (Moss and Deven 1999). Reduced hours and working-from-home policies may help retention over the child rearing years, but there is a growing body of evidence about negative long-term effects on wages, and the reinforcing of stereotypes held by employers about women's lack of commitment.

Reflecting this, there is evidence from the US that many women are wary of taking up WLB policies because they assume negative effects on pay and promotion (Hochschild 1997; Fried 1998). Glass (2004) studied women who had taken advantage of these policies over a seven-year period from childbirth onwards. The results show a benign or neutral effect for women in clerical, service or manual jobs for policies relating to childcare assistance and schedule flexibility, and a negative effective for those in professional and managerial positions, especially for those policies that reduced visibility in the workplace (working from home or working fewer than 30 hours per week). Glass concludes that these policies may be reinforcing traditional caring responsibilities and giving the impression to employers of less commitment.

The WLB rhetoric may thus ignore the gendered nature of the workplace. Gendered assumptions within organizations may perpetuate the assignment of higher-ranking jobs to those who appear to be fully committed to the work (Acker 1990). Swanberg (2004) argues on the basis of case studies of firms that gender role assumptions prevent organizational attempts to bring about family-friendly policies. Employers may make the assumption that committed people are those whose lives are arranged around their jobs – and these are most likely to be men. Less desirable jobs go to those whose jobs appear to be arranged around their lives. Thus occupational sex segregation is reproduced.

Looking specifically at parental leave policies, Moss and Deven (1999) conclude that long periods of leave in some countries may prove a 'poisoned chalice' that increases gender inequalities in the workplace, home and society. They argue that if they are not to reinforce traditional gender roles in the home and the workplace, parental leave policies must be used equally by men and women. However, this seems unlikely to happen, since the financial penalty for the household of the man taking parental leave may be greater, in view of his likelihood of earning more. Employees also feared that they would be overlooked in the succession planning process and felt that a move from full-time to flexible working was a one-way move which could not be reversed (CIPD 2003; Houston and Waumsley 2003).

There may therefore be unintended consequences of women taking advantage of family-friendly measures. In terms of some aspects of quality of life, such as lack of stress, it could be argued that these measures are to their advantage (Houston and Waumsley 2003). The take-up of these policies is gendered and because the normative view of employment is continuous full-time employment, these policies could end up being disadvantageous to women in the long run; for example, they could contribute markedly to women's poverty in old age. Whilst the existence of such policies can contribute to retention and arguably help recruitment, they may be particularly negative in terms of career progression.

Shortening working time for all workers may be the most promising way of bringing about a more egalitarian division of domestic labour (Mutari and Figart 2001). Fagnani and Letablier's (2004) study of the impact of a reduction in working hours in France reveals that some couples were enthusiastic about the effect on their work–life balance, but the traditional gendered domestic division of labour did not change significantly. Gender cultures are no doubt very slow to change. It seems important to acknowledge that there is a major difference between a context where all are subject to a statutory reduction in working hours and one where such a thing is left to individual decision-making, as in the liberal social regimes of the UK and the US.

Take-up of WLB policies

The issue here is whether all types of employees take up what can be seen as new opportunities for flexible working and whether all types of jobs are equally amenable to these. Is WLB only for well-qualified people or is it only for those in jobs with lower levels of responsibility and status? There is conflicting evidence here. Taylor (2002) argues that highly qualified women in professional and managerial occupations are best able to achieve work–life balance. But Crompton *et al.* (2003) found that low-paid workers in the retail sector were the best able to achieve this. From the perspective of the US, Lambert and Haley-Lock (2004) argue that there is inequality in the distribution of these opportunities and that there are therefore implications for social justice in the workplace. They conclude that US employers direct work–life balance policies to better qualified employees and the result is: 'jobs at the top and jobs at the bottom may thus look very different in terms of the challenges facing working parents' (Lambert and Haley-Lock 2004: 190).

In the UK, it appears that employers are more likely to accede to requests for flexible working if employees work fewer than 40 hours per week (DTI 2005a). The request is also more likely to be accepted if it comes from a woman, although men are less likely to make a request – only 12 per cent of eligible fathers have applied for flexible working under the Employment Act 2002 (EOC 2005). Requests for flexible working were highest amongst those working in sales, customer services and administrative jobs; they were lowest amongst managers (DTI 2005a).

This might indicate that in some occupations, perhaps those that demand high levels of qualification, there may be particular dangers of taking up WLB policies. In a study of accountants in the UK, Smithson *et al.* (2004) conclude that women who worked flexibly in order to combine working with caring commitments risked damaging their career prospects. Smithson *et al.* showed that men's use of flexible working was quite different: they typically deferred working flexibly to a later stage when their career progressed further. There was therefore a clear impact on current and future salary for women taking up flexible working arrangements, which was not equivalent for the men who did so. Smithson *et al.* argue that in this context, the promotion of flexible working arrangements is reinforcing the gender pay gap, as Walby and Olsen (2002) also conclude. Epstein *et al.*'s (1998) study of women in professional occupations casts similar doubt on flexible working. Part-time work, they argue, carries with it considerable stigma within organizations and there are major consequences for the careers of individuals who take it. They argue that professionals define themselves, in part, by their commitment to overtime.

Policy effectiveness

In order to measure effectiveness, an agreed definition needs of course to be arrived at. If the definition is subjective, as Guest (2002) suggests, there may be some difficulty in measurement: what may seem like balance to one individual may not do so to his or her partner or boss. One individual's balance could be regarded by another person as imbalance. This leads to the possibility that the success or otherwise of so-called work–life balance policies cannot be measured easily; organizations can advertise themselves as good employers from the point of view of WLB, but this cannot be verified by comparison with some kind of yardstick. This difficulty is compounded by the fact that few organizations keep data on requests for flexible working (Yeandle *et al.* 2003).

The issue of measurement raises also the issue of effectiveness. There is some evidence that the presence of family-friendly practices was not associated with a reported work–life balance (CIPD 2003). Despite the establishment of gender equality and work–family reconciliation policies in Sweden, Cousins and Tang (2004) report that a higher proportion of both mothers and fathers than in the UK report a conflict between their work and family lives. This implies that policies were either ineffectively implemented or that they may have lessened but did not eliminate the problem. This leads to the possibility that firms use these policies as a recruitment tool, branding themselves as good employers from this point of view, for example through the league tables discussed below. The presence of such policies can easily be established, but their effectiveness much less so, particularly if a definition of effectiveness is individually determined and subjectively arrived at.

Plantenga (2004) concludes that it is not yet clear whether the combined result of increasing women's employment levels and increasing flexibility favour gender equality. The reality is that this could only be shown through longitudinal data that tracked over time the effects of people taking up flexible working. This would need to be for the medium term – for example access to promoted posts – and for the longer term – for example income in old age.

Conclusions

In social regimes that continue to espouse a male breadwinner ideology, women's employment is considered a strain on the family; men's employment assumes little or no domestic responsibilities. Thus, work–life balance policies will be seen as the domain of women, possibly reinforcing gendered attitudes at work and in the home. The gendered attitudes of both employees and employers may be at the root of this prognosis of little change (Houston and Waumsley 2003). Lewis (1997: 13) casts doubt on the embeddedness of WLB policies; her view is that employers are often 'playing about at the margins'. It is revealing that in the UK employers were more likely to agree to requests for flexible working if such requests came from women (DTI 2005a). This implies an acceptance from employers that the policies are aimed at women, although Smithson and Stokoe (2005) argue that employers routinely deny that gender makes a difference within their organizations. Only 12 per cent of eligible fathers have applied for flexible working under the Employment Act 2002 (EOC 2005).

There is a growing body of literature that seeks to put emphasis on the possible short-term and long-term disadvantages of women taking up such policies. Although these adaptations may help women accommodate multiple roles in the short run – and thus improve their quality of life at least in terms of time management – they have the potential to reduce employment opportunities and income in both the short and the long term. Plantenga (2004: 121) implicitly refers to the distinction between short-term opportunities and long-term effects by concluding that 'flexibilization can offer opportunities, but also take them away'. At the same time there is increasing public policy concern about the negative effects on children of the lack of balance between work and family life experienced by large numbers of parents.

One of the questions taxing policy-makers is how to convince management and organizations that they stand to gain from establishing work–life balance policies. Publicly available and widely publicized league tables are a key tool in bringing about change which is not legislated for. Swanberg (2004) discusses the use in the US of the 'Family Friendly Index' citing studies that have benchmarked top companies against this. In a liberal regime where cultural change is seen as lying outside the realm of government, such league tables have a key role. State regulation is replaced by self-regulation. It is nevertheless unclear whether there is a connection between a company's success and its ranking against league tables of this sort. Evidence that shareholders take notice of such issues is unclear.

In the public sector, there is the theoretical possibility of contract compliance, where contracts are only given to companies that can demonstrate their efforts and success in terms of equality and diversity. But in the private sector, this is less obvious, unless the link can be made between the existence of such policies and greater productivity, recruitment and retention. Swanberg (2004) cites studies that have compared employees in less and more family-supportive workplaces. Employees with more supportive workplaces were shown to have higher levels of job satisfaction, more commitment to their organization's success, greater loyalty to their employers and a stronger likelihood to stay with the company. Thus, productivity could be argued to be enhanced in supportive workplaces. However, studies are typically small-scale and need to be carried out longitudinally in order to evaluate outcomes.

It may be that the 'corporate social responsibility' (CSR) perspective – emphasizing the broader social goals of organizations – is the means of bringing the moral arguments to the fore in the private sector so that there is less concern with measuring the precise and short-term impact of WLB policies on performance and productivity. Within CSR is the idea that organizations have responsibilities towards a range of stakeholders, not simply shareholders, including employees, families and the wider community. WLB policies could be one internal lever to promote reconciliation between the rights of various stakeholders.

Another issue facing organizations is that whilst policies may be put in place by senior managers with a genuine commitment to change, a key person in implementing policy is the line-manager. There is evidence that there may be a weak link here. Research on line-managers in a range of public and private sector organizations has revealed that the majority had only a limited understanding of their organization's policy framework and a minority were ignorant of the framework (Yeandle et al. 2003). Yeandle et al.'s research found that managers wanted to be able to treat employees fairly, and to be perceived as acting unfairly by giving some employees concessions was a 'real worry' for the managers. Many decisions about flexible working requests were made by reference to the past performance of employees, something that in itself is affected by the employee's domestic situation. Yeandle *et al.*'s argument is that by making decisions on these grounds, those who had been able to be adaptable workers in the past continued to be favoured. However, this perspective was rarely conceded by the managers. Line-managers appeared to value employees who were able to respond to unpredictable increases in work demands – thus implicitly valuing a model that people without caring commitments were more able to fulfil.

Note

1   In 2005, the average cost of a day nursery place for a child under two in inner London averaged over £8700 per year, over 30 per cent higher than the England average (Greater London Authority 2005). In outer London costs are 20 per cent higher. These are average costs across all providers, including subsidized places, so the actual cost for a parent attempting to find a private day nursery place could well exceed £200 per week. Daycare Trust surveys, carried out annually, show that costs have risen by more than inflation to around £7000 per year per child, with costs in some parts of the country, particularly London, being considerably higher (*The Guardian*, 26 January 2005).

References

Acker, J. (1990) 'Hierarchies, jobs, bodies: a theory of gendered organizations', *Gender and Society*, 4 (2): 139–58.

Anderson, M., Bechhofer, F. and Gershuny, J. (1994). *The Social and Political Economy of the Household*, Oxford: Oxford University Press.

Bailyn, L. and Harrington, M. (2004) 'Redesigning Work for Work–Family Integration', *Community, Work and Family*, 7: 197–208.

Beck, U. (1992) *Risk Society*, London and California: Sage.

Blair-Loy, M. and Wharton, A. (2002) 'Employees' use of work–family policies and work-place social context', *Social Forces*, 80 (3): 813–45.

Blumberg, R. L. (ed.) (1991) *Gender, Family and Economy: the Triple Overlap*, California: Sage.

Brayfield, A. (1995) 'A bargain at any price? Childcare costs and women's employment', *Social Science Research*, 24: 188–214.

CBI (1996) *A Winning Strategy – The Business Case for Equal Opportunities*, London: Confederation of British Industry.

CIPD (2003) *Managing Employee Careers*, London: Chartered Institute of Personnel and Development.

Clark, S. C. (2000) 'Work/family border theory: 'a new theory of work/life balance', *Human Relations*, 53 (6): 747–70.

Coser, L. (1974) *Greedy Institutions: Patterns of Undivided Commitment*, New York: Free Press.

Cousins, C. and Tang, N. (2004) 'Working time and work and family conflict in the Netherlands, Sweden and the UK', *Work, Employment and Society*, 18 (3): 531–50.

Crompton, R. and Harris, F. (1999) 'Attitudes, women's employment and the changing domestic division of labour: a cross-national analysis' in R. Crompton (ed.)

Restructuring Gender Relations and Employment, Oxford: Oxford University Press, 105–27.

Crompton, R., Dennett, J. and Wigfield, A. (2003) *Organisations, Careers and Caring*, Bristol: Policy Press and Joseph Rowntree Foundation.

Croner Consulting (2004a) *Flexible Working*, brief issue 129, Kingston upon Thames: Croner Consulting.

Croner Consulting (2004b) *Flexible Working*, brief issue 121, Kingston upon Thames: Croner Consulting.

Daycare Trust (2006) *2006 Childcare Costs Survey*, London: Daycare Trust, <www.daycaretrust.org.uk>.

Dex, S. and Scheibl, F. (2002) *SMEs and Flexible Working Arrangements*, Bristol: Policy Press and Joseph Rowntree Foundation.

DfEE (1998) *Meeting the Childcare Challenge*, London: Department for Education and Employment.

DTI (2005a) *Results of the Second Flexible Working Employee Survey*, London: Department for Trade and Industry.

DTI (2005b) *Choice and Flexibility: A Consultation Document*, London: Department for Trade and Industry.

Edwards, C. and Robinson, O. (2004) 'Evaluating the business case for part-time working amongst qualified nurses', *British Journal of Industrial Relations*, 42 (1): 167–83.

EOC (2005) *Part-time is No Crime: So Why the Penalty?* Manchester: Equal Opportunities Commission.

Epstein, C. F., Seron, C., Oglensky, B. and Saute, R. (1998) *The Part-time Paradox: Time Norms, Professional Lives, Family, and Gender*, London: Routledge.

Fagnani, J. and Letablier, M.-T. (2004) 'Work and family life balance: the impact of the 35-hour laws in France', *Work, Employment and Society*, 18 (3): 551–72.

Fisher, K. and Layte, R. (2002) *Measuring Work–Life Balance and Degrees of Sociability: A Focus on the Value of Time Use Data in the Assessment of Quality of Life*, Colchester: University of Essex.

Fried, M. (1998) *Taking Time: Parental Leave Policy and Corporate Culture*, Philadelphia: Temple University Press.

Glass, J. (2004) 'Blessing or curse? Work–family policies and mothers' wage growth over time', *Work and Occupations*, 31 (3): 367–94.

Glover, J. (2002) 'The "balance model": theorising women's employment behaviour', in A. Carling, S. Duncan and R. Edwards (eds) *Analysing Families*, London: Routledge.

Gornick, J. and Meyers, M. (2004) 'Welfare regimes in relation to paid work and care', in J. Giele and E. Holst (eds) *Changing Life Patterns in Western Industrial Societies*, Oxford: Elsevier.

Gottlieb, B., Kellaway, E. and Barham, E. (1998) *Flexible Work Arrangements*, Chichester: John Wiley.

Guest, D. (2002) 'Perspectives on the study of work–life balance', *Social Science Information*, 41 (2): 255–79.

Haicault, M. (1984) 'La gestion ordinaire de la vie en deux', *Sociologie du Travail*, 3: 268–77.

Haicault, M. (1994) 'Pertes de savoirs familiaux, nouvelle professionnalité du travail domestique: quels sont les liens avec le système productif?' *Recherches Féministes*, 7 (1): 125–38.

Himmelweit, S. (2002) 'Making visible the hidden economy: the case for gender-impact analysis of economic policy', *Feminist Economics*, 8 (1): 49–70.

Hochschild, A. (1989) *The Second Shift*, Harmondsworth: Viking Penguin.

Hochschild, A. (1997) *The Time Bind: When Work Becomes Home and Home Becomes Work*, New York: Henry Holt.

Home Office (1998) *Supporting Families*, London: Stationery Office.

Houston, D. and Waumsley, J. (2003) *Attitudes to Flexible Working and Family Life*, Bristol: Policy Press.

Jones, A. (2004) *Work Life Diversity: Rising to New Challenges*, paper presented at the Department for Trade and Industry Employment Relations Seminar Series, London.

Kingsmill, D. (2001) *Kingsmill Review of Women's Pay and Employment*, London: Stationery Office.

Kossek, E., Colquitt, J. and Noe, R. (2001) 'Caregiving decisions, well-being, and performance: the effects of place and provider as a function of dependent type and work–family climates', *Academy of Management Journal*, 44 (1): 29–44.

Lambert, S. and Haley-Lock, A. (2004) 'Stratification of opportunities for work–life balance', *Community, Work and Family*, 7 (2): 179–95.

Lewis, S. (1997) '"Family friendly" employment policies: a route to changing organizational culture or playing about at the margins?' *Gender, Work and Organization*, 4 (1): 13–23.

McGlynn, C. (2003) 'Strategies for reforming the English solicitors' profession: an analysis of the business case for sex equality', in U. Schultz and G. Shaw (eds) *Women in the World's Legal Professions*, Portland, OR: Hart Publishing, 159–74.

Moss, P. and Deven, F. (1999) *Parental Leave: Progress or Pitfall?* Netherlands Interdisciplinary Demographic Institution/CBGS.

Mutari, E. and Figart, D. (2001) 'Europe at the crossroads: harmonization, liberalization and the gender of work time', *Social Politics*, 8 (1): 36–64.

OECD (2001) *Employment Outlook*, Paris: OECD.

Parcel, T. and Cornfield, D. (2000) *Work and Family: Research Informing Policy*, Thousand Oaks, CA: Sage.

Persson, I. and Jonung, C. (1997) *Economics of the Family and Family Policies*, London: Routledge.

Pfau-Effinger, B. (2004) *Development of Culture, Welfare States and Women's Employment in Europe*, Aldershot: Ashgate.

Plantenga, J. (2004) 'Changing work and life patterns: examples of new working-time arrangements in the European member states', in J. Giele and E. Holst (eds) *Changing Life Patterns in Western Industrial Societies*, Oxford: Elsevier, 119–35.

Purcell, K. (2002) *Qualifications and Careers: Equal Opportunities and Earnings Among Graduates* (Working Paper Series No 1), Manchester: Equal Opportunities Commission.

Rapoport, R. and Bailyn, L. (2002) *Beyond Work–family Balance: Advancing Gender Equity and Work Place Performance*, San Francisco, CA: Jossey Bass, Wiley.

Robeyns, I. (2003) 'Sen's capability approach and gender inequality: selecting relevant capabilities', *Feminist Economics*, 9 (2/3): 61–92.

Rubery, J., Smith, M. and Fagan, C. (1998) 'National working-time regimes and equal opportunities', *Feminist Economics*, 4 (1): 71–101.

Sichtermann, B. (1988) 'The conflict between housework and employment', in J. Jenson, E. Hagen and C. Reddy (eds) *Feminization of the Labour Force*, Oxford: Polity, 276–87.

Skinner, C. (2005) 'Coordination points: a hidden factor in reconciling work and family life', *Journal of Social Policy*, 34 (1): 99–119.

Smithson, J. and Stokoe, E. (2005) 'Discourses of work–life balance: negotiating "gender-blind" terms in organizations', *Gender, Work and Organization*, 12 (2): 147–68.

Smithson, J., Lewis, S., Cooper, C. and Dyer, J. (2004) 'Flexible working and the gender pay gap in the accountancy profession', *Work, Employment and Society*, 18 (1): 115–36.

Sullivan, O. (2000) 'The division of domestic labour: twenty years of change', *Sociology*, 34 (3): 437–56.

Spain, D. and Bianchi, S. (1996) *Balancing Act: Motherhood, Marriage and Employment among American Women*, New York: Russell Sage Foundation.

Swanberg, J. (2004) 'Illuminating gendered organization assumptions', *Community, Work and Family*, 7 (1): 3–28.

Taylor, R. (2002) *Future of Work Life Balance*, Swindon: ESRC Future of Work Programme.

TUC (2005a) 'The UK's long hours problem', http://www.tuc.org.uk/work_life/tuc-11005-f0.cfm, accessed May 2006.

TUC (2005b) *Challenging Times*, London: Trades Union Congress.

Walby, S. and Olsen, W. (2002) *The Impact of Women's Position in the Labour Market on Pay and Implications for UK Productivity: Report to Women and Equality Unit*, London: Department of Trade and Industry.

Yeandle, S., Phillips, J., Scheibl, F., Wigfield, A. and Wise, S. (2003) *Line-managers and Family-Friendly Employment*, Bristol: Policy Press, Joseph Rowntree Foundation.

Chapter 8

Women and trade unions

Introduction

It is important that any attempt to understand women, employment and organizations considers the role of trade unions in advancing or holding back the gender equality project. It is argued that trade unions have 'helped shape the contours of inequality' (Dickens 1997: 287), but that they can also be part of the solution to the problem. Dickens (1997: 287) argues for a multi-pronged, articulated approach to equality policy-making involving the three key industrial relations actors – the state, employers and trade unions. Within the context of a discussion of women and organizations, trade unions also make an interesting case study of the possibilities for gender transformation of structures and cultures.

However, trade unionism is not traditionally associated with women. Historically, unions have generally concentrated on organizing and representing the interests of male workers in heavy industry. Consequently women workers in Britain and North America have had far lower rates of union membership and the unions have neglected women's interests. Today the picture has altered somewhat, in response to a gradually changing economic, social and political context. Overall union membership has been falling across the industrialized world in recent decades, largely as a consequence of economic restructuring; in particular the decline in the traditionally highly unionized, male dominated manufacturing sector, a growth in the less unionized, female dominated service sector and increasing levels of 'atypical' employment (Howell 1996). British trade union density has fallen massively and is now around 29 per cent (Grainger 2006), while density in Canada is also about 30 per cent (Statistics Canada 2004) and in the US about 12 per cent (Bureau of Labor Statistics 2005). The gender composition of membership has also shifted significantly so that women and men are now more evenly represented. Today, the 'typical' British trade unionist is just as likely to be female as male, more likely to be a non-manual than manual worker, more likely to work in services than production and in the public sector, but the one constant characteristic, more likely to work full-time (Brook 2002). These relatively new member characteristics are also now dominant in North American unions (Chao and Utgoff 2005).

Not only has the composition of trade union membership altered, but the long period of decline has also prompted fundamental reassessment of the traditional modus operandi of the trade unions. Of particular note, in some countries, including North America and the UK, the unions have increased the level and scope of their organizing efforts, now seeking to reach previously unorganized workers and groups of workers with historically and/or currently lower rates of unionization, such as 'atypical' workers, women, black and minority ethnic, and young workers. There have been both 'top-down' union leadership initiatives to recruit under-represented groups and 'bottom-up' membership pressure on unions to become more inclusive and representative of diverse constituencies, especially women. There is now widespread recognition in the British, European and North American trade union movements that membership growth and even union survival involves recruiting and retaining a greater diversity of members and also revitalizing policies and agendas to represent membership diversity effectively (Colgan and Ledwith 2002a; Hunt and Rayside 2000).

Women and trade union membership

As stated in the introduction, North American and British women are now almost as likely as are men to be union members. In the US 11 per cent of women compared with 14 per cent of men are union members (Bureau of Labor Statistics 2005) and in Canada the proportions are 30 per cent of women compared with 31 per cent of men (Statistics Canada 2004). Union density among women is variable though, with individual characteristics such as class, age and ethnicity, and employment factors such as sector, industry, occupation and employment status (full- or part-time) all influencing propensity to unionize. Table 8.1 shows union density in the UK by various individual characteristics that cross-cut gender.

People who work in unionized workplaces are far more likely to join a union than those who do not, meaning that the gendered membership patterns are, at least in part, due to variable rates of unionization and union presence across industries and sectors. In Britain, women with higher-level qualifications working in the public sector are the most likely to be union members, part-time workers are among those least likely to be members, and black British women are more likely than white women to be members (Brook 2002).

Women's attitudes to trade unionism

Despite historically lower levels of union membership, women are found to be supportive of trade unionism. For example, a poll conducted in the US in 1997 found that women are more favourably inclined towards trade unions than men. Forty-nine per cent of unionized women said they would vote for union representation compared to 40 per cent of men (Cobble and Bielski Michal 2002).

Table 8.1 Union density in the UK by individual characteristics

	All (%)	Women (%)	Men (%)
Age group			
20–29 years	19	20	18
30–39 years	30	30	30
40–49 years	38	36	39
50 years and over	35	32	37
Ethnic group			
White	29	28	30
Non-white	26	28	24
Highest qualification			
Degree or equiv.	37	44	31
Other higher ed.	44	52	33
A-level or equiv.	28	21	31
GCSE or equiv.	28	21	31
Other	25	21	29
No qualifications	24	20	29
All employees	29	28	30

Source: adapted from Brook (2002) (based on *Labour Force Survey* data).

However, general support for trade unionism does not necessarily translate into actually joining. It is instructive to look at why people join unions. Waddington and Whitston's (1997) survey of new union members in the UK has been influential in establishing the main reasons. They identify two broad categories: (i) collective reasons (including mutual support, improved pay and conditions, peer pressure and belief in unionism); and (ii) individual benefits (including training and education, professional and financial services). The greatest gender difference that Waddington and Whitston find is that women emphasize support issues more than men, and that men are more likely than women to mention a belief in trade unions. However, it should be noted that Waddington and Whitston's survey established belief from the statement, 'I believe in trade unions and want to take part', whereas it has been argued that a distinction is needed between women believing in unions and actually wanting to participate, for reasons that will be discussed later. A number of authors have found that the male–female membership differential is partly attributable to women's lower favourability to trade unions based on their dissatisfaction with their actual experiences of unions, especially the unions' approaches to part-time workers (Sinclair 1995; Walters 2002).

In addition, although women tend to be lower paid than male new members, in Waddington and Whitston's survey (1997), they were less likely to cite improved pay and conditions as a reason for union joining. If we marry this with the data in

Table 8.1, showing high levels of union membership among highly qualified women, it is possible to conjecture that this group of women still feels vulnerable (and in need of support) despite being relatively privileged on account of their highly qualified status.

Different jobs, different rates of union membership

As discussed, the data reveal differential union membership rates among women, dependent on occupation and employment status. It is interesting to compare the group with the highest level of membership – professional and highly qualified women (discussed more broadly in Chapter 5) – with the group with the lowest level – part-time women workers (discussed more broadly in Chapter 4).

Given their relatively privileged position, the typical profile of a female trade union member as a highly qualified or professional worker might strike one as odd and perhaps contrast with an expectation that the most deprived workers (e.g. part-time women) would be the most likely to sign up to trade unionism in the hope of improving their employment conditions. It is interesting that the literature on women in the professions and management (such as that drawn upon in Chapter 5) rarely mentions trade unions and the conventional wisdom is that the processes involved in becoming a professional or manager might militate against or even be in conflict with a collective orientation (Healy and Kirton 2002).

In the Canadian context, Armstrong (1993) discusses tensions between union and professional values and commitment. The underlying premise of trade union-ism is that there is a division of interests between employers/managers and workers and a relatively antagonistic relationship between the two. This is often referred to as 'them' and 'us'. Professions demand vocational commitment that is structured into work organization and the employment relationship (e.g. the requirement to work unpaid overtime) and this might be at odds with traditional trade union demands. Reflecting this tension, nurses initially (in the early part of the twentieth century) chose to form professional associations to represent their professional and employment interests, rather than join unions because they did not identify with the male-dominated, working-class union movement. They saw union tactics such as aggressive bargaining and strikes as unprofessional. A legal ruling in the early 1970s separating the bargaining process from the other activi-ties of the professional associations led to the rapid growth of female-dominated unions for nurses operating alongside the professional associations. Based on a model of male, industrial unionization, Armstrong argues that the unions achieved gains for nurses, but failed to recognize the degree of women's profes-sional commitment to their work. The separation of professional and union issues proved to be a false divide in this case.

Healy and Kirton (2002) argue that while there might well be tensions between professional and union values and commitment, the unions (especially in the pub-lic sector) can and do play a role in upholding professional standards, as well as in improving pay and conditions. For example, the female-dominated teachers' union in Britain, the National Union of Teachers, has used the media to voice its members' concerns about standards in schools and about various educational reforms. Similarly, the female-dominated health sector unions in Britain have campaigned against National Health Service reforms that many employees see as detrimental to service provision and overall professional standards. In this way the union acts as a conduit for articulating collective grievances about threats to professionalism and puts those grievances into the public domain and onto the political agenda. Therefore, in practice there is no necessary conflict between professional and union commitment and the fact that British unions have been willing to pursue professional issues might explain, at least in part, high levels of membership among highly qualified and professional employees.

In contrast, as stated earlier, the category of women least likely to be trade union members is that of part-time workers; yet arguably they have the most to gain from collective organization, since they are more likely to be low paid, low skill and vulnerable in times of change (see Chapter 4). It is commonly argued that structural factors mean that part-time workers have less opportunity to join a union as they are concentrated in industries and occupations with low levels of unionization (Walters 2002). However, it has been shown that even when part-timers are employed in unionized workplaces they are still less likely to be union members (Sinclair 1995). An alternative explanation for lower union membership among female part-timers is the approach that unions have taken towards part-time workers, rather than women's individual characteristics and attitudes towards trade unions. It has been suggested that part-time women workers do not lack commitment or belief in trade unionism (Cunnison and Stageman 1995; Walters 2002). Cunnison and Stageman (1995) argue that the negative attitudes of male trade unionists towards female part-time workers provide a better explanation of their low rates of union membership. They argue that the trade union movement still holds as its ideal the full-time worker, resulting in unions prioritizing bargaining on issues most likely to be of benefit to full-timers. In her study, Tomlinson (2005) highlights how British women typically move in and out of part-time work over the life course. While their fundamental attitudes to trade unionism might not alter, their actual experiences of trade unions might vary according to employment status. This in turn might affect whether or not a woman remains in a union or joins one in the future.

Women and the trade union agenda

This brings the discussion to the question of the trade union agenda and the extent to which it addresses the issues that most concern women. It is argued that through much of their history unions have been sceptical of and even hostile to women, regarding them as threatening higher wages, job security and union solidarity (Cockburn 1991; Cunnison and Stageman 1995).The global trade union movement has been subjected to extensive feminist criticism for failing to bargain and campaign vigorously enough on behalf of women (e.g. Briskin 2002; Cobble and Bielski Michal 2002; Cockburn 1991). Munro (2001: 457) suggests that 'the trade union agenda is embedded in the hierarchical nature of the labour market in which the interests of skilled white male workers have been prioritized and presented as general class interests, to the detriment of other workers'. Male domination has resulted in a limited range of issues being identified as union ones, particularly those associated with full-time work, such as overtime payments and the length of the working week. Issues having a greater bearing on women, such as flexible working and pro rata pay and conditions for part-timers, have generally been neglected. A survey by the European Trade Union Confederation (ETUC 2002) sheds some light on union activity in the area of women's employment. The survey found that while the principle of equal pay for equal work is incorporated into the collective agreements of a number of countries, the issue does not seem a central one in collective bargaining. Many European trade unions believe that gendered wage differences are more likely to be resolved through legislation than collective bargaining. However, the majority of European trade union confederations claim to mainstream gender in all trade union employment policies.

The extent to which gender should be central to collective bargaining is contested. Numerous studies in the UK and North American contexts have found that whilst women share many bargaining concerns with men, they prioritize issues differently (e.g. Cobble and Bielski Michal 2002; Healy and Kirton 2002; Waddington and Kerr 2002). For example, women trade union members give a higher priority to bargaining on certain specific issues such as equal pay, maternity leave and pay, childcare arrangements, sexual harassment, measures to reduce gendered barriers to career progression and part-time work; all issues that have a greater bearing on women's lives. There has been a noticeable shift over the past 20 years in the understanding of what constitutes a trade union issue and unions in many countries now have gender equality issues on the policy agenda. On the whole it is trade union women who have brought to the agenda a range of issues that point to the connection between work and home/family life. For example, childcare, domestic violence and women's health issues are now more likely to feature in trade union policy in many countries (Briskin 2002). Heery and Kelly's (1988) study of British female paid union officials showed that female presence did make a difference to the conduct of trade union work because women prioritize issues such as equal pay, childcare, maternity leave and sexual harassment in collective bargaining that men typically do not.

One recent turn has been the questioning of the notion of a unitary set of 'women's issues', where trade union women and researchers have highlighted class and ethnic differences among women as significant in determining their concerns and needs (Colgan and Ledwith 2000; McBride 2001). For example, it is clear that the employment conditions of part-time, low-paid women are entirely different from those of professional and managerial women and while issues such as the 'glass ceiling' and career progression might be the pressing ones for the latter group, part-time and low-paid women are more likely to be concerned with basic terms and conditions. However, it is also argued that while it is important to acknowledge women's diversity, there are sufficient common experiences among women to make it possible to identify a range of work interests specific to women that need to be firmly on the trade union agenda (Munro 2001). These would include 'women's issues' such as sexual harassment, the gender pay gap and gender segregation that cross status and occupational divides, impacting on all working women to some extent, as Chapters 2 and 3 indicate.

Most feminist industrial relations writers, even if they are critical, see unions as having at least the potential to act to improve women's employment conditions (Cobble and Bielski Michal 2002; Hunt and Rayside 2000) and it is recognized that the agenda has changed over time in response to the feminization of the labour market and to the demands of women trade union activists themselves (Kirton and Healy 1999). Briskin (2002) contends that over the past couple of decades in the Canadian context women trade unionists have successfully pressured unions to take up issues of childcare, reproductive rights, sexual harassment and violence against women, pay equity and other issues of concern to women. For example, half of Canadian women covered by major collective agreements now have the protection of a formal sexual harassment clause (up from 20 per cent in 1985); about 60 per cent of major Canadian collective agreements contain a non-discrimination clause (Briskin 2002: 34). This kind of activity by trade union women has pushed the boundaries of what is considered a trade union issue so that the agenda is now more likely to transcend the workplace and acknowledge the connection between work and home/family that is so fundamental to many women's employment. The general consensus is that women's position inside trade unions has an impact on the trade union agenda because once in positions of influence and power, women are able to act in ways that influence the content and processes of union bargaining and campaigning.

Women inside trade unions

Unions are democratic organizations and this makes them particularly instructive as case studies for the possibilities and limitations of gender equality policies. Theoretically every union member has the opportunity to participate by voting in elections for representatives and officers and on policy issues, by attending meetings and voicing opinions. Participation in these kinds of union activities is important because this is where a trade union career begins. The reality is that generally speaking unions are managed and run by men, even though in many individual unions they are now in a minority in membership terms. This has resulted in a situation where many women argue that although they are not actually excluded from trade unions, they do not feel included (Kirton 2005: 396).

In many ways women's position inside the unions across the developed world mirrors their position in other types of organization. The general picture is one of women's under-representation in senior decision-making positions relative to their share of membership (see Colgan and Ledwith 2002a), indicating a 'glass ceiling' mirroring that experienced by women in managerial positions in main-stream organizations (discussed in Chapter 5). Women are under-represented at every level from local workplace representatives, to paid union officials, to members of executive committees. Table 8.2 shows that in Europe women are generally not represented in union confederations' highest level structures of power in proportion to their share of membership. Similarly, in the US 40 per cent of union members are female, but there is still significant under-representation of women in decision-making positions (Cobble and Bielski Michal 2002). Women are also noticeably absent among the figureheads of unions, just as they are from the boardrooms of mainstream organizations (see Chapter 5). In the UK women head up just two of the Trade Union Congress's (TUC) 20 largest unions – both teaching unions – but it is well over a decade since a woman led any of the country's ten largest unions where women's membership is concentrated (Labour Research Department 2004). However, it is important to note that the current picture of women's under-representation is actually a major improve-ment on the situation up until about 20 years ago. The past two decades have witnessed a significant jump in the number of women on union executive boards in Europe and North America (Healy and Kirton 2000; Cobble and Bielski Michal 2002).

Table 8.2 Women's representation in trade union confederations in 15 European Union countries

Country	Trade union membership (% Women)	Women delegates to Congress (%)	Executive committee (% Women)
Austria	32	34	13
Belgium	48	18	27
Denmark	48	30	19
Finland	46	38	20
France	42	41	26
Germany	30	34	19
Ireland	45	31	17
Italy	38	30	23
Luxembourg	32	15	18
Netherlands	29	25	21
Norway	45	37	27
Portugal	47	22	22
Spain	32	27	24
Sweden	52	38	53
UK	40	35	32

Source: adapted from European Trades Congress (ETUC) (2002).

There has been a great deal of academic interest in gendered patterns of union participation. A traditional (patriarchal) argument was that women are inherently more passive (see Purcell 1979) or uninterested in unions because of their lack of attachment to paid work and lesser belief in the principles of trade unionism (Cunnison and Stageman 1995). More recently it has been argued that although overall women are less willing to participate in unions than are men, their reluctance is more prominent in certain aspects of union activism. In one study of Cypriot public sector unions (Metochi 2002), over one-third of women reported being willing to take part in collective action and/or frequently to attend union meetings, but a far smaller proportion said that they were willing to be elected onto the union's decision-making bodies or as union officials. This suggests complexity in women's orientations to union participation, rather than a straightforward lack of interest or commitment. The global feminist literature emphasizes a multitude of interrelated barriers and constraints for women, particularly the gendered division of domestic work, the organization of women's work, the organization of trade union work and the masculine culture of trade unions (e.g. Briskin and McDermott 1993; Colgan and Ledwith 2002b).

The gendered division of domestic work

As we discussed in Chapter 7, there is considerable evidence that women continue to take the main responsibility for running the home and caring for the family, whether they work full- or part-time and whether or not they have children. One consequence of women carrying the 'double burden' of paid work and household work is that they are 'time poor' with little spare time to participate in public life generally. Women's time poverty is particularly discussed in Chapter 7 in regard to 'work–life balance' policies.

It is now generally recognized that women's union participation is constrained by traditional gender roles in the home (Colgan and Ledwith 1996). In Britain, research has found that women who lead traditional lives are less likely to participate (especially to become representatives), in contrast to men in the same objective circumstances (Walton 1991; Lawrence 1994). It is important though to allow for a life-cycle effect and recognize that women might lead a traditional life for a period (probably during the family formation years) and a less traditional one later in the life course (perhaps after divorce). Reflecting this, research has found that most senior union women are 'atypical', meaning older, child-free and often partner-free (e.g. Kirton and Healy 1999). These women are more able to give the necessary time, effort and commitment to trade union participation, while women with dependent children and partners are more likely to be 'time poor'. On the other hand, women leading traditional lives are more likely to become active if they have supportive partners, especially during the child rearing phase (Lawrence 1994; Ledwith et al. 1990). For example, as discussed in Chapter 5, professional women have a greater tendency to retain full-time work continuity over the life course; they are more likely to share domestic work with their partners and perhaps reflecting this they constitute a larger proportion of British female union representatives (Cully *et al.* 1999). In contrast, women who work part-time are far less likely to participate in their union. This is unsurprising given that women who work part-time usually do so in order to balance work and family life when children are young and they are therefore unlikely to take on extra unpaid work.

The variability of household arrangements means that even when the unions implement enabling policy initiatives (such as meetings in places and at times to suit women, childcare provision at residential courses and conferences), women's increased participation does not necessarily follow. However, this is at least in part because these kinds of policy interventions are designed to help women manage their different roles in order to overcome domestic constraints, while accepting their existence. 'Family friendly' measures do not fundamentally challenge or alter gender relations either inside the family or inside the unions (McBride 2001). There is some evidence, though, that once women become politicized through union participation, they are less likely to comply with traditional gendered domestic arrangements (e.g. Cockburn 1994; Jones 2002).

The organization of women's work

To emphasize women's traditional role in the family as the main explanation for their lesser union participation risks falling into the trap of blaming women for their under-representation in union affairs. Some authors have argued that the organization of women's paid work can also act as a significant barrier to participation. For example, it is claimed that women's paid work is less likely than men's to develop skills necessary for trade union participation, including self-confidence, public speaking, participating in meetings, etc. (e.g. Cockburn 1991; Lawrence 1994). Consequently when women become active, they often talk of feeling 'out of their depth' and at a disadvantage compared to men (Kirton 1999) and there is therefore an interrelationship between the nature of women's work and the masculine culture of trade unions.

It is also argued that the organization of women's work provides fewer opportunities for the construction of a collective identity because their work is often socially isolated and closely supervised. Munro (2001) highlights the gendering of cleaning work and the way women cleaners might experience tighter supervisory control and can have less opportunity to move around in the workplace. In addition, part-time work in particular provides less opportunity to participate, because union meetings are more likely to be arranged to suit a full-time norm and part-time workers are less likely to receive paid time off for trade union duties (Munro 1999: 199). Thinking about the organization of women's work helps to explain why professional and highly qualified women are over-represented among union active women, particularly at the more senior levels of the union hierarchy. It is not because they are more committed or interested, but that their work and domestic life allow them to develop relevant skills and also the time to participate on male terms.

The organization of trade union work

Feminist scholars have drawn attention to the character of trade union organization itself in order to shift the blame for women's under-representation away from women themselves and onto the unions. Rather than providing childcare to enable women to adapt to the male norm, a better solution might be to make adaptations to the way trade union work is organized. Most British unions claim to have done this to some extent by, for example, changing meeting arrangements to make them more 'woman-friendly'. But the extent to which this high-level policy commitment is reflected in the practice of local union branches and workplaces is highly questionable; some women still appear to complain that meeting times and venues are not convenient (Munro 1999; Bradley *et al.* 2005).

Another aspect of the organization of trade union work reflecting men's relative 'time wealth' and the assumption of the trade union official as a man is the high level of time commitment required for both paid and voluntary union roles, particularly senior ones (Watson 1988; Cockburn 1991; Colgan and Ledwith 1996; Kirton and Healy 1999; Franzway 2000). Trade union officials are expected to work in the evenings and at weekends and frequently travel around the country attending meetings and conferences (Bradley 1999). Writing about the Australian union movement, Franzway (2000: 259) draws on the concept of the 'greedy institution' to underscore that union activism demands not only a considerable time commitment, but also a commitment to particular sets of values, which demand 'libidinal' energy. Since the family is another greedy institution, and by definition it is only possible to serve one greedy institution at a time, women especially face conflicting demands and find it difficult to combine trade union work with conventional family life.

Watson's (1988) classic study of British trade union officers exposes the 'long hours culture' of paid trade union work, one of the gendered consequences of which is women's relative under-representation in the ranks of paid officials. In the UK women make up approximately 27 per cent of national paid officials in the ten largest unions in comparison to approximately 43 per cent of membership. In only one union – female dominated retail trade union USDAW – does the proportion of female national officials match or exceed the proportion of women in membership (Labour Research Department 2004). However, this is a considerable increase over the past decade – in 1993 women's share of national official positions in the ten largest unions was about 10 per cent, compared to 33 per cent of membership (Labour Research Department 1994).

Similarly, in none of ten selected US trade unions with large numbers of women members does women's share of officers and executive members equal their share of membership, with an average gap of 29 per cent in 2000 (Cobble and Bielski Michal 2002). Table 8.3, showing the proportion of women in membership and in senior positions in five selected large UK unions at two points in time – 1993 and 2003 – reveals the nature and degree of change that has occurred in the UK. Overall, women are also now better represented in leadership positions in US unions compared with 1990, when the gap was about 36 per cent (Cobble and Bielski Michal 2002).

Table 8.3 Women in membership and senior positions in five selected large UK trade unions

	UNISON (public services)	TGWU (general union)	GMB (general union)	USDAW (retail trade union)	NUT (teaching union)
Women in membership					
1993	950,000	177,000	300,000	189,000	121,000
2003	925,000	170,000	260,000	196,000	191,000
Women as %					
1993	68	18	38	60	74
2003	72	20	40	59	76
Women as % Executive Committee					
1993	42	5	36	69	27
2003	64	33	36	59	40
Women as % national paid officials					
1993	20	4	13	0	30
2003	48	5	14	71	11
Women as % regional paid officials					
1993	31	7	12	21	11
2003	36	10	14	31	23

Source: adapted from *Labour Research* (1994, 2004).

The masculine culture of trade unions

Within the feminist critique of trade union organization, a number of authors explore the masculine character of trade union culture (e.g. Kirton 1999; Healy and Kirton 2000; McBride 2001; Williams 2002) and how it deters women from participating, but also how women seek to cope with or to challenge it (e.g. Colgan and Ledwith 2000, 2002b). It is argued that unions have failed to attract women into participation in equal numbers with men because of the masculine image associated with them.

Cunnison and Stageman (1995) identify the main masculine characteristics of trade unions as (i) an 'anti-femininity', (ii) a strong association with paid work and the achievement of status and independence, and (iii) a positive valuing of mental and physical toughness, competition and aggression. By 'anti-femininity' it is meant that stereotypically feminine behaviour such as the free expression of emotion is repudiated in favour of dispassionateness. Greene and Kirton's (2002) study of women-only trade union courses addresses this point. Women trade unionists reported that they had found it liberating and refreshing to be able to openly display emotions and tell personal stories in the women-only environment, without fear of dismissal of their views and arguments. On the second point, the dominant image of a trade union representative or official is of a full-time male worker who is the provider for a family and who is free to do as he pleases outside of work hours. This image underpins the organization of trade union work discussed earlier, but stands in stark contrast to the dominant model of the female worker, whose work life is closely bound up with family. Finally, the dominant image of the trade union official is of a 'hard-nosed, thrusting, aggressive and competitive man' (Cunnison and Stageman 1995: 14). It is often argued that women reject the stereotypically 'macho table-thumping style' associated with male trade unionists (Bradley 1999). The sex-typing of the trade union officer as male has echoes of the debates surrounding the gendered nature of management more generally (see Chapter 5).

While, as Cunnison and Stageman (1995) acknowledge, this depiction of trade union culture might be over-simplified, even a caricature, they argue that there is truth behind it and that women trade unionists find values and behaviour that do not fit with their own experiences and identities. For example, many women still report that sexist remarks and language, heckling and derisive comments are features of trade union meetings that are particularly frequent when women are speaking. This leaves many women feeling uncomfortable and alienated in the trade union environment (Kirton 1999).

Strategies for addressing women's under-representation

The unrepresentativeness of union leadership has been the subject of much debate among scholars around the globe (e.g. Colgan and Ledwith 2002a). It is argued that the issues that most concern women are easy for unions to neglect or ignore when women are absent from or marginal within the union hierarchy. In the words of Colling and Dickens (1989: 32), 'the absence of women *at* the table has to be part of the explanation for the absence of women *on* the table'. With women beginning to make inroads into union leadership positions, research has shown that their presence does appear to bring 'women's issues' to the union agenda and to contribute to incremental transformation of union culture. For example, research within one large male dominated British union (Kirton and Healy 1999) demonstrated that senior union women had adopted woman-conscious strategies with the twin objectives of transforming patriarchal union culture and union bargaining agendas.

Of course not all women experience and respond to the barriers and constraints in the same way. Some women are deterred while others 'battle against the odds' (Dorgan and Grieco 1993) and participate anyway. As shown earlier, women can and do sometimes reach the higher levels of the union hierarchy. On average though, women do participate to a lesser extent and are under-represented in union decision-making bodies and therefore it is now widely recognized by the unions that this necessitates action. Many unions have now developed a raft of gender equality strategies. It is important to emphasize though that the male dominated union movement established gender equality strategies in response to a widespread and sustained feminist campaign dating back to the early 1970s in North America and the UK, rather than simply by its own volition.

Positive action strategies have been widely used to redress gender inequalities inside trade unions and to increase the representativeness of decision-making structures. According to a liberal understanding of equality (Jewson and Mason 1986), positive action is concerned with removing the obstacles to 'free and equal competition among individuals' (1986: 222) (see Chapter 6). In the union context this approach has produced a range of measures, often coordinated by specialist women's officers, to enable the participation of individual women, such as childcare provision at union conferences and residential training courses, and women-only courses to empower women. There are also initiatives to attract and interest women members such as research and literature on 'women's issues' (Kirton and Greene 2002).

However, the debate within unions is not simply about how to facilitate the participation of individual women. One fundamental claim is that women's under-representation spells a gendered 'democracy deficit' (Cockburn 1995). The global trade union movement is seeking to tackle this with a review of traditional union structures and practices (e.g. Cobble and Bielski Michal 2002; Trebilcock 1991; ETUC 2002). A radical conception of equality is more concerned with outcomes than with processes and therefore more interventionist measures flow from this approach (Jewson and Mason 1986), including reserved committee seats for women, and separate women's groups, committees and conferences (Kirton and Greene 2002). It is the more radical initiatives that are thought to offer the greatest promise of gendered transformation (Colgan and Ledwith 1996; McBride 2001; Kirton and Greene 2002; Parker 2002).

Women's separate organizing

The more radical gender equality measures are all forms of women's separate organizing, which has become a widespread strategy within trade unions in Europe, North America, and Australia (Colgan and Ledwith 2002a). In Europe the overwhelming majority of trade union confederations have a women's committee and department with an advisory and decision-making role and around half have women's conferences (ETUC 2002). In 2000 13 of 27 UK unions provided some form of women-only groups (SERTUC 2000). This all suggests widespread acceptance in the union movement of the strategy of women's separate organizing, which has delivered gains for women. A comparison of UK trade unions between 1987 and 1997 shows a shift from a liberal approach towards more radical forms of separate organizing and a greater representation of women in union structures over time (Healy and Kirton 2000).

The transformative potential of women's separate organizing flows from two key ideas. First, it allows women to come together in a safe environment to develop their own priorities and agendas, which can then be fed into the mainstream (Briskin 1993). Second, it legitimates the representation of women as an oppressed social group, which is key to changing the nature of what counts as trade union business (Cockburn 1995). The rationale for women's separate organizing is that women have common concerns because there are issues that bear more on them as a disadvantaged social group. In order to pursue these concerns women need a separate space in which to reflect and be empowered (Parker 2002). Parker (2002: 25) identifies a range of objectives of women's groups including: advancing women's interests by lobbying on (bargaining) issues; issuing recommendations of concern and developing policy for women; helping women's recruitment, representation and involvement in unions; providing a 'space' in which to mobilize, disseminate information and exchange ideas; challenging discriminatory attitudes and practices; and developing leadership and assertiveness skills. It is argued that women's separate organizing has contributed to a redefining of union interests and a widening of the union agenda and to mobilizing women and encouraging their activism (Parker 2002).

However, women's separate organizing is not without its critics. Measures such as women's committees and conferences are sometimes charged with being tokenistic and with using patronizing gestures that imply that women are somehow deficient and in need of extra help. In addition, the separation of women from the mainstream, critics claim, results in marginalization of women and their concerns. It is also sometimes argued that women's separate organizing dilutes union solidarity and strength (Greene and Kirton 2005). Reflecting the controversy, unions in some countries have moved away from women's separate organizing. For example, after developing in the 1970s, separate organizing has recently declined in Italy as rivalries among women and between women's groups and the mainstream union progressively emerged and different political orientations grew in importance (Beccalli and Meardi 2002). In order to build on the strengths and opportunities of separate organizing, but to minimize the weaknesses and threats, coalition strategies are increasingly called for. Here, diverse constituencies within unions make links internally (e.g. women's groups with black and minority ethnic groups, etc.), as well as externally (with community groups, political groups, etc.) (Briskin 2002; Ledwith and Colgan 2002).

Conclusions

The examination of women and trade unions throws up a number of challenges for management and organizations. It is argued that 'trade unions have helped shape the contours of inequality' and that 'collective regulation has served often to reinforce rather than challenge inequalities' (Dickens 1997: 287). However, the labour market context in which the trade union movement determines its priorities has irreversibly changed. It is absolutely clear that the trade union movements of North America and Europe now need women workers to join if they are to survive. In this sense it could be argued that unions have their own business case for diversity (see discussion in Chapter 6). Although British trade union membership declined through the 1980s and most of the 1990s, it has now stabilized and as has been shown women are now a substantial proportion of union members in the UK and in other countries. One question is what this context means for the management of the employment relationship.

It is argued that in the UK context, influenced by the developing social agenda in Europe, notions of partnership working have been imported implying an expanding role for trade unions in their relations with employers. Further, regulations emanating from the European Union have helped shift the UK context in favour of joint engagement and regulation (Colling and Dickens 2001). While many organizations have developed gender equality strategies without any pressure from trade unions, it is the case, in the UK context at least, that formal equality policies are more commonplace in workplaces with recognized unions (Kersley *et al.* 2005). Combined with gendered changes inside trade unions, there is now a stronger platform for unions to influence gender equality policy and practice in organizations. Women's growing representation in the running of unions points to an increasingly feminized union agenda that management and organizations need to respond to. It is also an indication that the notion of the passive woman worker should finally be buried. In some feminized occupations such as teaching and nursing, unionization in the UK remains strong and it is clear that the unions are voicing members' concerns about various changes in policy and working practices in these areas. Further, the feminization of labour markets and organizations in many industrialized countries should also signal to employers and unions the need to develop gendered policies of attraction and retention.

Another question raised in this and other chapters in this book relates to the way forward for gender equality strategies. The history of the trade union movement's problematic relationship with women workers bears witness to the dangers of a 'gender-blind' approach to organizational policy-making. Ignoring the realities of women's working lives – in particular the intersection between work and family – is not the way to positively attract and retain women, either in employment or in trade unions. The barriers that women face in making progress in management and occupational hierarchies are similar to those faced by women attempting to pursue paid or voluntary careers in the trade union movement. The union movement represents an example of the kinds of outcomes that can be achieved, in terms of gendered redistribution of power, by employing more radical equality initiatives, such as women's separate organizing. There is also a call within the trade union movement for gender equality issues to be mainstreamed within collective bargaining so that gender dimensions to traditional bargaining issues might be brought to the fore. This has echoes of the wider debates about the potential benefits of mainstreaming equality promoted by the European Union

(Rees 1998). The question that has not yet been answered is whether within a mainstreaming strategy the voices of the most marginalized are heard. Again, within the trade union context, more radical equality initiatives such as rules on proportional representation of women and reserved committee seats for women have been used as devices to make sure that women have a place at the table where policy agendas are debated. However, as discussed earlier and in Chapter 6, there is resistance to 'special measures' and to quotas from trade unions as organizations and also from women whom such initiatives are designed to benefit. Whatever approach is adopted it is clear that trade unions will only realize their potential to be partners in advancing gender equality in employment if they can reverse membership decline and embrace strategies towards internal gender equality.

References

Armstrong, P. (1993) 'Professions, unions or what? Learning from nurses', in L. Briskin and P. McDermott (eds), *Women Challenging Unions*, Toronto: University of Toronto Press, 304–21.

Beccalli, B. and Meardi, G. (2002) 'From unintended to undecided feminism? Italian labour's changing and singular ambiguities', in F. Colgan and S. Ledwith (eds) *Gender, Diversity and Trade Unions*, London: Routledge, 113–31.

Bradley, H. (1999) *Gender and Power in the Workplace*, Basingstoke: Macmillan.

Bradley, H., Healy, G. and Mukherjee, N. (2005) 'Multiple burdens: problems of work–life balance for ethnic minority trade union activist women', in D. Houston (ed.) *Work–Life Balance in the 21st Century*, Basingstoke: Palgrave Macmillan, 211–29.

Briskin, L. (1993) 'Union women and separate organizing', in L. Briskin and P. McDermott (eds) *Women Challenging Unions*, Toronto: University of Toronto Press, 89–108.

Briskin, L. (2002) 'The equity project in Canadian unions: confronting the challenge of restructuring and globalization', in F. Colgan and S. Ledwith (eds) in *Gender, Diversity and Trade Unions*, London: Routledge, 28–47.

Briskin, L. and McDermott, P. (1993) (eds) *Women Challenging Unions*, Toronto: University of Toronto Press.

Brook, K. (2002) 'Trade union membership: an analysis of data from the Autumn 2002 LFS', *Labour Market Trends* (July): 343–54.

Bureau of Labor Statistics (2005) *Union Members in 2005*. www.bls.gov/newsrelease/pdf/union1.pdf (accessed June 2006).

Chao, E. and Utgoff, K. (2005) *Women in the Labor Force: A Databook*, Washington: Department of Labor.

Cobble, D. and Bielski Michal, M. (2002) 'On the edge of equality? Working women and the US labour movement', in F. Colgan and S. Ledwith (eds) *Gender, Diversity and Trade Unions*, London: Routledge, 232–56.

Cockburn, C. (1991) *In the Way of Women*, Basingstoke: Macmillan.

Cockburn, C. (1994) 'Play of power: women, men and equality initiatives in a trade union', in S. Wright (ed.) *Anthropology of Organizations*, London: Routledge, 95–114.

Cockburn, C. (1995) *Strategies for Gender Democracy: Women and the European Social Dialogue*, Brussels: European Commission.

Colgan, F. and Ledwith, S. (1996) 'Sisters organising – women and their trade unions', in S. Ledwith and F. Colgan (eds) *Women in Organizations*, Basingstoke: Macmillan: 152–85.

Colgan, F. and Ledwith, S. (2000) 'Diversity, identities and strategies of women trade union activists', *Gender, Work and Organization* ,7 (4): 242–57.

Colgan, F. and Ledwith, S. (eds) (2002a) *Gender, diversity and trade unions*, London, Routledge.

Colgan, F. and Ledwith, S. (2002b) 'Gender and diversity: reshaping union democracy', *Employee Relations*, 24 (2): 167–89.

Colling, T. and Dickens, L. (1989) *Equality Bargaining – Why Not?* Manchester: Equal Opportunities Commission.

Colling, T. and Dickens, L. (2001) 'Gender equality and trade unions: a new basis for mobilization?' in M. Noon and E. Ogbonna (eds) *Equality, Diversity and Disadvantage in Employment*, Basingstoke: Palgrave, 136–55.

Cully, M., Woodland, S., O'Reilly, A. and Dix, G (1999) *Britain at Work*, London: Routledge.

Cunnison, S. and Stageman, J. (1995) *Feminizing the Unions*, Aldershot: Avebury.

Dickens, L. (1997) 'Gender, race and employment equality in Britain: inadequate strategies and the role of industrial relations actors', *Industrial Relations Journal*, 28 (4): 282–9.

Dorgan, T. and Grieco, M. (1993) 'Battling against the odds: the emergence of senior women trade unionists', *Industrial Relations Journal*, 24 (2): 151–64.

ETUC (2002) *Women in Trade Unions: Making the Difference*, Brussels: European Trade Union Confederation.

Franzway, S. (2000) 'Women working in a greedy institution: commitment and emotional labour in the union movement', *Gender, Work and Organization*, 7 (4): 258–68.

Grainger, H. (2006) *Trade Union Membership 2005*. London: DTI.

Greene, A. M. and Kirton, G. (2002) 'Advancing gender equality: the role of women-only trade union education', *Gender, Work and Organization*, 9 (1): 39–59.

Greene, A. M. and Kirton, G. (2005) 'Trade unions and equality and diversity', in A. Konrad, P. Prasad and J. Pringle (eds) *Handbook of Workplace Diversity*, London: Sage: 489–510.

Healy, G. and Kirton, G. (2000) 'Women, power and trade union government in the UK', *British Journal of Industrial Relations*, 38 (3): 343–60.

Healy, G. and Kirton, G. (2002) 'Professional and highly qualified women in two contrasting trade unions', in F. Colgan and S. Ledwith (eds) *Gender, Diversity and Trade Unions*, London: Routledge, 186–204.

Heery, E. and Kelly, J. (1988) 'Do female representatives make a difference? Women FTOs and trade union work', *Work, Employment and Society*, 2 (4): 487–505.

Howell, C. (1996) 'Women as the paradigmatic trade unions? New work, new workers and new trade union strategies in Conservative Britain', *Economic and Industrial Democracy*, 17 (4): 511–43.

Hunt, G. and Rayside, D. (2000) 'Labor union response to diversity in Canada and the United States', *Industrial Relations*, 39 (3): 401–44.

Jewson, N. and Mason, D. (1986) 'The theory and practice of equal opportunities policies: liberal and radical approaches', *Sociological Review*, 34 (2): 307–34.

Jones, S. (2002) 'A woman's place is on the picket line. Towards a theory of community industrial relations', *Employee Relations*, 24 (2): 151–66.

Kersley, G., Alpin, C., Forth, J., Bryson, A., Bewley, H., Dix, G. and Oxenbridge, S. (2005) *Inside the Workplace: First Findings from the 2004 Workplace Employment Relations Survey* (WERS 2004), London: Department of Trade and Industry.

Kirton, G. (1999) 'Sustaining and developing women's trade union activism: a gendered project' *Gender, Work and Organization*, 6 (4): 213–23.

Kirton, G. (2005) 'The influences on women joining and participating in unions', *Industrial Relations Journal*, 36 (5): 386–401.

Kirton, G. and Healy, G. (1999) 'Transforming union women: the role of women trade union officials in union renewal', *Industrial Relations Journal*, 30 (1): 31–45.

Kirton, G. and Greene, A. M. (2002) 'The dynamics of positive action in UK trade unions: the case of women and black members', *Industrial Relations Journal*, 33 (2): 157–72.

Labour Research Department (1994) 'Still a long road to equality', *Labour Research*, March: 5–7.

Labour Research Department (2004) 'Women's rise in unions patchy', *Labour Research*, March: 10–12.

Lawrence, E. (1994) *Gender and Trade Unions*, London: Taylor and Francis.

Ledwith, S. and Colgan F. (2002) 'Tackling gender, diversity and trade union democracy: a worldwide project?' in F. Colgan and S. Ledwith (eds) *Gender, Diversity and Trade Unions: International Perspectives*, London: Routledge, 1–27.

Ledwith, S., Colgan, F., Joyce, P. and Hayes, M. (1990) 'The making of women trade union leaders', *Industrial Relations Journal*, 21 (2): 112–25.

McBride, A. (2001) *Gender Democracy in Trade Unions*, Aldershot: Ashgate.

Metochi, M. (2002) 'The influence of leadership and member attitudes in understanding the nature of union participation', *British Journal of Industrial Relations*, 40 (1): 87–111.

Munro, A. (1999) *Women, Work and Trade Unions*, London: Mansell.

Munro, A. (2001) 'A feminist trade union agenda? The continued significance of class, gender and race', *Gender, Work and Organization*, 8 (4): 454–71.

Parker, J. (2002) 'Women's groups in British unions', *British Journal of Industrial Relations*, 40 (1): 23–48.

Purcell, K. (1979) 'Militancy and acquiescence amongst women workers', in S. Burman (ed.) *Fit Work for Women*, Oxford: Blackwell.

Rees, T. (1998) *Mainstreaming Equality in the European Union: Education, Training and Labour Market Policies*, London: Routledge.

SERTUC (2000) *New Moves Towards Equality – New Challenges*, London, Southern and Eastern Region TUC.

Sinclair, D. (1995) 'The importance of sex for the propensity to unionise', *British Journal of Industrial Relations*, 33 (2): 239–52.

Statistics Canada (2004) *The Union Movement in Transition*. http://www.statcan.ca/Daily/English/040831/do4083b.htm (accessed June 2006).

Tomlinson, J. (2005) 'Women's attitudes towards trade unions in the UK: a consideration of the distinction between full- and part-time workers', *Industrial Relations Journal*, 36 (5): 402–18.

Waddington, J. and Whitston, C. (1997) 'Why do people join trade unions in a period of membership decline?' *British Journal of Industrial Relations*, 35 (4): 515–46.

Waddington, J. and Kerr, A. (2002) 'Unions fit for young workers?' *Industrial Relations Journal*, 33 (4): 298–315.

Walters, S. (2002). 'Female part-time workers' attitudes to trade unions in Britain', *British Journal of Industrial Relations*, 40 (1): 49–68.

Walton, J. (1991) 'Women shop stewards in a county branch of NALGO', in N. Redclift and M. Sinclair (eds) *International Perspectives on Labour and Gender Ideology*, London: Routledge, 149–71.

Watson, D. (1988) *Managers of Discontent*, London: Routledge.

Williams, C. (2002) 'Masculinities and emotion work in trade unions', in F. Colgan and S. Ledwith (eds) *Gender, Diversity and Trade Unions*, London: Routledge, 292–311.

Chapter 9

Conclusion

Prospects for women's employment

Introduction

The major themes in women's employment that this book has addressed are relevant to one extent or another to all industrialized countries. Certainly women's increased employment participation coupled with continuing gender inequalities are global phenomena. This concluding chapter concentrates largely on the UK and summarizes the main areas of change and continuity in women's employment. In the final section we turn our attention to a consideration of the current and future policy directions by examining the efforts being made by the social partners – the state, trade unions and employers – to make progress on women's employment equality in the UK.

Change and continuity in women's employment

As we have seen in the preceding chapters, the increase in women's participation in the labour market over the past 50 years or so is a particularly significant feature of the economies of industrialized countries (Garcia *et al.* 2003). Some 50 years ago women made up 30 per cent of the UK workforce (Wilson 1994), compared with 46 per cent today (EOC 2005a). It is in response to a changing industrial structure that women's employment has grown while men's has shrunk. Men have traditionally been dependent on jobs in heavy industry and they have been hit hardest by the long period of decline of the manufacturing sector in Western Europe and the US at least. In contrast, the service sector, an area of traditional female employment, has expanded and women have benefited. Indeed, it is argued that most of the increase in women's employment can be linked to changes in industrial structure, favouring feminized sectors such as business and health and education services (Wilson 1994).

As shown in Chapters 2 and 5, women have also moved increasingly into areas of employment previously regarded as male strongholds, especially professional and managerial work. In its 2006 publication, *Sex and Power: Who Runs Britain?*, the Equal Opportunities Commission outlines the changes that have occurred since the early 1970s prior to the Sex Discrimination Act (1975). In 1974 just 2 per cent of managers were women and less than 1 per cent of directors were women – the equivalent figures are now 33 per cent and 14 per cent. In 1971 only 3 per cent of top managers in the Civil Service were women, compared to a quarter now. In 1975, there were no women senior police officers, whereas one in ten is now a woman (EOC 2006b). However, there has been less change in lower level occupations, where gender segregation remains more or less intact. We return later to this issue of a growing polarization between highly qualified and less qualified women.

It is also clear that women in many ways receive different and better treatment in the labour market of the 2000s compared to that of the 1970s, due in part at least to woman- and family-friendly legislative changes. As an indication of this, in 1979 only around half of pregnant women were in employment and of those only 24 per cent went back to work within eight months of giving birth. Around two-thirds of pregnant women now work and about 70 per cent of these return to work within the first year (EOC 2006b). Progress has also been made on women's pay. In 1975 the full-time gender pay gap was 29 per cent and the part-time gender pay gap 42 per cent, compared to 17 per cent and 38 per cent respectively in 2005 (EOC 2006b). Here it should be noted that the pay situation has changed very little for part-time women workers, which we return to below.

If we assume women's increasing economic independence to be a good thing, then these changes look positive. However, before celebrating too heartily, beneath the surface we can observe seemingly intractable patterns that signal continuing gender inequalities in employment.

The persistence of horizontal gender segregation has meant that traditionally feminized employment, associated with relatively low pay and few prospects, has changed little. For example, in 1971, women comprised 76 per cent of those in clerical and secretarial occupations and 72 per cent of those in 'other sales occupations' (Wilson 1994). In 2004 the equivalent figures were 80 per cent and 69 per cent (EOC 2005a). So there is little change here: women continue to be concentrated in a narrow range of feminized occupations, just as they were in the mid 1950s. In Western Europe, over half of all employed women work in just two sectors – sales, hotels and catering, and health and education (Fagan and Burchell 2002). The changing opportunities and prospects for more highly qualified women therefore contrasts with the continuity and poor quality in lesser qualified women's employment patterns.

On the one hand, horizontal segregation has underpinned women's employment growth, since the sectors that have grown are those traditionally seen as suitable for women (Rubery *et al.* 1998). On the other hand it both produces and reproduces gender inequalities. Part of the explanation for the persistence of horizontal occupational segregation lies in the prevalence of part-time work among women and the fact that employers construct only certain types of jobs as part-time – generally low-skill, low-paid, low-status ones in feminized sectors. This means that women who 'choose' to work part-time often experience 'downward occupational mobility' (Blackwell 2001) and are to be found working 'below their potential' (EOC 2005a). Part-time jobs tend to be of low quality in Europe and the US and as discussed in Chapter 4, there is little opportunity for professionals and managers to work part-time (Hoque and Kirkpatrick 2003; Smithson *et al.* 2004). Even if they would like to, they realize that there are penalties in terms of being perceived by employers and colleagues as uncommitted (McGlynn 2003). Women who 'choose' to work part-time typically do so because of childcare responsibilities. In 2002 40 per cent of women in the UK who returned to work after childbirth changed from full-time to part-time work (WEU 2004). Women who make this 'choice' usually pay a heavy price in terms of their financial security in the medium to longer terms.

Women employed part-time have the highest risk of being low paid in the US and Europe when compared with full-time women and men (Robson *et al.* 1999). As discussed in Chapter 3, the gender pay gap in the UK is also far wider for part-time than for full-time women workers (WEU 2004). Therefore, any further growth in part-time work is likely to reinforce the gender pay gap, unless attention is paid to improving the quality and prospects of part-time work. We return to the concept of 'quality part-time work' below.

Occupational segregation is thought to be a major cause of the gender pay gap (Crompton 1999). In addition, the belief now is that at least some elements of the gender pay gap (and by extension of occupational segregation) reflect discriminatory social norms or indirect discrimination (Rubery *et al.* 2005). However, the gender pay gap is seen not only as an equality issue, but also as one of national economic importance (Walby and Olsen 2002). This is because it is not in governments' interest to have low-paid workers who pay low levels of taxation and who will require welfare support, particularly in old age. It is also an issue for individual employers, argues Kingsmill (2001), since a reduction in the gender pay gap will increase organizations' morale, efficiency, productivity and competitiveness. It will also avoid risks to reputation, of litigation and of poor recruitment. There are clear implications here for organizations' policy and practice.

Even in the area of employment where the picture looks most positive for women – professional and managerial work – there is evidence of continuing gender inequalities. Being in an occupation that requires high levels of qualification does not guarantee equal pay either. As we show in Chapters 3 and 5, women professionals and managers are more commonly found in lower-paying sectors and niches that often offer no pathway to the more senior or lucrative levels of the occupation or organization (ILO 2004). They may also encounter a 'glass ceiling' when seeking promotion or a 'glass cliff' when they reach top leadership positions (Ryan and Haslam 2005).

No discussion of change and continuity in women's employment can be complete without consideration of the gendered division of domestic labour. In Chapter 1 we discussed the changing nature of the household, in particular the dramatic decline in the number with a male full-time breadwinner and a woman out of the labour market. However, as we show in Chapter 4, while women's increased employment has undoubtedly destabilized this traditional model, in the UK it has been replaced by the 'one and a half breadwinner model', where the man works full-time and the woman part-time (Crompton *et al.* 2005). What have these changes meant for women's traditional roles in the home and family? As we discuss in Chapter 7, research in industrialized countries generally shows that women and men persist in spending markedly different amounts of time on childcare and other domestic activities, even when both are in full-time paid work. It is of course possible that this will change over time with greater numbers of women participating in full-time employment through the child rearing phase. However, based on a study of young graduates, Purcell (2002: 28) states that 'young women still accept the cultural mandate that has allocated the primary parenting responsibility to females'. But some changes have been observed in the UK in terms of 'who does what' in the household: there is some evidence that young men have fewer traditional ideas about the domestic division of labour (Gershuny 2000). There is abundant research in different national contexts confirming that family and domestic responsibilities constrain – or at least contextualize – women's paid work careers. An unequal domestic division of labour is agreed by many commentators to be a major factor in women's inequalities in the labour force.

Gender cultures (which as we have seen can vary cross-nationally) are strongly rooted and it is unlikely that the domestic division of labour can be seen as the concern of governments. Nevertheless, it is possible that some statutory policies have the potential to impact upon these household decisions. We know from time budget studies (see Chapter 7) that the more time that is spent in the labour market, the less time is spent on domestic activities. Following on from this, we might argue that a more equal domestic division of labour could result from shorter working hours for all – a short-hours full-time model. A reduction in working hours is not utopian, since the limiting of hours is the official position of the European Union, despite its resistance by the UK. This would be a major change for many men for whom the long-hours culture is probably engrained. Crompton *et al.* (2005) point out that men cannot be more involved in domestic and caring activities if their work hours are long. But would a reduction in hours necessarily imply a change in the domestic division of labour? The gender culture, as commentators such as Pfau-Effinger (2004) have pointed out, is deeply rooted. There is little evidence from France that the 35-hour working week has changed 'who does what' in the home (Fagnani and Letablier 2004). A more optimistic – and complex – scenario in the UK, however, is suggested by Warren (2003). Based on secondary analysis of large nationally representative survey data, Warren shows that working-class couples are more likely to share childcare than middle-class couples. There is a long tradition of working-class fathers' involvement in childcare, dating back to the 'twilight shifts' (see Chapter 4) of the 1950s. Low-income families have always had to depend on 'household childcare'. However, Warren shows that in these households the domestic tasks other than childcare were still firmly female-dominated.

Overall, if there have been some positive changes in the position of women in the labour market, white, well-qualified women are the chief winners. Ethnic differences in women's employment patterns and achievements in the UK are notable. One stark indicator of this is that white women have higher employment and lower unemployment rates than black and minority ethnic women (EOC 2005a). The unemployment rate of white women is 4 per cent, while that of all black and minority ethnic women is 10 per cent. However, within the latter category there are large differences ranging from an unemployment rate among Indian women of 7 per cent, among black Caribbean women of 8 per cent and among Bangladeshi women of 20 per cent.

These differences within women's employment are indicative of an increased polarization of women, especially between those who are highly qualified and able to access higher level occupations and those who are less well qualified and who remain in highly segregated feminized employment (Glover and Arber 1995; Walby 1997). As we discuss in Chapter 7, highly qualified, highly paid women are also more able to buy in replacement domestic labour so that they are able to pursue their employment and achieve some sort of reconciliation of work and family life, crucially without depending on the actions of government and employers. A further polarization is growing between older women and older men: at various points in this book we have documented the considerable evidence of financial insecurity that particularly hits older women. This is the case in the UK and the US, but much less so in the Nordic countries. A pension system that is based on employment record, type of employer and size of salary is not at all to the advantage of older women, who constitute one of the poorest groups in the UK. The Nordic system of economic security based on citizenship and not employment history is much more to the advantage of older women.

Current and future policy directions

This section turns to the policies being pursued by the social partners – government, trade unions and employers – that might improve women's employment prospects.

Government policies

There are a number of significant developments in UK government policy that are intended to address gender inequality in employment. We have seen in our examination of different social and welfare regimes that government policy can make a difference. One such development is the forthcoming establishment of a new Commission for Equality and Human Rights (CEHR) incorporating all the existing equality commissions (gender, race, disability) by 2008/09. This is similar to the approach taken in other countries including Australia, Canada and the US, where all strands of equality are dealt with within a single body. The EOC has stated that it supports the principle of the CEHR on grounds that single-strand bodies are more effective at dealing with inter-sectional or multiple discrimination issues (EOC

2004). In addition, as the EOC contends, recent research and experience has shown that gender equality is an increasingly subtle and complex issue that cannot be tackled by a simple one-dimensional approach. This stance reflects the criticisms that have long been made by black feminist writers that the discrimination experienced by black women cannot be understood by reference to a single theory of inequality or oppression (hooks 1989; Anthias and Yuval-Davis 1993). Having separate commissions for gender and race equality implies a separation of sex and race discrimination that does not match up to black and minority ethnic women's actual experiences. In addition, the CEHR will include age, sexual orientation and religion or belief; areas in which the UK now has legal regulations and which also intersect with gender. The establishment of the CEHR may go some way to meeting the manifold criticisms of the British approach to equality policy-making.

As discussed in Chapter 6, one of the fundamental criticisms of the British policy approach to equality centres on conceptual flaws contained in the 'equal opportunity' concept reflected in legislation and in turn in employer policies. Fredman (2002) argues that the most basic concept of equality – the 'equal treatment principle' – assumes that it is possible to detach individuals from their gender (or race) and treat them simply as individuals. The legal formulation in the UK of this principle is direct discrimination, the underlying aim of which is a gender-neutral society. However, it is well established, as Fredman states, that this approach has had limited value in addressing gender inequalities. The 'equal opportunities principle' – the aim to identify and remove barriers to equality – has its legal formulation in indirect discrimination. Indirect discrimination also has its limitations because often indirectly discriminatory barriers can be justified by reference, for example, to job-related criteria, even if such criteria mean that under-represented groups remain excluded. In any case, the UK legislation is complaints-based and seeks to provide redress to individual victims of discrimination. Thus, discrimination is reduced to individual acts of prejudice perpetrated against individual victims (Fredman 2002).

As discussed in Chapter 7, the UK has avoided more radical conceptions of equality that might have brought about more substantive change, such as 'affirmative action' used in the US to tackle gender and race inequalities. The fundamental problem is that the UK government's approach does not recognize structural discrimination. Structural discrimination can be defined as 'sources of group-patterned disadvantage and inequality that are neither a consequence of the voluntary choices of individual members of the disadvantaged group nor a product of particular social agents' bias against that group' (Williams 2000). So, for example, if an individual employer does not promote a suitably qualified woman because of explicit assumptions about her experiencing a conflict between work and family commitments, then a charge of discrimination might be faced. However, the same employer is not required to consider how it might encourage more women to apply for promotions (i.e. remove gendered barriers).

In Chapter 6, we discuss the changing public and political discourses that underpin contemporary organizational equality policies, which now generally draw on the concept of diversity. Flowing from this, although the 'business case' for equality has always featured in the discourse of the social partners, it has now become much more prominent within government and employer policies. The existing evidence on employer equality policies indicates a reluctance to take responsibility for structural equality issues and there is no solid evidence that employers are persuaded into doing so by the business case for diversity. Employers seem to be more convinced by the idea that individuals are responsible for balancing work and family and that while individual acts of discrimination and displays of prejudice need to be dealt with, the organization has no responsibility to intervene in order to directly influence employment outcomes. We drew attention in earlier chapters to the view that 'preference theory' had given academic legitimacy to employers' assumptions of freely chosen decisions (Sommerlad and Sanderson 1998).

Another turn in discourse is the gender-neutral language that infuses organizational (and government) equality policies. This is particularly apparent in work–life balance and flexibility policies that are often presented as 'for everyone'. In this way, so the argument goes, work–life balance becomes an issue for all that employers will then take up more enthusiastically (Smithson and Stokoe 2005). However, despite employers insisting on a gender-neutral environment, many of the policy initiatives are implicitly aimed at women and/or those with primary responsibility for children, just as under the former label of 'family-friendly' policies. As we show in Chapter 7, there is a continued focus on enabling women to balance work with family roles and the positioning of the work–life balance debate as primarily about women. After all, 'work–life balance' does not tackle structural gender inequalities such as segregation and the pay gap, which produce the material inequalities that push women towards privileging family roles and men towards privileging paid work. The problem is that whilst we still have a marked gender pay gap it will continue to make rational economic sense for most households to privilege the male career. Thus the reality is that women are the main users of these policies.

As we show in Chapter 7, the evidence so far of employer policy and practice in the area does not point far beyond strategies to recruit and retain female workers in a tight labour market. This view is reflected by Smithson and Stokoe, whose analysis of work–life balance policies in banking and accountancy organizations suggests that 'masking or minimizing gender differences within gender-neutral language does not, as a strategy, appear to be working as a means for advancing gender equality' (2005: 164). 'WLB' discourse also risks throwing back the decision-making onto the household, where a traditional domestic division of labour is produced and reproduced.

Trade union policies

As discussed in Chapter 8, it has been argued that trade unions have 'helped shape the contours of inequality' (Dickens 1997: 287), as well as potentially being part of the solution.[1] Colling and Dickens (2001) have argued that in the context of a Labour government in Britain and a strong commitment among EU member states to tackle social inequalities, there is now a strengthened platform for collective bargaining. If this is true, then now is the time for the unions to seize the opportunity to bargain on equality issues. As we discussed in Chapter 8, unions have their own business case for tackling inequalities in the sense that since women are now an important source of members, unions need to make themselves more attractive to women by dealing with their specific employment concerns.

Certainly, the British Trade Union Congress (TUC) is now giving a stronger steer to unions to develop strategies for tackling equality issues. As part of this and following a recommendation from the TUC's Stephen Lawrence Task Group,[2] at its 2001 conference the TUC agreed a rule change that involved a commitment to undertaking biennial equality audits of affiliated trade unions and their activities. The audits are very detailed and provide a window on the activities of unions in the equality area. The second audit in 2005 (TUC 2005) focused on collective bargaining, covering information on the unions' bargaining and equality structures, the process of introducing an equality dimension into collective bargaining and the results of collective bargaining in terms of their equality impact.

The main way that unions identify priorities for equality bargaining is through conference or executive committee decisions. This is problematic because women are under-represented among conference delegates and on executive committees. However, recommendations from union equality bodies also influence the agenda for about two-thirds of unions. Listening to equality bodies such as women's committees is particularly important in order to overcome the lack of influence women have in mainstream decision- and policy-making forums in unions. A large amount of research over the past 20 years or so has argued that this is a major reason for the slow progress on equality bargaining and a major issue for unions to tackle. There is certainly evidence that the increased efforts to ensure women have a voice are paying off – according to the 2005 audit unions are now taking up issues that have a greater bearing on women. Among the top equality bargaining goals identified by the unions were: measures to achieve equal pay, particularly for women; work–life balance and flexible working; and parental rights, including maternity and paternity leave and pay.

The extent of success is difficult to assess, though, because the audit finds that most unions do not monitor the results of equality bargaining at local level, although at national level there is closer monitoring. From the available information, it appears that it is easier to negotiate on some issues than others; for example there is a greater degree of success on flexible working and work–life balance and childcare than on women's pay. This indicates that employers are more willing to make concessions where they see some benefit for themselves, for example in flexible work arrangements, than on the harder and potentially more costly issue of pay.

Organizational policies

Nearly a decade ago Dickens (1997: 285) characterized the approach of the UK government to employment inequalities as inadequate, arguing that 'there is no legal requirement to *do* anything to promote equality' (original emphasis). This is set to change, at least in the public sector. From early 2007 public authorities will be required by law for the first time to *promote* gender equality. The so-called 'gender equality duty' will mean that public sector employers will have to set gender equality goals and consider the different needs of women and men at work. Specifically, there are three key components requiring public sector employers to: draw up and publish a scheme identifying specific gender equality goals and showing how they will be implemented; develop and publish an equal pay statement; and conduct gender impact assessments to provide understanding of the impact that new policies and services may have on women and men and allow any negative effects to be mitigated. It is suggested that these key components will involve measures to ensure fair promotion and development opportunities and tackle occupational segregation. The policy will have to be reviewed at regular intervals and monitoring and evaluation will take place (WEU 2005). These requirements have major data-gathering implications, a point that we take up below.

There will also be a challenge to organizations to ensure that such measures are not merely treated as requiring compliance, but that they will be the basis of proactive measures to promote gender equality, alongside similar legal requirements for disability and ethnicity. The challenge for the government will be to ensure that organizations have sufficient support to carry out procedures which, anecdotally, seem to be particularly demanding in administrative terms. In this light, it may be unsurprising that so few organizations appear to have carried out equal pay reviews (Browne 2004; EOC 2006b).

The Equal Opportunities Commission (EOC) states that the introduction of the duty on public sector organizations to promote gender equality should mean that we will see increased childcare provision and more flexible working as employers respond to the needs of parents and carers (EOC 2006a). However, the government has stated that public authorities will have 'a good deal of discretion' on how they meet the duty, stating that it 'does not wish to prescribe' how this should be done (WEU 2005: 15). Although the EOC welcomes the duty as 'the most significant change to sex equality legislation in 30 years' (EOC 2006a), it is not uncritical. In its response to the proposals, the EOC makes it clear that it would like to see more enforceable specific and action-focused duties and a stronger steer on creating a government-wide gender equality strategy (EOC 2005b). At the time of writing, the formulation of the duty has yet to be finalized and how and whether the EOC's criticisms will be taken on board remains to be seen. Cunningham (2000) argues that the climate in the public sector has changed and the advent of 'new public management' has meant that even public sector employers cannot be relied upon to adopt voluntarily the rigorous approach to tackling gender inequalities that the EOC is arguing is necessary. If the government is serious about the business case for gender equality and about tackling the gender pay gap and occupational segregation, the EOC's concerns need to be taken on board.

Of course, this still leaves the question of the lack of action required of private sector employers to promote equality. The available evidence suggests that private sector employers are far less likely to have in place the kind of measures that would help to remove some of the barriers to women's employment opportunities and choices. For example, they are far less likely to offer paid parental leave, special paid leave for family emergencies or leave for carers of older adults (Kersley *et al.* 2005). They are much less likely than the public sector to carry out equal pay reviews.

Although there is no legal requirement to have a formal written equality policy in the UK, there is evidence that an increasing proportion of employers have such policies. A major representative survey found that in 2004 73 per cent of workplaces had a policy, compared with 64 per cent in 1998 (Kersley *et al.* 2005). Equality policies were more commonly found in larger workplaces and were almost universal in public sector workplaces and in workplaces with a recognized trade union. At first sight, this looks quite positive, but when it comes to *action* to give effect to the policy, the use of specific policy initiatives is less widespread. For example, only around 30 per cent of workplaces with a policy had mechanisms in place for monitoring recruitment and selection processes by sex, 13 per cent monitored promotion processes and 9 per cent reviewed relative pay rates. Again, appropriate and systematic data-gathering is at issue here.

However, the incidence of flexible working arrangements for non-managerial employees had increased from 1998. Generally though, this was from a low base, so that arrangements such as flexitime, homeworking and term-time only working remained relatively uncommon. The survey also found that managers commonly considered it to be up to the individual to balance their work and family responsibilities (69 per cent in the private sector and 47 per cent in the public sector) (Kersley *et al.* 2005).

On balance the evidence indicates a willingness to accept the principle of gender equality, particularly on the part of private sector employers, but a reluctance to develop policy initiatives that might go some way towards making the principle become a reality. Based on an analysis of an earlier survey, Hoque and Noon (2004) argue that in many workplaces equality policies are nothing more than an 'empty shell'. They also point out that even where there are initiatives in place, these tend to be targeted at women managers and professionals, so that for the majority of non-managerial women, the policies may be particularly meaningless.

This emphasis on professional and managerial women is evident even in the more proactive policies in the public sector. The UK Civil Service has produced a 'Ten Point Plan' for delivering a diverse labour force (Civil Service 2006). Within this, two of the key targets are for 37 per cent of the Senior Civil Service to be women and 30 per cent of top management posts to be filled by women by 2008. (Current figures are 29 per cent and 26 per cent respectively.) Delivering these targets involves getting women better represented in the feeder grades, for example, by using 'positive action' recruitment methods. While the Ten-Point Plan does not focus exclusively on the senior grades, it appears that the primary goals are focused in this area. Other goals are less clearly defined. For example, under 'measurements and evaluation' one 'deliverable' is the plan to carry out staff surveys to 'capture issues related to culture change and barriers to inclusivity', which has a 'continuous' timescale. What will be done with the information gathered from these surveys is not specified.

This leads on to a general point about data-gathering. Many of the initiatives described above, whether statutory or not, have clear data requirements. For example, gender impact assessments have a 'monitoring' requirement, yet the guidelines about how to do this appear obscure. Browne's (2004) conclusion about the pay audits that were the result of the Kingsmill Report, covered in Chapter 3, merits repetition here. Her view is that analyses were generally poorly done and because the data were not gathered systematically using agreed methods, there is very little possibility of comparing across organizations. This means that any evaluation of impacts or indeed of trends over time will be largely impossible. If clarification is not forthcoming, then it appears likely that organizations will go along with these procedures merely because they have to (i.e. the compliance approach) and not because they believe that organizational improvements will come out of it.

Final comments

Women's labour force participation is sought by governments, both pan-European and national, primarily for economic reasons. There are argued to be social and economic advantages for individuals, households and governments, as well as moral arguments relating to fairness. We started this book with Giele and Holst's (2004) view of 'lags' between the reality of women's lives and societal institutions and cultural beliefs. One lag is that although women's participation in the labour market has changed a lot, the institutional context in which families and individuals live has changed rather little. As Moen (2003) points out, workplaces, schools, service providers and so on tend to assume that a full-time (female) homemaker is available. Yet, households tend less and less to have such a person 'on call'; the model of the male breadwinner and the full-time carer is now particularly unusual in industrialized countries.

A second lag referred to by Giele and Holst (2004) relates to policy: the needs of individuals and families resulting from women's presence in the labour market are not generally matched by public support to meet those needs. The result of this is the 'do-it-all' woman, trying to fit in many roles; the term 'time squeeze' seems apt. In the context of a domestic division of labour that is changing only very slowly, one solution has been for women in the UK to work fewer hours. As a large body of literature shows, this is not to the economic advantage of women, either in the short or long term. Part-time working (even amongst the highly qualified) is poorly paid and not associated with posts of responsibility. There are also long-term effects of this type of work, in terms of financial insecurity in old age, leading to a major 'gender income gap'.

As a solution to the 'time squeeze', part-time working may appear to many women as the solution. This might not matter if quality part-time working was available. By this we mean part-time work that is relatively high-hours, that can be in senior positions, where there is not a wage penalty, where women are not overqualified, where there is training and where there are not long-term consequences for economic wellbeing. In policy terms, it seems particularly important to focus on developing quality part-time working. Gender equality might then be advanced if this was taken up by both women and men, as appears to be happening in the Netherlands. Work–life balance for all would be improved and children's needs could probably be better catered for. Nevertheless, even this aim is not straightforward: in Chapter 8 we pointed out that trade union support for improving the prospects and conditions of part-time workers is at odds with a traditional focus on safeguarding the number of hours worked. If (in an admittedly utopian world) quality part-time working was achieved and this became attractive to men in terms of work–life balance and possible participation in child rearing, there would inevitably be lower pay for men, something that trade unions have traditionally fought against.

Employers appear to be focusing on recruitment and retention, but less on advancement; therefore little attention is paid to vertical segregation and there seems to be an acceptance that employees 'choose' whether or not to seek advancement. Thus very little attention is paid to equality of outcome, which would go against the traditional equal opportunities approach and also against the meritocratic philosophy of the diversity management approach. A focus on retention is justifiable in terms of bottom-line arguments, since retaining people avoids wastage. In contrast, a focus on advancement would move employers towards the moral arguments of fairness, something that private sector employers are probably loath to do, in view of the primacy of the market. It would also imply that if advancement was shown to be unevenly distributed, measures would need to be put in place. Realistically, these would be positive action policies. A focus on advancement would also imply major investment in data-gathering, since longitudinal, highly diversity-disaggregated information would be required.

Intervening in the often choppy waters of the choice/constraint argument is not an aim of this book, since we are not focusing on what underpins women's decision-making about their employment. Nevertheless, we have cast light on the various obstacles that women face in the labour market and to that extent it is clear that we have come down on the side of those who argue for a constrained or at least a 'situated' choice. But we also recognize the importance of women as agents and not as victims; for example we have discussed work that highlights 'moral rationalities' as a basis for women's decision-making about the prioritization of the domestic sphere, thus casting a new light on the traditional 'rational choice' approach.

We have highlighted the possibility that different types of approaches to welfare may create a context where choice is more freely arrived at. Bonke and Koch-Weser (2004) claim that a social democratic model (as found in the Nordic social model) underpinned by strong state measures (e.g. on childcare, eldercare and citizens' economic security) gives citizens more freedom of choice. In other types of welfare regimes, there is considerable social and private responsibility assigned to families and this decreases the amount of individual choice available. Cultural ideas about appropriate gender roles – the 'gender culture' – will also constitute a factor that underpins women's decision-making. In contexts with traditional ideas about appropriate roles, this will constitute a constraint in terms of women's freedom to make choices about paid work. Not only will the cultural expectations serve as a brake, but they will also exacerbate a 'time squeeze'. Fitting in large amounts of paid work with taking the major responsibility for domestic labour, including caring work, is simply not viable. In contexts – which could be countries or social groups – where there is an acceptance of egalitarian values and of households financed by dual breadwinners, there is likely to be more genuine choice about women's paid work.

Bonke and Koch-Weser's argument counters the claim that women make employment choices freely since they argue that some countries, but by implication not others, are good at providing their male and female citizens with 'relatively ample margins of choice in designing their life projects' (2004: 252). But the generous Nordic social model comes at a price – that of high personal and employer taxation. It seems realistically very unlikely that the electorates that have supported the liberal low-taxation model of the UK and the US will move rapidly towards the Nordic model.

Thus, the UK is left with seeking a range of piecemeal solutions. Most of these have focused on the pay gap; whilst it can be argued that women 'choose' part-time working and perhaps to a lesser extent that they seek employment in sectors and occupations where other women work (i.e. gender segregation), it is much harder to argue that they choose to be paid less than men. It is unsurprising therefore that the Women and Work Commission, set up by the Department for Trade and Industry, has focused on this (DTI 2006). Its proposals focus on training and advice issues. Crucially, it has not advised that pay audits should be compulsory for the private sector, despite advice from trade unions and the Equal Opportunities Commission. Whether its proposals will have an effect is of course a matter of conjecture, although there is a suggestion that some formal evaluation will be carried out. It appears from the report that the public sector will continue on its course of mandatory organizational change, reporting to a Ministerial Committee about progress on a range of fronts, including equal pay reviews. By contrast, the private sector is given guidelines for good practice. The report merely says that private sector companies should 'consider the implications of the report for how they operate in order to make the most difference to the most women' (DTI 2006: Executive Summary p. 8). One rather more concrete recommendation is that the Department for Trade and Industry should provide funds to support a new initiative, the Quality Part-Time Work Change Initiative, that will pilot the development of quality part-time work. This concept – which insists that part-time workers can hold senior positions – is one that we have supported in this book. A clear example is the Netherlands where part-time work has been promoted as a basis for greater equality between women and men; there 28 per cent of women and men working part-time are in professional jobs (Rubery *et al.* 1998).

In our final section, we make two points about globalization and women's employment. A first issue is that of the liberalization of labour markets and its effect on the UK. The 2004 entrants to the European Union from Central and Eastern Europe and the Baltic states are now able to find employment freely in the UK. These are likely to be young people who are child-free, possibly well trained, mobile and willing to work long hours. We discussed in Chapter 7 Yeandle *et al.*'s (2003) conclusion that line-managers appeared to value employees who were able to respond to unpredictable increases in work demands – thus implicitly valuing a model that people without caring commitments were more able to fulfil. If we link this to the reality of greater inward migration to the UK we could make the prognosis that private sector employers will favour this new labour force over women who are increasingly expecting their domestic lives to be taken into consideration in the arrangement of their working lives. The 'new business case' for diversity that we discussed in Chapter 6 may well be put under strain in this context. Employees who make demands about flexible working patterns – or whom employers think may do so in the future because they are of childbearing age – may become less desirable in a liberalized labour market. In this context we may see an increasing polarization between the private and public sectors in terms of women's employment, with women finding that the private sector is increasingly an inhospitable place to be in terms of reconciling paid work and domestic commitments. It is relevant to remind ourselves of McGlynn's (2003) view that the private sector's 'bottom line' arguments for diversity are on shaky ground unless they are underpinned by the moral arguments of fairness and equality of outcome.

A second point relates to the globalization of caring work. Hochschild (2003) has written about the concept of the 'nanny chain' where women from poor countries provide childcare, and increasingly care of older people, for people in the rich countries. Hochschild focuses particularly on the 'chain' between the Philippines and the US. In the Philippines, older children and relatives look after the children of women who have migrated to the US to look after children there, often for several years at a time. The money that they send back to care for their children and to educate them has become the second largest source of foreign currency in the Philippines. Since the early 1990s, 55 per cent of migrants out of the Philippines have been women. Immigration rules in the US do not allow them to take their children with them. Thus, globalization may not just be increasing inequalities in terms of access to money, but also in terms of access to care.

This example is salutary since it reminds us that many of the inequalities that we have discussed in this book could be considered to be minor. From this perspective, it would be hard to deny this, but this does not mean that women's employment in the industrialized countries does not pose challenges. There are major challenges for the state, especially in terms of who cares for children and older people, now that women are subject to such a 'time squeeze'. There are wider challenges such as the falling birth rate, and the associated 'demographic time bomb' relating to fewer children and an ageing population. And there are challenges for social justice, since despite the many advances that women have made, many inequalities persist. There is indeed a lag between the changes that have taken place in women's employment especially over the past half-century, and state and societal responses to these changes.

Notes

1   This complexity is illustrated by recent allegations that the major public services union in the UK, Unison, is alarmed at the size of an equal pay deal achieved by health workers at two hospitals in the north of England (Campbell 2006). The fear, allegedly, is that if equal pay claims of this size were achieved across the sector, both the union and the public sector would lose government support.

2   Black teenager Stephen Lawrence was murdered in a racist attack in April 1993 in London. An inquiry, led by Sir William MacPherson, into the police handling of the murder investigation characterized the Metropolitan Police Service as institutionally racist. The MacPherson report, published in 1999, also argued that institutional racism was endemic in the UK. The TUC subsequently established the Stephen Lawrence Task Group in order to step up its campaign to tackle racism in Britain (<http://www.tuc.org.uk/sltg>).

References

Anthias, F. and Yuval-Davis, N. (1993) *Racialised Boundaries: Race, Nation, Gender, Colour and Class and the Anti-Racist Struggle,* London: Routledge.

Blackwell, L. (2001) 'Occupational sex segregation and part-time work in modern Britain', *Gender, Work and Organization*, 8 (2): 146–63.

Bonke, J. and Koch-Weser, E. (2004) 'The welfare state and time allocation in Sweden, Denmark, France and Italy', in J. Giele and E. Holst (eds) *Changing Life Patterns in Western Industrial Societies*, Oxford: Elsevier, 231–53.

Browne, J. (2004) 'Resolving gender pay inequality? Rationales, enforcement and policy', *Journal of Social Policy*, 33 (4): 553–72.

Campbell, B. (2006) 'Embarrassment of riches', *Guardian Weekend*, 18 February.

Civil Service (2006) *Delivering a Diverse Civil Service: A Ten Point Plan*, London: Home Civil Service.

Colling, T. and Dickens, L. (2001) 'Gender equality and trade unions: a new basis for mobilization?' in M. Noon and E. Ogbonna (eds) *Equality, Diversity and Disadvantage in Employment*, Basingstoke: Palgrave Macmillan.

Crompton, R. (ed.) (1999) *Restructuring Gender Relations and Employment*, Oxford: Oxford University Press.

Crompton, R., Brockman, M. and Lyonette, C. (2005) 'Attitudes, women's employment and the domestic division of labour: a cross-national analysis in two waves', *Work, Employment and Society*, 19 (2): 213–33.

Cunningham, R. (2000) 'From great expectations to hard times? Managing equal Opportunities under new public management', *Public Administration*, 78 (3): 699–714.

Dickens, L. (1997) 'Gender, race and employment equality in Britain: inadequate strategies and the role of industrial relations actors', *Industrial Relations Journal*, 28 (4): 282–9.

DTI (2006) *Shaping a Fairer Future*, London: Women and Work Commission.

EOC (2004) *Fairness For All: A New Commission for Equality and Human Rights: A Response from the Equal Opportunities Commission*, Manchester: Equal Opportunities Commission.

EOC (2005a) *Facts about Women and Men in Great Britain*, Manchester: Equal Opportunities Commission.

EOC (2005b) *Advancing Equality for Men and Women: Government Proposal to Introduce a Public Sector Duty to Promote Gender Equality: Response to Department for Trade and Industry*, Manchester: Equal Opportunities Commission.

EOC (2006a) 'Different lives, different needs, different services', http://www.eoc.org.uk/Default.aspx?page=17686 (accessed May 2006).

EOC (2006b) *Sex and Power: Who Runs Britain? 2006*, Manchester: Equal Opportunities Commission.

Fagan, C. and Burchell, B. (2002) *Gender, Jobs and Working Conditions in the European Union*, Dublin: European Foundation for the Improvement of Living and Working Conditions.

Fagnani, J. and Letablier, M.-T. (2004) 'Work and family life balance: the impact of the 35-hour laws in France', *Work, Employment and Society*, 18: 551–72.

Fredman, S. (2002) *The Future of Equality in Britain*, Manchester: Equal Opportunities Commission.

Garcia, B., Anker, R. and Pinnelli, A. (eds) (2003) *Women in the Labour Market in Changing Economies: Demographic Issues*, Oxford: Oxford University Press.

Gershuny, J. (2000) *Changing Times: Work and Leisure in Postindustrial Society*, Oxford: Oxford University Press.

Giele, J. and Holst, E. (2004) 'New life patterns and changing gender roles', in J. Giele and E. Holst (eds) *Changing Life Patterns in Western Industrial Societies*, Oxford: Elsevier, 3–22.

Glover, J. and Arber, S. (1995) 'Polarization in mothers' employment', *Gender, Work and Organization*, 2 (4): 165–79.

Hochschild, A. (2003) 'The nanny chain', in R. Ely, E. Foldy and M. Scully (eds) *Reader in Gender, Work and Organization*, Malden, MA: Blackwell, 401–7.

hooks, B. (1989) *Talking Back*, London: Sheba.

Hoque, K. and Kirkpatrick, I. (2003) 'Non-standard employment in the management and professional workforce: training, consultation and gender implications', *Work, Employment and Society*, 17 (4): 667–89.

Hoque, K. and Noon, M. (2004) 'Equal opportunities policy and practice in Britain: evaluating the "empty shell" hypothesis', *Work, Employment and Society*, 18 (3): 481–506.

ILO (2004) *Breaking through the Glass Ceiling: Women in Management*, Geneva: ILO.

Kersley, B., Alpin, C., Forth, J., Bryson, A., Bewley, H., Dix, G. and Oxenbridge, S. (2005) *Inside the Workplace: First Findings from the 2004 Workplace Employment Relations Survey (WERS 2004)*, London: Department of Trade and Industry.

Kingsmill, D. (2001) *Kingsmill Review of Women's Pay and Employment*, London: Stationery Office.

McGlynn, C. (2003) 'Strategies for reforming the English solicitors' profession: an analysis of the business case for sex equality', in U. Schultz and G. Shaw (eds) *Women in the World's Legal Professions*, Oxford and Portland, OR: Hart Publishing, 159–74.

Moen, P. (ed.) (2003) *It's About Time: Couples and Careers*, Ithaca, NY: IRL Press.

Pfau-Effinger, B. (2004) *Development of Culture, Welfare States and Women's Employment in Europe*, Aldershot: Ashgate.

Purcell, K. (2002) *Qualifications and Careers: Equal Opportunities and Earnings among Graduates* (Working Paper Series No. 1), Manchester: Equal Opportunities Commission.

Robson, P., Dex, S., Wilkinson, F. and Salido Cortes, O. (1999) 'Low pay, labour market institutions, gender and part-time work: cross-national comparisons', *European Journal of Industrial Relations*, 5 (2): 187–207.

Rubery, J., Grimshaw, D. and Figueiredo, H. (2005) 'How to close the gender pay gap in Europe: towards the gender mainstreaming of pay policy', *Industrial Relations Journal*, 36 (3): 184–213.

Rubery, J., Smith, M., Fagan, C. and Grimshaw, D. (1998) *Women and European Employment*, London: Routledge.

Ryan, M. and Haslam, S. A. (2005) 'The glass cliff: evidence that women are over-represented in precarious leadership positions', *British Journal of Management*, 16 (2): 81–90.

Smithson, J. and Stokoe, E. (2005) 'Discourses of work–life balance: negotiating "genderblind" terms in organizations', *Gender, Work and Organization*, 12 (2): 147–68.

Smithson, J., Lewis, S., Cooper, C. and Dyer, J. (2004) 'Flexible working and the gender pay gap in the accountancy profession', *Work, Employment and Society*, 18 (1): 115–36.

Sommerlad, H. and Sanderson, P. (1998) *Gender, Choice and Commitment: Women Solicitors in England and Wales and the Struggle for Equal Status*, Aldershot: Ashgate.

TUC (2005) *TUC Equality Audit 2005*, London: Trades Union Congress, <http://www.tuc.org.uk/extras/auditfinal.pdf>.

Walby, S. (1997) *Gender Transformations*, London: Routledge.

Walby, S. and Olsen, W. (2002) *The Impact of Women's Position in the Labour Market on Pay and Implications for UK Productivity: Report to Women and Equality Unit*, London: Department of Trade and Industry.

Warren, T. (2003) 'Class- and gender-based working time? Time poverty and the division of domestic labour', *Sociology*, 37 (4): 733–52.

WEU (2004) *Interim Update of Key Indicators of Women's Position in Britain*, London: Women and Equality Unit, Department of Trade and Industry.

WEU (2005) *Advancing Equality for Men and Women: Government Proposal to Introduce a Public Sector Duty to Promote Gender Equality*, London: Women and Equality Unit.

Williams, M. (2000) 'In defence of affirmative action: North American discourses for the European context?' in E. Appelt and M. Jarosch (eds) *Combating Racial Discrimination*, Oxford: Berg.

Wilson, R. (1994) 'Sectoral and occupational change: prospects for women's employment', in R. Lindley (ed.) *Labour Market Structures and Prospects for Women*, Manchester: Equal Opportunities Commission.

Yeandle, S., Phillips, J., Scheibl, F., Wigfield, A. and Wise, S. (2003) *Line-managers and Family-friendly Employment*, Bristol: Policy Press, Joseph Rowntree Foundation.

Index